Contents

WITH PASSIONATE VOICE

WITH PASSIONATE VOICE

Re-Creative Singing in Sixteenth-Century England and Italy

Robert Toft

OXFORD
UNIVERSITY PRESS

OXFORD
UNIVERSITY PRESS

Oxford University Press is a department of the University of Oxford.
It furthers the University's objective of excellence in research, scholarship,
and education by publishing worldwide.

Oxford   New York
Auckland   Cape Town   Dar es Salaam   Hong Kong   Karachi
Kuala Lumpur   Madrid   Melbourne   Mexico City   Nairobi
New Delhi   Shanghai   Taipei   Toronto

With offices in
Argentina   Austria   Brazil   Chile   Czech Republic   France   Greece
Guatemala   Hungary   Italy   Japan   Poland   Portugal   Singapore
South Korea   Switzerland   Thailand   Turkey   Ukraine   Vietnam

Oxford is a registered trademark of Oxford University Press
in the UK and certain other countries.

Published in the United States of America by
Oxford University Press
198 Madison Avenue, New York, NY 10016

Library of Congress Cataloging-in-Publication Data
Toft, Robert.
With passionate voice : re-creative singing in 16th-century England and Italy / Robert Toft.
pages cm
Includes bibliographical references and index.
ISBN 978–0–19–938202–6 (hardback)—ISBN 978–0–19–938203–3
(pbk.)—ISBN 978–0–19–938204–0 (electronic text)—ISBN 978–0–19–938206–4
(online file)   1. Vocal music—England—16th century—History and criticism.
2. Vocal music—Italy—16th century—History and criticism.
3. Singing—England—History—16th century.   4. Singing—Italy—History—16th century.
5. Vocal music—Interpretation (Phrasing, dynamics, etc.)   6. Performance practice
(Music)—History—16th century.   I. Title.
ML1620.2.T64 2014
783'.01409031—dc23
2014003118

1 3 5 7 9 8 6 4 2
Printed in the United States of America
on acid-free paper

Acknowledgments

I first became interested in researching the performance of sixteenth-century song a number of years ago as a lutenist who, like the singers I accompanied, had begun to search for historically secure ways of turning mute manuscripts and prints into passionate musical declamation. This quest took me on a long and rewarding journey to root my approach to performing lute songs within the musical culture of the late Renaissance, and along the way I incurred innumerable debts. I would like to thank the pioneering performers who dared to venture onto that murky bog we now call historically informed performance, for without their concerts and recordings, I never would have been drawn to this music. I would also like to express my gratitude to all those singers with whom I have worked for their willingness to embrace historical principles, especially since our approaches to performance usually conflicted with modern thinking. Many years ago, the late Robert Spencer generously shared his research with me, and over the past few years, I have benefited greatly from discussions with Jacob Heringman, Robert Meunier, and John Potter.

I have been most fortunate to have had the opportunity to coach a large number of students, and the courses and master classes I have given provided me with the sort of workshop a researcher of performing practices needs. Beyond Western University, my home base, I would like to thank, in particular, Emma Kirkby and Nicholas Clapton (Dartington International Summer School), Anthony Rooley and Evelyn Tubb (Schola Cantorum, Basel), Jacob Heringman and Peter Seymour (University of York), Paul Elliott (Early Music Institute, Indiana University, Bloomington), Deborah Kelleher and Kathleen Tynan (Royal Irish Academy of Music, Dublin), Mary O'Neill (University of

Birmingham), and Daniel Taylor (University of Toronto) for giving me an opportunity to work with some of their students.

This book is based on my earlier study of English lute song, *Tune thy Musicke to thy Hart: The Art of Eloquent Singing in England 1597–1622* (University of Toronto Press, 1993), long out of print, and draws on some of the material I published in *Aural Images of Lost Traditions: Sharps and Flats in the Sixteenth Century* (University of Toronto Press, 1992); "An Approach to Performing the Mid 16th-Century Italian Lute Fantasia," *The Lute, The Journal of the Lute Society* 25 (1985); and "Limitations of Meaning: Text and Context in Monteverdi's 'Baci soavi e cari' (1587)" in *The Sounds and Sights of Performance in Medieval and Renaissance Music: Essays in Honour of Timothy McGee,* ed. Brian Power and Maureen Epp (Ashgate, 2009). All passages have been used with permission of the publishers.

Except for the correction of obvious errors, the music examples faithfully represent the sources from which they were taken, especially with regard to note values, textual punctuation, spelling of words, and diacritical marks. All translations, unless stated otherwise, are my own, but Marinella Lacchini (Milan) generously helped me with several aspects of sixteenth-century Italian. Specific pages in period sources are cited in the following manner: Sancta Maria 1565: I, 25, fol. 74v, in which the numerals after the colon indicate part, chapter, and folio or page number.

About the Companion Website

www.oup.com/us/withpassionatevoice
Oxford University Press has created a password-protected website to accompany *With Passionate Voice: Re-Creative Singing in Sixteenth-Century England and Italy,* and the site contains demonstrations of some of the principles discussed in the book (username: Music3; password: Book3234).

The annotated scores housed on the site illustrate how singers might complete the creative process the composer began by realizing Renaissance notation from within the musical culture of the sixteenth century. Readers are encouraged to use these scores, as well as recordings that will eventuate, in conjunction with the book, as a starting point for their own explorations of the old methods of interpretation/re-creation.

WITH PASSIONATE VOICE

Introduction

THIS BOOK ESTABLISHES THE PRINCIPLES OF PERFORMANCE SINGERS USED in England and Italy between c. 1500 and c. 1620 and explains how vocalists today can bring secular music from those countries to life from within the musical culture of the period. Recent research on past approaches to singing reveals that performers of the era did not deliver the notated texts of *frottole*, madrigals, and lute songs as literally as their modern counterparts (see, in particular, Toft 1993). Indeed, vocalists today typically render the music of composers from Marchetto Cara (c. 1470–c. 1525) to John Dowland (1563–1626) much closer to the way it survives on paper than performers four and five hundred years ago did, the common modern practice being one of interpreting the notation within a narrow range of parameters so as to minimize the creative contribution of the singer, leaving the composer's score to speak for itself. Several scholars have noted the inclination of performers over the last sixty or seventy years to revere the sanctity of the written text (see, for example, Brown 1999, Crutchfield 1989, and Freitas 2002), and Robert Philip (1992: 207–40), in a fascinating study of early recordings, documents the trend in the first half of the twentieth century toward, among other things, "literalness" and "evenness of expression," two important aspects of the then-emerging modern style prized by musicians who desired greater clarity and precision in the delivery of notated texts (229).

In the sixteenth and early seventeenth centuries, however, singers viewed scores quite differently, and for them to transform inexpressively notated compositions into passionate musical declamation, they treated texts freely and personalized songs through both minor and major modifications. In other words, vocalists saw their role more as one of re-creation than of simple interpretation, and because the final shaping of the music was their responsibility, the songs listeners heard often differed substantially from what appeared in print.[1] Renaissance scores, whether individual vocal part books, lute songs, tablatures, or keyboard partituras, reduce expression to a set

1

of symbols that at best can only approximate the unwritten nuances that constitute a performing style, and since singers in the sixteenth and early seventeenth centuries do not seem to have adhered to the notation strictly, knowledge of the strategies vocalists of the time employed to liberate music from the written page will enable us to complete the creative process the composer had merely begun.

AN AGE OF RHETORICAL PERSUASION

Although attitudes toward the performance of music from earlier cultures have changed greatly over the past several decades, the task of historically minded singers remains the same. If vocalists wish to re-create the performing practices of older societies, they must extrapolate from the surviving documents to bridge the gap that exists between those documents and actual performance. The more distant the culture, the more difficult the problem becomes, especially if we take the subject of this book, the performance of solo and part songs in England and Italy between c. 1500 and c. 1620, as an example. At first glance, the musical culture of this period might appear to be nothing more than an earlier manifestation of modern practices, but on closer examination, we quickly discover that Renaissance musicians embraced quite a different set of values. Obviously, musical style and the aesthetic underlying that style have changed significantly over the past four to five hundred years, and this makes us foreigners in their society. Presumably, we do not have an intuitive understanding of the music from this era or of approaches to its performance, and for us to recover the performing practices of the time, we must reconstruct those customs from the surviving artifacts, that is, from the music itself and from both musical and nonmusical treatises. Moreover, we probably should take care to thicken the context of our discussion and place musical activity in its broader cultural perspective. By doing this, we can at least make an attempt to avoid, to use the words of the historian Robin Collingwood (1961: 155), "the mistake of arranging in the past what is actually all present experience."

In the sixteenth century, performers communicated through a dramatic display of passion that not only inflamed the minds of listeners but also moved their emotions. In fact, both solo and consort singers made a magnificent impression, and several fascinating statements from the late fifteenth and sixteenth centuries attest to the marvelously persuasive effect of singing. In a letter to Pico della Mirandola (written c. 1488 and published in 1498), Angelo Poliziano described the performance of Fabio Orsini, a young singer who at the time was only eleven years old:

> As soon as we sat at the table, [Fabio], together with other experts, was ordered to sing some songs notated with those little signs of music. At once, a certain most

agreeable voice flowed into our ears or rather truly into our hearts, so that in fact (I know not about the others), I was almost transported outside of myself, moved no doubt by an unspoken feeling of some utterly divine pleasure. He then delivered a heroic song that he himself had recently composed to honor our Pietro dei Medici. . . . The voice itself was not entirely that of someone reading aloud nor entirely that of someone singing, but yet both could be discerned, neither separated from the other. Nevertheless, it was varied according to what the passage required, either even or modulated—now punctuated, now continuous, now raised, now restrained, now subdued, now vehement, now slow, now swift, always faultless, always clear, always delightful, the gesture neither indifferent nor sluggish but yet not affected or offensive. Anyone would have said that a young Roscius [the ancient Roman actor] was on the stage.

Ut ergo discubuimus canere quaedam iussus notata musicis accentiunculis carmina, simul cum peritis aliis, statim suavissima quadam voce sic in aures nostras illapsus, immo vero in praecordia est, ut me quidem (caeteros nescio) pene extra me rapuerit, certe sensu tacito divinae prorsus cuiusdam voluptatis affecerit. Pronuntiavit heroicum deinde carmen, quod ipse met nuper in Petri Medicis nostri laudem composuerat, . . . Vox ipsa nec quasi legentis, nec quasi canentis, sed in qua tamen utrunque sentires, neutrum discerneres, varie tamen prout locus posceret, aut aequalis, aut inflexa, nunc distincta[,] nunc perpetua, nunc sublata, nunc deducta, nunc remissa, nunc contenta, nunc lenta, nunc incitata, semper emendata[,] semper clara, semper dulcis. Gestus non ociosus, non somniculosus, sed nec vultuosus tamen ac molestus. Rosciolum prorsus aliquem diceres in scaena versari. (Poliziano 1498: Bk. 12, fol. pvii^v–pviii; cited in Abramov-van Rijk 2009: 363–64)

Somewhat later, Baldassare Castiglione, in his *Il libro del cortegiano* (first edition, 1528), described the similar effects made by the Frenchman Bidon (dates unknown) and the Italian Cara:

Consider music, the harmonies of which are now solemn and slow, now very quick and of novel moods and means: yet all are pleasing, but for different reasons, as one perceives from the way Bidon sings: which is so skillful, nimble, vehement, excited, and of such varied melodies, that the spirits of his hearers all are so moved, so inflamed; and thus entranced, it seems as if they are lifted up to heaven. No less does our Marchetto Cara move with his singing, but with a more tender harmony: that by a delectable way, and full of plaintive sweetness, moves and penetrates the soul, gently imprinting in it a delightful passion.

Vedete la Musica, l'armonie della quale hor son gravi e tarde, hor velocissime, e di novi modi e vie: nientedimeno tutte dilettano, ma per diverse cause: come si comprende nella maniera del cantare di Bidon: la quale è tanto artificiosa, pronta, vehemente, concitata, e di cosi varie melodie, che i spiriti di chi ode, tutti si commovono, s'infiammano, et cosi sospesi par che si levino in sino al cielo. Ne men commove nel suo cantar il nostro Marchetto Cara, ma con piu molle harmonia: che per una via placida, & piena di flebile dolcezza intenerisce, & penetra l'anime, imprimendo in esse soavemente una dilettevole passione. (1588: I, 37, fol. F4v)

One of the most striking features of these accounts is the degree to which the performers moved the affections or passions of their listeners, but as Sir Thomas More reminds us (1516: 420; trans. 1559: 182–83), by the early sixteenth century, this had become a principal object of both instrumental and vocal music:

For all their musike bothe that they [the Utopians] playe upon instrumentes, and that they singe with mannes voyce dothe so resemble and expresse naturall affections, the sound and tune is so applied and made agreable to the thinge, that whether it bee a prayer, or els a dytty of gladnes, of patience, of trouble, of mournynge, or of anger: the fassion of the melodye dothe so represente the meaning of the thing, that it doth wonderfullye move, stirre, pearce, and enflame the hearers myndes.

Quod omnis eorum musica: sive quae personatur organis: sive quam voce modulantur humana: ita naturales affectus imitatur & exprimit: ita sonus accommodatur ad rem, seu deprecantis oratio sit, seu laeta, placabilis, turbida, lugubris, irata, ita rei sensum quendam melodiae forma repraesentat, ut animos auditorum mirum in modum afficiat, penetret, incendat.

One can readily understand, of course, that singers like Bidon and Cara could inflame the minds of their hearers when performing solo songs, for writers such as Castiglione (1588: II, 13, fol. L2v) had acknowledged the superiority of single voices for moving listeners:

all the sweetness consists, as it were, in one alone [that is, in one singer accompanied by a "viola"], and we observe and understand the fine manner and air [of the song] with much greater understanding when the ears are not occupied by more than a solo voice; and besides you will also better discern every little error [the singer makes]; which does not happen in singing with company, for one [voice] helps the other.

tutta la dolcezza consiste quasi in un solo: & con molto maggior attention si nota & intende il bel modo, & l'aria non essendo occupate le orecchie in piu che in una sol voce: & meglio ancor vi si discerne ogni piccolo errore; il che non accade cantando in compagnia perche l'uno aiuta l'altro.

But part songs could move listeners to the same degree, and two midcentury writers attest to the persuasiveness of consort music. In fact, as the preceding quotations intimate, musicians had come to regard their art as a sister to oratory and poetry, and both Gioseffo Zarlino (1517–1590) and Nicola Vicentino (1511–c. 1576) reveal just how closely related these three arts actually were. Zarlino (1558: 192–93) noted that composers wrote counterpoint in the same way that others constructed orations, poems, and paintings, and Vicentino (1555: IV, 42, fol. 94r–v), in a chapter of his treatise called "A method for singing in consort every kind of composition" ("Regola da concertare cantando ogni sorte di compositione"), advised singers to use the orator as a model for persuading listeners. Vicentino also suggested that the more one understood learned compositions the more one would be moved by them, and therefore singers needed to be aware of what the musical poet, that is, composer, had in mind. Gaspar Stoquerus (c. 1570: ch. 2, fol. 3) agreed, for he maintained that when composers wrote music that matched the subject matter of the words, performers could wondrously move listeners to love, hate, wrath, pity, piety, and so forth: "If it [the alignment of music and text] is properly managed, the souls of men are wondrously moved to love, hate, wrath, pity, piety, and so forth, conformably with the subject matter contained in the words."/"Haec si aptè fiat, mire hominum animos ad amorem, odium, iram, misericordiam, pietatem, etc. pro subiecta verbis materia commovet." Along these lines, Giovanni del Lago (1540: 39) noted that whenever composers wished

to compose a madrigal, or a sonnet, or a barzelletta, or any other song, they first needed to think [it] over in the mind, and in that searching find a tune appropriate to the words, so the song will correspond to the words, that is, suit the subject, because how many times when learned composers have to compose a song, are they accustomed first to consider carefully among themselves to what end and to what purpose they chiefly invent and compose it, that is, which affections of the soul they should move with that song, that is, in which mode they should compose it.

. . . comporre un madrigale, o sonetto, o barzalletta, o altra canzone, prima bisogna considerare nelle mente, & in quella investigando ritrovare uno aire conveniente alle parole, ut cantus consonet verbis, cioe, che convenga alla materia, perche quante volte, che i dotti compositori hanno da comporre una cantilena, sogliono prima diligentemente fra se stessi considerare a che fine, & a che proposito quella potissimamente instituiscono, & componghino, cioe quali affetti d'animo con quella cantilena movere debbino, cioe di qual tuono si deve comporre.

Other writers active in the sixteenth and early seventeenth centuries confirm the oratorical basis of singing, and a number of authors root vocal practices in the art of rhetoric, that is, in the art of persuasive speech. Statements connecting rhetoric and music occur with increasing frequency between the sixteenth and eighteenth centuries, and by the early seventeenth century, the connection had become so well established that Henry Peacham the Younger, in *The Compleat Gentleman* (1622: 96), began the section devoted to the place of music in a gentleman's life with the words "Musicke a sister to Poetrie." The prominent position afforded these words reaffirms the link between rhetoric and music that was in Europe by this time at least two centuries old.[2] Peacham did not merely mention superficial similarities, however, and in the course of his discussion of music, he listed some of the links between poetry and music: "Yea, in my opinion, no Rhetoricke more perswadeth, or hath greater power over the mind; nay, hath not Musicke her figures, the same which Rhetorique? What is a *Revert* but her *Antistrophe*? her reports, but sweete *Anaphora's*? her counterchange of points, *Antimetabole's*? her passionate Aires but *Prosopopoea's*? with infinite other of the same nature" (103). Other English writers commented on the close connections between poetry and music as well. Francis Bacon (1627: 38) contended that "there be in *Musick* certaine *Figures*, or *Tropes*; almost agreeing with the *Figures* of *Rhetoricke*; And with the *Affections* of the *Minde*, and other *Senses* [Peacham had listed some of the figures shared by music and rhetoric]"; and Thomas Campion (1614: no. 5) asserted that in songs music enhances the persuasive qualities of the texts:

> Happy is hee whose words can move,
> Yet sweet Notes help perswasion.
> Mix your words with Musicke then,
> That they the more may enter.

As these writers clearly demonstrate, the capacity to persuade or move the minds of listeners, that is, their affections or passions, had become the primary function of music, along with its sister arts oratory and poetry. Passions, to quote Thomas Wilson (1553: 266), "are none other thyng, but a stirryng, or forcyng of the mynde, either to desier, or elles to detest, and lothe any thyng, more vehemently then by nature we are commonly wonte to doe." Certain internal acts or operations of the soul caused this increased vehemence, and by altering the humors of the body, these operations produced affections, such as, love, pain, ire, joy, fear, hope, flight, hatred, etc. (Wright 1604: 8, 33–34).

The concept of the affections and passions and the discipline of rhetoric were inseparable during the sixteenth and early seventeenth centuries. Thomas Elyot (1546: fol. 41v) defined rhetoric as "the science, wherby is taughte an artificiall fourme of spekyng, wherin is the power to perswade, move, and delyte." Numerous textbooks on the subject survive, and the writers dealt fully not only with the construction of impassioned discourse but also with the various devices speakers could use to capture the minds of listeners. Traditionally, rhetoricians divided their art into five areas: *inventio, dispositio, elocutio* or *decoratio, memoria*, and *pronunciatio. Inventio* entailed finding the subject matter, and in *dispositio*, orators arranged or ordered the material to suit their purpose. Once the material had been arranged, *elocutio* involved amplifying and decorating the discourse with fine words and sentences. Speakers then memorized (*memoria*) and delivered the speech, *pronunciatio* being concerned with the techniques of delivery orators employed to move the passions of listeners.

Within these five areas, some sixteenth-century English rhetoricians considered *pronunciatio* to be preeminent. Thomas Wilson's remarks (1553: 33, 432) typify the period:

> Demosthenes therfore, that famouse Oratour beyng asked what was the chiefest point in al Oratorie, gave the chiefe and onely praise to Pronunciation, being demaunded, what was the seconde, and the thirde, he still made answere, Pronunciation, and would make none other aunswere. . . . For though a manne can finde out good matter, and good woordes, though he canne handsomely set them together, and cary them very well awaie in his mynde, yet it is to no purpose, if he have no utteraunce [delivery]. . . . Arte without utteraunce can dooe nothyng, utteraunce without Arte can dooe right muche.

But, of course, by Thomas Wilson's day the attributes of persuasive delivery had been known for centuries. Quintilian (first century A.D.), for example, mentioned not only the characteristics of good reading but also the fundamental role a knowledge of *elocutio* played when orators prepared their delivery:

> Reading [aloud] remains for consideration. In this connexion there is much that can only be taught in actual practice, as for instance, when the boy should take breath, at what point he should introduce a pause into a line, where the sense ends or begins, when the voice should be raised or lowered, what modulation should be given to each phrase, and when he should increase or slacken speed, or speak with

greater or less energy. In this portion of my work, I will give but one golden rule: to do all these things, he must understand what he reads.

> Superest lectio, in qua puer ut sciat, ubi suspendere spiritum debeat, quo loco versum distinguere, ubi claudatur sensus, unde incipiat, quando attollenda vel summittenda sit vox, quo quidque flexu, quid lentius, celerius, concitatius, lenius dicendum, demonstrari nisi in opere ipso non potest. Unum est igitur, quod in hac parte praecipiam: ut omnia ista facere possit, intelligat. (Trans. in Quintilian I, 147)

In other words, to speak eloquently one must understand the structure of the text and use the techniques of *pronunciatio* (some of which Quintilian lists) to impress the figurative language of the text (*elocutio*) upon listeners. In fact, *pronunciatio* and *elocutio* had become so closely related by the early seventeenth century that Thomas Heywood (1612: fol. C4r) commented on the importance of rhetoric for teaching actors how to fit their pronunciation to the phrase (and by "phrase" Heywood presumably meant *elocutio*). The function of *pronunciatio* and *elocutio*, and hence the goal of persuasive discourse, then, was to imprint the affections of the text in the souls of listeners (Wright 1604: 124).

The art of eloquent speaking[3] during the sixteenth and early seventeenth centuries presupposed a knowledge of *elocutio* and *pronunciatio*, and in some quarters, writers viewed speaking and singing as closely related arts, particularly, one might hypothesize, because of the similarity between the tessitura of many songs and the speaking range of the voice. Roger Ascham (1545: I, fol. 11v), for example, maintained that preachers and lawyers should receive instruction in singing so that they would learn how to adapt their voices to the affections present in their texts:

> Preachers and lawiers, bycause they shalnot without this [singinge], be able to rule their brestes, for every purpose. For where is no distinction in telling glad thinges and fearfull thinges, gentilnes & cruelnes, softenes and vehementnes, and suche lyke matters, there can be no great perswasion. For the hearers, as Tullie sayeth, be muche affectioned, as he is that speaketh. At his wordes be they drawen, yf he stande still in one facion, their mindes stande still with hym: If he thundre, they quake: If he chyde, they feare: If he complayne, they [be] sory with hym: and finally, where a matter is spoken, with an apte voyce, for everye affection, the hearers for the moste parte, are moved as the speaker woulde. But when a man is alwaye in one tune, lyke an Humble bee, or els nowe up in the top of the churche, nowe downe that no manne knoweth where to have hym: or piping lyke a reede, or roring lyke a bull, as some lawyers do, whiche thinke they do best, when they crye lowdest, these shall never greatly moove, as I have knowen many wel learned, have done, bicause theyr voyce was not stayed afore, with learnyng to synge.

Somewhat later, William Byrd (1588: preface), in listing the reasons everyone should learn to sing, suggested that singing "is the best meanes to procure a perfect pronunciation [delivery], and to make a good Orator."

In other countries, the arts of speaking and singing were intertwined as well. Both Italian and German writers advise singers to use the orator as a model, Vicentino (1555: IV, 42, fol. 94v) expressing the relationship between the two arts explicitly:

> The experience of the orator teaches this [the value of changing tempo (mutare misura) within a song], for one sees how he proceeds in an oration—for now he speaks loudly and now softly, and more slowly and more quickly, and with this greatly moves his auditors; and this way of changing the tempo has a great effect on the soul. And for this reason one sings the music from memory ready to imitate the accents and effects of the parts of the oration, [for] what effect would the orator make if he recited a fine speech without regulating his accents, pronunciations, fast and slow motions, and soft and loud levels of speaking? That would not move his hearers. The same should occur in music, for if the orator moves his auditors with the aforesaid devices, how much more powerfully would music, recited with the same devices, accompanied by well-united harmony, make a greater effect.

> La esperienza, dell'Oratore l'insegna, che si vede il modo che tiene nell'Oratione, che hora dice forte, & hora piano, & più tardo, & più presto, e con questo muove assai gl'oditori, & questo modo di muovere la misura, fà effetto assai nell'animo, & per tal ragione si cantarà la Musica alla mente per imitar gli accenti, & effetti delle parti dell'oratione, & che effetto faria l'Oratore che recitasse una bella oratione senza l'ordine dei suoi accenti, & pronuntie, & moti veloci, & tardi, & con il dir piano & forte quello non muoveria gl'oditori. Il simile dè essere nella Musica. perche se l'Oratore muove gli oditori con gl'ordini sopradetti, quanto maggiormente la Musica recitata con i medesimi ordini accompagnati dall'Armonia, ben unita, farà molto più effetto.

In 1619, Michael Praetorius (229) reaffirmed the close connections between speaking and singing:

> Just as the concern of an orator is not only to adorn an oration with beautiful, pleasant, and vivid words and magnificent figures but also to pronounce correctly [that is, to use good delivery] and to move the affections: now he raises his voice, now he lets it fall, now he speaks with a voice sometimes intense and soft, sometimes whole and full: so must a musician not only sing but sing with art and grace so that the

heart of the listener is stirred and the affections are moved, and thus the song may
achieve the purpose for which it was made and toward which it is directed.

Gleich wie eines Oratoris Ampt ist/nicht allein eine Oration mit schönen anmu-
tigen lebhafftigen Worten/unnd herrlichen Figuris zu zieren/sondern auch recht
zu pronunciiren, und die affectus zu moviren: In dem er bald die Stimmen erhe-
bet/bald sinken lesset/bald mit mächtiger und sanffter/bald mit ganzer und voller
Stimme redet: Also ist eines Musicanten nicht allein singen/besondern künstlich
und anmütig singen: Damit das herz der Zuhörer gerühret/und die affectus bewe-
get werden/und also der Gesang seine Endschafft/dazu er gemacht/und dahin er
gerichtet/erreichen möge /

These writers clearly identify the ability to move the affections of listeners as the main
purpose of both singers and speakers. Vocalists, we learn, made the passions of the
poem manifest through their persuasive delivery, and they adopted many of the orator's
techniques to inflame and capture the minds of their listeners. But to move the passions
of others, singers literally had to tune their music to their hearts, for the heart was "the
very seate of all Passions." And if one intended to "imprint a passion in another, it is
requisit first it be stamped in our hearts: for thorow our voices, eies, and gestures, the
world will pierce and thorowly perceive how we are affected." In other words, speakers
and singers regarded the external actions of voice and gesture as the windows through
which listeners pass to discover the "secret affections" of a performer's heart (Wright
1604: 33, 172, 174).

This book, then, extrapolates from historical documents, both musical and nonmusical, to reconstruct the style of sung delivery known in England and Italy between
c. 1500 and c. 1620, that is, from the *frottole* of Marchetto Cara and Bartolomeo
Tromboncino, to the early madrigals of Claudio Monteverdi, to the monodies of Giulio
Caccini and the lute songs of John Dowland. My approach to resurrecting old methods of performing secular music, most of which fell into neglect long ago, stems from
two questions I asked myself: "What would a Renaissance listener have expected from
a vocalist?" and "At this great distance, can we determine with some degree of accuracy what those expectations would have been?" I would answer the second question
affirmatively, but only if we look broadly in sixteenth- and early seventeenth-century
culture for information. In reconstructing performing practices, I like to use the anal-
ogy of concentric circles. The innermost circle contains the song or part song intended
for performance, but since the sources of the music offer virtually no commentary on
questions of phrasing, articulation, tempo, dynamics, tonal quality of the voice, etc.,
we must look to the next circle, writings about music, for information. Unfortunately,

treatises on music frustrate us almost as much as the sources of the music themselves, and we must proceed to the next circle. In this circle, I place those documents that deal with spoken discourse, the performing art most closely related to singing. Here we find information that allows us to reconstruct important principles of sixteenth- and early seventeenth-century eloquent singing. But the question we need to ask at this point is "Should we apply information from an outer circle to the center?" I would also answer this question affirmatively, because the observations of Ascham, Byrd, Castiglione, Lago, Poliziano, Praetorius, and Vicentino quoted above suggest that the arts of speaking and singing shared many of the same characteristics. Moreover, the teaching of rhetoric and oration lay at the heart of grammar-school education, particularly in the later sixteenth century, and from the time they were quite young, educated people, including singers, would have studied the principles of eloquent delivery from books on rhetoric and oration.

Initially, we probably should learn to understand poems and their musical settings in the same way that Renaissance schoolchildren understood poetry, orations, etc.; that is, we should develop the ability to recognize "every trope, every figure, aswell of words as of sentences" (Kempe 1588: 233), taking note of the "Rhetoricall placing of the words" (Brinsley 1612: 104). Having achieved this, we will then be in a position to discover "the Rhetoricall pronounciation and gesture fit for every word, sentence, and affection" (Kempe 1588: 233). By dividing the topic into these two categories, *elocutio* and *pronunciatio*, I follow traditional rhetorical teaching, a method I have found most useful for training vocalists to sing eloquently and act aptly. The restoration of song delivery to its rhetorical roots not only places the art of eloquent singing in a broad cultural context but also allows music to take its rightful position beside its sister arts, poetry and oratory. After all, Thomas Campion (1613/1: "To the reader") likened short ayres to quick and good epigrams in poetry, many songs showing as much artifice as larger poems. To this end, I endeavor to thicken the context of the discussion of sixteenth- and early seventeenth-century solo and part song by exploring those aspects that music shares with her sister arts, as well as those unique to music. Hence, the book focuses on *elocutio* and *pronunciatio*, drawing on treatises devoted to rhetoric and oration to reconstruct many of the principles I believe formed the foundation of both spoken and sung discourse. The close relationship between speaking and singing, as already noted, makes treatises on oration a natural reservoir for the historically minded modern singer to explore, especially since treatises devoted to music do not offer as much information as we would like. I will concentrate, then, on those techniques that transfer easily from one medium to the other. The principles of delivery relating to the voice, written about so extensively in the language arts, pervade every aspect of utterance, and in using books on rhetoric and oration to reconstruct principles of singing—the books that educated Renaissance musicians would have studied in school—we can begin to approach the performance of song from a broader cultural context. This permits us to formulate a style of delivery consistent with known tenets of the time, an interpretive/re-creative framework that remained remarkably consistent throughout the sixteenth century. For example, singers based their approach to phrasing directly on principles of grammar and punctuation (pausing), and discussions of these matters did not change substantially as the century progressed. Indeed, in many respects, an account of a performance by Orsini from around 1488 is virtually identical to Vicentino's recommendations for consort singing in 1555 and Caccini's description of speaking in tones from 1602. Put simply, I aim to discuss the music in the context of late Renaissance rhetoric, modal theory (and its antecedents in language), and traditions of performing, free from as much modern thinking as possible. Because this requires us to gain a detailed knowledge of an earlier, and in many respects unexplored, musical culture, the book adopts terms and concepts from the period, most of them unfamiliar today, to shed light on old principles of performing that fell into disuse long ago. As we gradually become proficient in this musical language, we can begin to perform Renaissance music more as native speakers, or at least with less of a modern accent. The process is much like learning a foreign language—the acquisition of vocabulary and an understanding of grammar are crucial for mastering the language. Regrettably, no easy modern equivalents exist for most of the terms and concepts used in this book.

My arrangement of the material has been inspired by the method of schooling William Kempe (1588: 233) prescribed for children. Kempe suggested young scholars study "grammar," "rhetoricall ornaments," "pronounciation and gesture," and "logike" in the course of their education. But as this book primarily concerns the techniques of delivery, I have narrowed Kempe's plan to suit my purpose, omitting "logike." I place the discussion of the rudiments of musical grammar in an appendix, for even though Zarlino noted in 1558 (345–46) that musicians should gain "a complete knowledge of all manner of things concerning music"/"cognitione perfetta delle cose della Musica," many readers will already be secure in their technical understanding of sixteenth-century compositional structure and notational practices. For them, the appendix may be regarded as a review of core concepts, but for other readers who are new to the music of this era, the appendix provides essential information (in the form of basic vocabulary and grammatical precepts) that will allow them to comprehend easily discussions in the book that rely on an awareness of older principles of composition. The first section of the appendix concentrates on fundamental matters (modes, cadence structure, mimetic procedures, *supplementum*, and fantasia), while the second considers one of the main ambiguities of Renaissance notation, the addition of unnotated sharps and flats. Familiarity with these facets of musical grammar will assist singers when planning phrasing, tempo relations between sections, the final shaping of melodic lines, and the precise coloring of vertical sonorities. In short, the appendix will help vocalists become "native speakers" of sixteenth-century musical language.

The book begins with a discussion of the foremost task every singer must undertake when performing sixteenth-century music: find an appropriate way to fit the words to the notes, particularly when period sources do not place individual syllables or entire words as accurately as performers require. The second part of the book focuses on *elocutio* ("rhetoricall ornaments"), principally in English lute song, for as Quintilian maintains, students must understand what they read before they can read well (I, 146–47). Part 3 considers *pronunciatio* and concentrates on the tangible characteristics of eloquent delivery. My treatment of phrasing, which explores the role of punctuation in speaking and singing, appears at the beginning of this section, and I follow it not only with a discussion of the important role accent and emphasis played in determining note length (in relation to the *frottola* repertoire) but also with a consideration of how singers made the rhetorical structure of the text evident to listeners through voice and gesture. The section also includes an examination of that aspect of delivery peculiar to music, the art of improvised melodic embellishment. The fourth part of the book concerns the practical application of this reconstructed style of delivery to both solo and part songs. I use works by Dowland and Caccini as case studies, as well as a madrigal by Monteverdi.

If we today wish to master the re-creative processes Renaissance musicians learned from a young age, we probably need to adopt the persona of a musical orator who arouses passions in listeners through a manner of performance designed to approximate the intuitive understanding of delivery singers had in the sixteenth and early seventeenth centuries. Because composers did not write down their ideas exactly as they intended them to be expressed, literal readings of notated music will fail to produce performances worthy of the praise writers from the period lavished on singers. Indeed, if we want to turn skeletally written music into persuasive communication, we need to complete the creative process the composer had begun by realizing those aspects of the music that remain hidden in the score until we release them. In other words, we should assume more of a re-creative role than an interpretive one.

This book establishes the principles that govern this re-creative style of singing, and it provides vocalists with the tools they need to free the music from the written page. Singers in the sixteenth century had a number of strategies available to them for liberating solo and part songs from their inexpressive notation, and even though most of these practices, along with the vocabulary necessary for understanding them, will take time to master, knowledge of the old techniques allows us to develop personal styles based on whatever mixture of principles suits us best. The broad range of methods singers employed to tell their stories convincingly were well established by the time of the composers considered in this book, for Quintilian had employed the same sorts of principles that Renaissance orators relied on to effect an imitation of people "appassionate," to borrow a word from Thomas Wright (1604: 179). Performers achieved perfection, then, only through the combination of words, voice, and gesture: "And, indeed, since words in themselves count for much and the voice adds a force of its own to the matter of which it speaks, while gesture and motion are full of significance, we may be sure of finding something like perfection when all these qualities are combined"/"Et hercule cum valeant multum verba per se, et vox propriam vim adiiciat rebus, et gestus motusque significet aliquid, profecto perfectum quiddam fieri, cum omnia coierunt, necesse est" (trans. in Quintilian: XI, 247).

The book offers many suggestions to help singers find the perfection Quintilian idealized, and I urge readers to view these suggestions simply as that, possibilities for adding subtleties of performance in historically informed ways that try to remain within the musical culture of the period. They are not meant to be prescriptive; nor should the music examples be read too literally. Still, the examples provide models for singers to follow, not to copy slavishly but to vary in a thousand ways, the ultimate goal being to re-create the music with a passionate voice while remaining, as much as possible, within Renaissance musical culture.

NOTES

1. John Potter (1998: 167–68) distinguishes interpretation from re-creation through the notion that "the generation of meaning in rock music . . . is an additive process in the sense that the added meanings are creative, rather than interpretive." He then goes on to contrast the Beatles' version of Chuck Berry's "Roll over Beethoven," complete with its reworked tune and added text, to recorded versions of Schubert's "Winterreise," "which reproduce identical notes and text and differ within a very narrow set of parameters." In this book, I use the terms *interpretation* and *re-creation* in Potter's restricted sense.

2. Johannes Nucius (1613: fol. A4r), names Dunstaple as one of the first rhetorically expressive composers, and Elders (1981) discusses the rhetorical implications of two works by Dufay; see also Brown (1982), who examines the rhetorical connotations of the term *imitatio* in the late fifteenth and sixteenth centuries, and LeCoat (1975), who discusses the rhetorical basis of poetry, painting, and music in Italy and France between 1550 and 1650.

3. Thomas Elyot (1546: fol. 40v) defined eloquence in relation to speaking: "Undoubtedly very eloquence is in every tonge where any matter or act done or to be done is expressed in wordes, cleane, propise, ornate, and comely, wherof sentences be so aptly compact, that they by a vertue inexplicable, do draw unto them the mindes and consent of hearers, beynge therewith either persuaded, meved, or to delectacion induced."

PART

1

PREPARING THE TEXT

Words Appropriately Fitted to the Notes

SIXTEENTH-CENTURY SOURCES OF VOCAL MUSIC RARELY ALIGN TEXT AND music with the precision modern performers would like, and scores from the period, whether handwritten or printed, present singers with a number of problems to solve. For instance, the copyists and publishers responsible for the editions of Clemens non Papa's "Fremuit spiritus Jesu," shown in Example 1.1a, place the words and phrases in their approximate locations without positioning the syllables exactly. Consequently, vocalists who perform from these copies have to determine the location of every syllable for themselves, despite the fact that three of the sources attempt to give singers a rough idea of where at least some of the words might begin and end (see Bru27088, Leip49, and 1555, which separate syllables in the words "Jesu," "turbavit," and "seipsum"). A manuscript like Kas91, however, offers vocalists very little assistance, for the copyist employed the sign "ij" to indicate word repetition instead of writing out the words again (see the first staff of Example 1.1a). Moreover, even the most accurately notated source, Bru27088, occasionally fails to guide performers precisely. Indeed, although singers might easily find an appropriate underlay for the notes on the first staff, particularly if they adhere to the copyist's positioning of the extra words, the initial phrase of the second staff certainly could be realized in more than one way (Example 1.1b). Undoubtedly, vocalists would place the word "et" under the first note of the passage, but where should they locate the initial syllable of "turbavit": under the D (as written in Bru27088), the previous F (as given in 1555), or the following D (as indicated in Leip49)? And what about the remaining syllables in the word? Should singers position them as in Bru27088 or as in Leip49 and 1555? Interestingly, the other sources contain fewer words than Bru27088, and because of this performers need to decide which syllables should carry melismas. For instance, in the opening phrase of the piece, Bru27088, Leip49, and 1555 clearly introduce a melisma on the first syllable of "Jesu," whereas 1554 and 1558 seem to suggest that singers should assign the melisma to the second syllable. Kas91, on the other hand, provides no guidance, for the copyist placed "Gesu" in the middle of the passage.

EXAMPLE 1.1 *Clemens non Papa, "Fremuit spiritu Jesu," superius part: (a) variant text placement; (b) realization of the relatively accurate text placement in Bru27088*

(a)

Bru27088:	Fremuit	spiritu	Je		su	fremuit	spiritu	Jesu	spiritu	Jesu
Kas91:	Fremuit	spiritus		Gesu		ij				
Leip49:	Fremuit	spiritus	Ie		su	fremuit	spiritus	ihesu	ij	Iesu
1554:	Fremuit	spiritus	ihesu			fremuit	spiritus	ihesu		
1555:	Fremuit	spiri tus	Ie		su,	Fremuit	spiritus	Iesu,		
1558:	Fremuit	Spiritus	Iesu			fremuit		Spiritus	Iesu,	

Bru27088:	et		turba-	vit seipsum	et	turbavit
Kas91:	&	Turbavit		seipsum		
Leip49:	et		turbavit	se	ipsum	
1554:	&	turbavit		seipsum		
1555:	&		tur	bavit seipsum		
1558:	&	turba		vit seipsum,		

Sources

Bru27088:	Brussels, Bibliothèque du Conservatoire Royal de Musique, MS 27088
Kas91:	Kassel, Murhard'sche Bibliothek der Stadt Kassel und Landesbibliothek, MS 4o Mus. 91/1-5
Leip49:	Leipzig, Universitätsbibliothek, Thomaskirche, MS 49 (1-4)
1554:	*Liber secundus cantionum sacrarum.* Louvain, 1554
1555:	*Tertius liber modulorum.* Geneva, 1555
1558:	*Novum et insigne opus musicum.* Nürnberg, 1558

(b)

Bru27088:	Fre- mu- it spi- ri- tu Je- su fre- mu- it spi- ri- tu Je- su spi- ri- tu Je- su

Bru27088:	et	tur- ba-	vit se- ip- sum et tur- ba- vit
Leip49:	et	tur- ba- vit	
1555:	et	tur-	ba- vit

This passage from "Fremuit spiritus Jesu" highlights some of the notational ambiguities present in Renaissance manuscripts and prints, and when a number of sources for a work survive, comparison between them can suggest solutions to problematic passages. But in addition to the musical sources themselves, several sixteenth-century treatises discuss text underlay, and modern scholars have extracted the principles governing the placement of text from those documents (see especially Harrán 1986 and the summary in Towne 1990/91). These principles, though few in number, offer welcome assistance to performers who wish to weigh the value of one solution over another, and an understanding of Renaissance procedures helps us realize the text from within known tenets of the time.

General advice from theorists follows a familiar pattern: because manuscripts and prints do not always convey the intentions of composers clearly, singers must alter the texts before them to produce eloquent performances. In fact, several writers advise composers not only to locate syllables with care but also to synchronize words and melody at cadences and rests (Harrán 1986: Appendix, 102, 107–10, 155, 158, 166). But if copyists or editors had placed the text inappropriately, at least one theorist, Gaspar Stoquerus, expected performers to correct the problems (Harrán 1986: Appendix, 171). The treatises regularly offer suggestions for novices, several writers recommending that singers place the first syllable on the initial note of a phrase and the final syllable on the last note of that phrase (Harrán 1986: Appendix, 238–41, 258–60). One exception to this practice seems to have been the final note of a *clausula*, which could be left without a separate syllable (Harrán 1986: Appendix, 206). In addition to these fundamental concepts, long notes should carry long or accented syllables, while short notes would receive short or unaccented ones (Harrán 1986: Appendix, 65–66). The metrical structure of the music governed both these principles, accented syllables falling on stressed beats and unaccented syllables on unstressed beats (Harrán 1986: Appendix, 235). Furthermore, several theorists stated that performers should assign a single syllable to notes bound by a ligature (two or more notes joined together in a compound symbol), and Stoquerus observed that singers could place another syllable within a ligature if the copyist had made an error (Harrán 1986: Appendix, 209, 215–16, 224–25, 230).

With regard to the words themselves, a number of writers counseled performers to elide vowels between words in Italian, but they also recommended separating them for musical reasons (Harrán 1986: Appendix, 184–86, 188). Pedro Cerone, however, felt singers should treat diphthongs as single syllables (Harrán 1986: Appendix, 151). In addition to discussing vowels, theorists maintained that vocalists could repeat either single words or complete phrases, as long as they did not overuse the practice (Harrán 1986: Appendix, 355, 366–68, 378n81).

One writer, Seth Calvisius, thought when singers performed melismatic passages, they should place the melisma on an accented syllable (Harrán 1986: Appendix, 247–49), while others suggested singing multiple notes to the penultimate syllable of a word (Harrán 1986: Appendix, 240–43, 247–48). Furthermore, theorists recommended delivering a series of semiminims (quarter notes) followed by a longer note to a single syllable, which would be placed under the first semiminim. But if a long note preceded the melisma, then it could carry the first syllable (Harrán 1986: Appendix, 232, 274–75, 278, 280–81). At the conclusion of a melisma, vocalists usually sang the next note to the same syllable; however, they could also introduce a new syllable on that note (Harrán 1986: Appendix, 281, 292–93, 298). But when performers found it necessary to assign more than one syllable to a melisma, each pair of notes could receive a separate syllable (Harrán 1986: Appendix, 283). Moreover, if a composer followed a series of semiminims with a group of smaller notes, that new series of notes should carry its own syllable (Harrán 1986: Appendix, 278). As a caution, Nicola Vicentino (1555: IV, 18, fol. 80v) reminded singers that if they reiterated the vowel on each note of a melisma in an "a.a.a.a.a.a" fashion, they ran the risk of reducing listeners to laughter, especially in plainchant.

In passages containing octave leaps, one theorist, Orazio Tigrini, thought that the upper note should not carry a new syllable; but Vicentino disagreed, particularly when the next word began on the upper note (Harrán 1986: Appendix, 336, 338–39). Other melodic profiles carried separate syllables, as well. For instance, in the dotted figure ♩. ♪♪ singers could place a syllable on each note, or they could retain the initial syllable on the second note (Harrán 1986: Appendix, 314–18, 323, 325). They could also divide the dotted note and put a syllable on a note equivalent in value to the dot (Harrán 1986: Appendix, 311–13). However, Stoquerus thought that syncopated notes in *clausulae* should not receive their own syllables (Harrán 1986: Appendix, 234, 333), and Vicentino warned singers to avoid introducing new syllables on dissonant notes, especially if they were syncopated (Harrán 1986: Appendix, 330).

One other point made by Gaspar Stoquerus concerns the number of notes available for underlaying the text. If performers found they had fewer notes than syllables, they could divide longer notes into a sufficient quantity of shorter ones (Harrán 1986: Appendix, 176–77), yet in passages containing repeated notes written by the composer, vocalists could also retain the first syllable on one or more of the subsequent notes (Harrán 1986: Appendix, cf. 342 and 343). The flexibility implied in Stoquerus's remarks, as well as many of the comments made by the other theorists cited here, reminds us that singers had considerable leeway when re-creating the vocal lines before them. In fact, the small number of surviving principles simply do not cover every situation a singer might encounter, and just like the application of unnotated sharps and flats discussed in the Appendix of this book, we need to combine theoretical information with the notational practices of copyists and printers if we wish to gain a broad understanding of the issues surrounding text underlay. For instance, in the problematic passage shown above in Example 1.1b, the placement of the word *turbavit* might follow either of the lower two solutions, for both find justification in theorists' discussions of melismas and octave leaps. Since each pair of notes in a melisma may carry a syllable, singers might wish to place "tur-" below the F instead of the D indicated in Bru27088, and as theorists permit performers to assign a syllable to the upper note of a leap when that syllable begins a new word, the solution in Leip49 seems feasible. Similarly, the realization from 1555 also follows at least one of the known theoretical principles, for the printer positioned the second syllable of "turbavit" one note after the leap, even though this location falls on the syncopated note of a *clausula*, thus conflicting with Stoquerus's views on cadences.

Nonetheless, despite the problems associated with "Fremuit spiritus Jesu," some sources do indicate the location of syllables quite accurately, and the edition of Bartolomeo Tromboncino's *frottola* "Ala guerra," published by Petrucci in 1509, unambiguously marks which notes belong to melismas by reiterating the syllables concerned (Example 1.2; mm. 6, 9, 11–12, 18–19, and 20–21). In two of these passages (mm. 5–6 and 18–19), Petrucci creates variety through different applications of the principles surrounding dotted figures. He regards both passages as 𝅗𝅥. 𝅗𝅥 𝅝 (in mm. 5–6, he divides the dotted note and reiterates the syllable on a repeated note equivalent in value to the dot), but either places a new syllable on the following short note ("pa-" in m. 6) or reiterates the previous syllable ("-u" in m. 19). In addition, he elides the vowels in the words "sempre e" (m. 8), and for singers to fit all the syllables under the notes, they occasionally have to split the values (mm. 4–5, 8–9). The only ambiguous passage occurs in measure 13. Here the performer must decide whether to place the final syllable of "tenace" on the first note of the measure or the second.

Text and translation:

Ala guerra ala guerra	To war, to war,
Ch'amor non vol piu pace	for love wants no more peace,
Ma sempre e piu tenace	but is ever more tenacious.
Questa guerra e mortale	This war is deadly,
Per un ardente strale	for a burning arrow,
Cagion d'ogni mio male	the cause of all my pain,
Per farme sempre guerra	makes me constantly war.
Ala guerra. . .	To war. . .
Io no trovo arma forte	I cannot find a powerful weapon
Che vetar possa morte	that can prevent death.
Io van batto a le porte	In vain, I beat at the gates,
Non di pace ma di guerra	not of peace but of war.
Ala guerra. . .	To war. . .
Hora son vinto un tutto	Now I am conquered in everything,
Preso arso e destrutto	captured, burnt, and destroyed.
Questo e d'amore il fructo	This is the fruit of love

Che sempre me fa guerra
    Ala guerra...

Ma la cagion vo dire
Poi ch'io deggio morire
E un secreto scoprire
Cagion di tanta guerra
    Ala guerra...

Una a chi servo fede
Che'l mio dolor non crede
Al fin per mia mercede
Mi fa con morte guerra
    Ala guerra...

Ma el tutto porto in pace
Per quel che nel cor face
Aspetta tempo e tace
Questa aspra e crudel guerra
    Ala guerra...

Ma sei tuo dur concetto
Non m'ha qualche respetto
Temo che po un dispetto
Finira l'aspra guerra
    Ala guerra...

Se altrove pur sei volta
E in tutto da me tolta

Ascoltame una volta
E a to posta fa po guerra

    Ala guerra...

that always makes me war.
    To war...

But I want to say the reason,
now that I must die,
is a secret to discover,
the reason for so much war.
    To war...

One whom I serve faithfully,
who does not believe my anguish,
in the end, for my reward,
makes me war to the death.
    To war...

But I bear it all peacefully,
for s/he who in my heart I make
wait for time and silence.
This harsh and cruel war.
    To war...

But is it your harsh opinion
not to have any regard for me.
I fear that a little spite
will end the harsh war.
    To war...

If you have turned elsewhere perhaps,
and have been taken away from me
    completely,
listen to me once,
and from your position make a
    little war.
    To war...

Ma non voler che in bando	But do not think that in banishment
Stia el tuo servo quando	your servant will stay, when
Tu el vedi lacrimando	you see him weeping,
Per la continua guerra	because of the never-ending war.
Ala guerra...	To war...

EXAMPLE 1.2 *Bartolomeo Tromboncino, "Ala guerra," lute song (1509) (in this and the following examples, ties with dotted lines indicate that the two notes were a single one in the original)*

(Continued)

EXAMPLE 1.2 (*Continued*)

ra ch'a- mor non vol piu- u pa- ce pa- a- a-

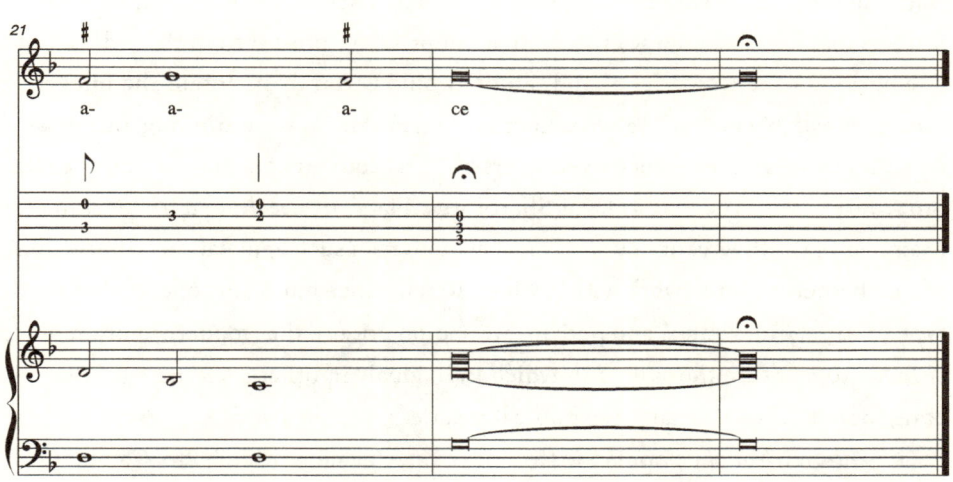

a- a- a- ce

Petrucci also published this *frottola* in a four-part version, with the complete text of the first verse underlain in just the *superius* (Example 1.3). As with many of the *frottole* Petrucci published as part songs, the lower voices often require a bit of adjustment in order for singers to underlay the syllables of the text. On two occasions in "Ala guerra," a pair of repeated notes need to be joined together to allow the text and music to coincide in the lower three parts (mm. 3–4, 21), and at another point in the piece singers may choose to place a new syllable on the short note of a dotted figure (mm. 18–19). Moreover, in two passages (mm. 4–7, 17–22) three ways of underlaying the text in the *superius* seem possible. In two of the options, vocalists might elide "che amor," as Petrucci did in the lute-song version of the piece from 1509 ("chamor"), while the third possibility would entail separating the vowels on the initial two repeated notes, as indicated in the part-song version from 1504 (in the *superius*, the printer elides "che amor" on the first utterance yet separates the two words in the next line of music, which changes the length of the poetic line from seven syllables to eight). These passages illustrate the inherent flexibility that pervades Renaissance procedures, and modern performers may wish to embrace the diversity of practices preserved in these documents. The elision of the words "che" and "amor" would certainly maintain the integrity of the seven-syllable poetic line on each utterance, but this way of thinking, one in which consistency takes precedence over diversity, runs counter to many sixteenth-century procedures (see "The Addition of Sharps and Flats" in the Appendix for numerous examples of the divergent practices one encounters in such application). The flexibility of the theoretical framework within which Renaissance musicians operated made this type of variety inevitable, and perhaps we should not use the (modern) notion of consistency to measure the skill with which individuals in other societies executed their craft, for it disallows variation in musical practices.

In another *frottola* popular with modern performers, Marchetto Cara's "O mia cieca e dura sorte," Petrucci's editions illustrate further choices singers may make. The lute-song version clearly compels vocalists not only to sing certain diphthongs to a single note but also to elide words so that all the syllables fit under the composer's notes (see, for instance, Example 1.4, mm. 1–2, "mia" and "cieca e"). But on other occasions singers can separate the syllables of "mia" and spread them across two or more notes (mm. 15, 18–19). Performers could also place the syllables of "dolente" in more than one way in measures 22–24. As the theorists maintain, every pair of notes in a melisma may carry a syllable, and so vocalists might position the text in either of the two manners shown in the example, both of which assign the accented syllable to the greatest number of notes.

EXAMPLE 1.3 *Bartolomeo Tromboncino, "Ala guerra," four-part version (1504)*

A- la guer- ra a- la guer- ra che a-
che
che a-

A- la guer- ra a- la guer- ra

A- la guer- ra a- la guer- ra

A- la guer- ra a- la guer- ra

mor non vol piu pa- ce ma sem- pre e piu
a- mor non vol piu pa- ce
mor non vol piu- u pa- a- ce

che a- mor non vol piu pa- ce ma sem-

che a- mor non vol pa- ce ma sem- pre e

che a- mor non vol pa- ce ma sem- pre e

(Continued)

EXAMPLE 1.3 (*Continued*)

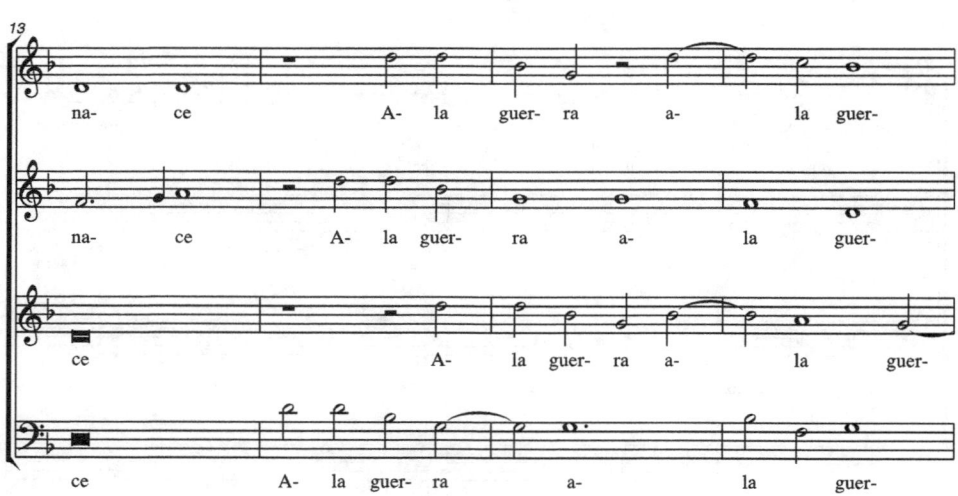

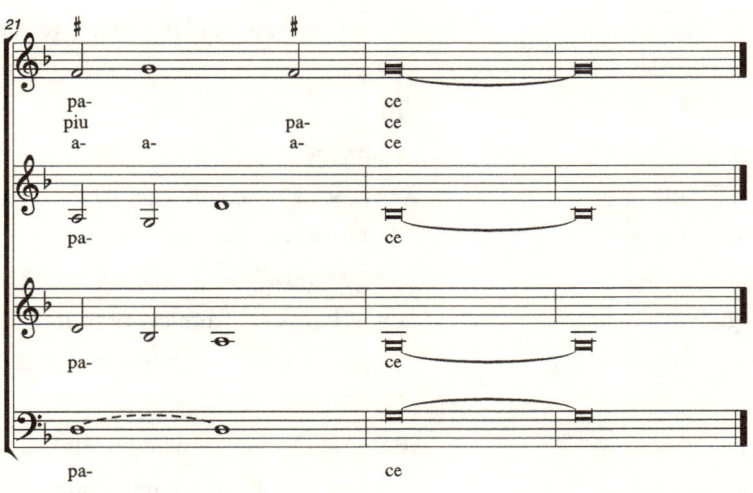

Text and translation:

O mia cieca e dura sorte | O my blind and lingering fate
Di dolor sempre nutrita | by grief ever nourished.
O miseria di mia vita | O wretchedness of my life
Tristo anuncio a la mia morte | sad omen of my death.

Piu dolente e piu infelice | More sorrowful and more unhappy
Son che alcun che viva in terra | am I than anyone who lives on earth.
L'arbor son che il vento atterra | I am the tree that the wind
| blows down,
Perche piu non ha radice | because it no longer has roots.
Vero e ben quel che se dice | It is certainly true what they say
Che mal va chi a mala sorte | that it goes ill for whomever has
| bad fortune.
O mia cieca e dura sorte... | O my blind and lingering fate...

La cagion de tanto male | The cause of so much grief
E fortuna e il crudo amore | is fortune and cruel love,
Per che sempre de bon core | because always with a good heart
Servit'ho con fe immortale | I have served with undying faith,
La qual hor sicato ha l'ale | she who now has shriveled wings
E bandita da ogni corte | and is banished from every court.
O mia cieca e dura sorte... | O my blind and lingering fate...

Perche un viver duro e grave | Because of a life hard and troubled,
Grave e dur morir conviene | troubled and hard is it necessary
| to die.
Finir voglio in pianti e pene | I want to end in tears and pain,
Come in scoglio fa la nave | as the boat does upon a rock,
Ch'al fin rompe ogni suo trave | until it breaks every one of its beams,
Poi che un tempo e stata forte | forasmuch as it once was sturdy.
O mia cieca e dura sorte... | O my blind and lingering fate...

Piglia exempio ognun che vede | Follow the example everyone sees
Scritto in la mia tomba obscura | written on my dark tomb:

Se ben son for di natura	If I should be good by nature
Morto son per troppo fede	I am slain by too much faith.
Per mi mai non fu mercede	For me there never was mercy;
Pieta m'ha chiuse le porte	pity has closed her doors to me.
O mia cieca e dura sorte...	O my blind and lingering fate...

EXAMPLE 1.4 *Marchetto Cara, "O mia cieca e dura sorte," lute song*

(Continued)

EXAMPLE 1.4 (*Continued*)

O mi- se- ria de mia vi- ta

tri- sto a- nun- cio a- la mi- a mor-

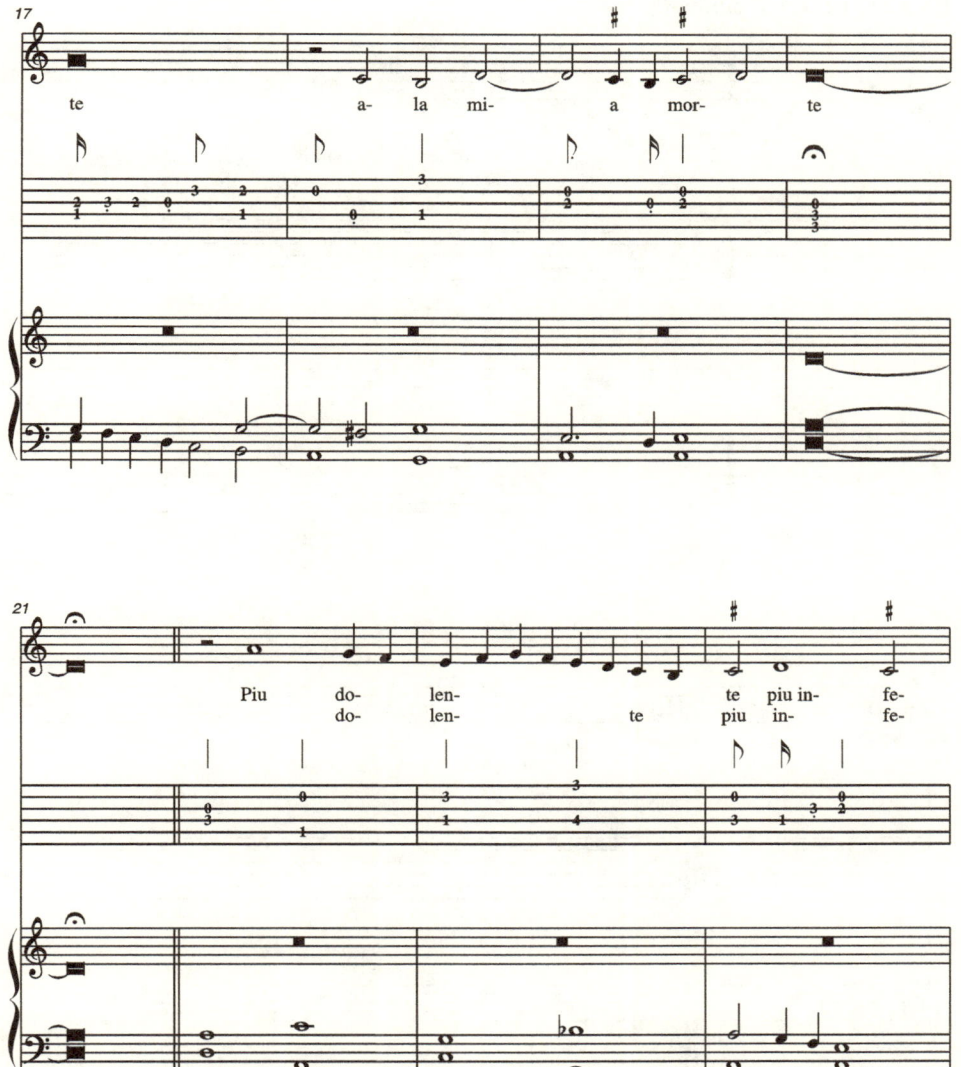

te   a- la mi-   a   mor-   te

Piu   do-   len-   te piu in-   fe-
      do-   len-   te piu in-   fe-

(Continued)

EXAMPLE 1.4 (*Continued*)

li-   ce   son   che al-   cun   che   vi-   va   in
L'ar-   bor   son   che il   ven-   to   at-

ter-   ra   per   che piu   non   ha   ra-   di-
ter-   ra   ve-   ro e ben quel   che   se   di-

The four-part version also presents singers with a number of issues to resolve, particularly with regard to the division of notes to make room for all the syllables (Example 1.5). For instance, if performers wish to regularize certain aspects of the text underlay, they must split some of the semibreves (whole notes) in two. In measures 14–17, singers may prefer to begin the descending scalar run in the *altus* and *tenor*, as well as the *bassus* phrase that commences on the high G in the middle of measure 16, on the first syllable of "morte." To do this, they must divide both the *altus*'s semibreve at the beginning of measure 15 and the *tenor*'s semibreve in the second part of the measure. Similarly, in the last section of the piece (mm. 34–40), a number of semibreves need to be split to accommodate the syllables.

EXAMPLE 1.5 *Marchetto Cara, "O mia cieca e dura sorte," four-part version*

O mi- se- ria de mia vi- ta

O mi- se- ria de mia vi- ta

O mi- se- ria de mia vi- ta

O mi- se- ria de mia vi- ta

tri- sto a- nun- tio a- la mi- a mor-

tri- sto a- nun- tio a- la mia mor-

tri- sto a- nun- tio a- la mia mor-

tri- sto a- nun- tio a- la mia mor-

(*Continued*)

EXAMPLE 1.5 (*Continued*)

li- ce son che al- cun che vi- va in
L'ar- bor son che'l ven- to at-

li- ce son che al- cun che vi- va in
L'ar- bor son che'l ven- to at-

li- ce son che al- cun che vi- va in
L'ar- bor son che'l ven- to at-

li- ce son che al- cun che vi- va in
L'ar- bor son che'l ven- to at-

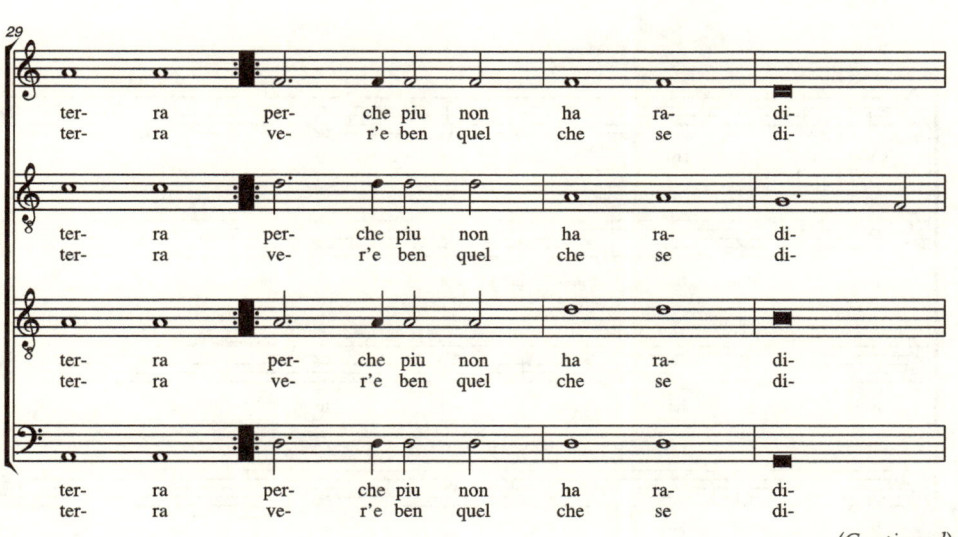

ter- ra per- che piu non ha ra- di-
ter- ra ve- r'e ben quel che se di-

ter- ra per- che piu non ha ra- di-
ter- ra ve- r'e ben quel che se di-

ter- ra per- che piu non ha ra- di-
ter- ra ve- r'e ben quel che se di-

ter- ra per- che piu non ha ra- di-
ter- ra ve- r'e ben quel che se di-

(Continued)

EXAMPLE 1.5 (*Continued*)

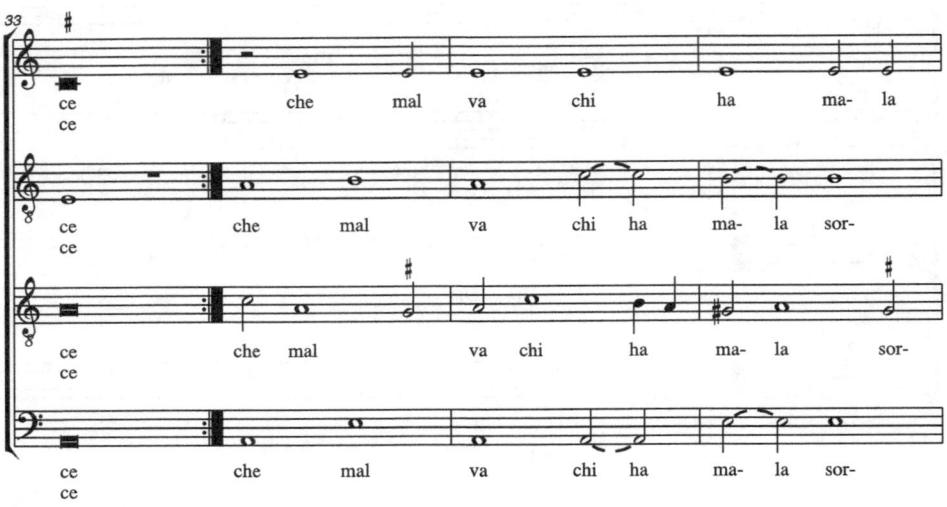

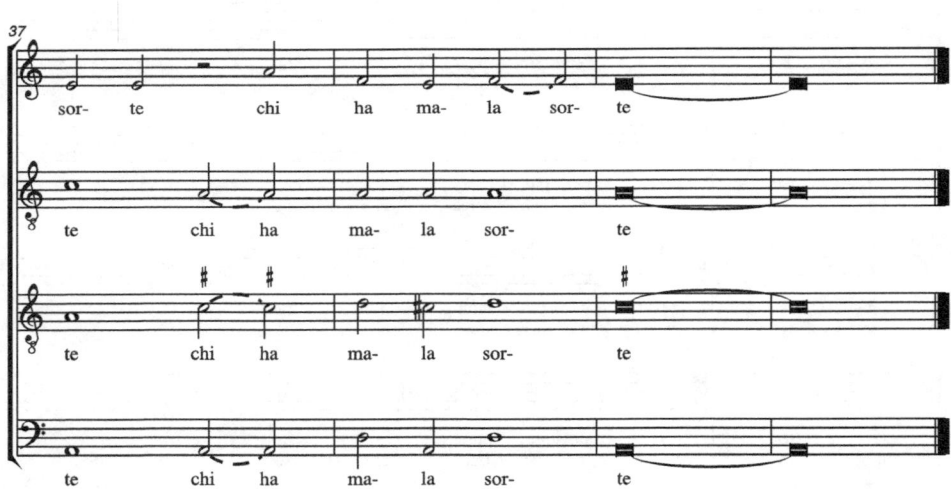

As these two *frottole* demonstrate, performers can resolve the issues surrounding the placement of text by combining theoretical principles with the clues sixteenth-century copyists and printers embedded in their editions. A careful consideration of the structural features of both the music and text will suggest a number of workable solutions to problematic passages, and the inherent flexibility of both the theorists' remarks and contemporary editorial practices allows modern singers to re-create the music in ways that reflect the breadth of earlier practices.

PART
2

ELOCUTIO: FINE WORDS AND MUSIC

Happy is hee whose words can move,
Yet sweet Notes help perswasion.
Mixe your words with Musicke then,
That they the more may enter.
(Campion 1614: no. 5)

Every Trope, Every Figure

I N ORDER TO PERFORM SIXTEENTH- AND EARLY SEVENTEENTH-CENTURY vocal music more from within the culture of the time, we probably should learn to comprehend poems and their musical settings in the same way that Renaissance schoolchildren understood poetry, orations, etc.; that is, we should develop the ability to recognize "every trope, every figure, aswell of words as of sentences" (Kempe 1588: 233), taking note of the "Rhetoricall placing of the words" (Brinsley 1612: 104). Having achieved this, we can then discover "the Rhetoricall pronunciation and gesture fit for every word, sentence, and affection" (Kempe 1588: 233). Nowhere is the rhetorical basis of texted music more apparent than in the English lute-song repertoire of the early seventeenth century, and I will use songs printed or copied in England to illustrate how closely intertwined the arts of music and language had become by the end of the Renaissance.

Henry Peacham the Younger's direct reference to the "passionate Aire" as a *prosopopoeia* not only establishes the rhetorical basis of lute song but also hints at the persuasive or affective performing style required by the singer. In rhetoric, *prosopopoeia* involves "a fayning of any person, when in our speech we represent the person of anie, and make it [him] speake as though he were there present" (Fraunce 1588: fol. G2r). Or to paraphrase Quintilian (IX, 390–91) and Henry Peacham the Elder (1577: fol. O2r–v), the orator personifies the inner thoughts and affections of an absent person, making that person actually seem to appear before the eyes of the hearer. It forms part of a larger group of figures, known generically as *hypotyposis* (*demonstratio* in Latin), directed toward lively description or counterfeit representation (Puttenham 1589: 199). In the case of *prosopopoeia*, the singer feigns the affections of the imaginary person in the poem, bringing forth the ruling passion of that person (often the poet). Singers in their musical orations must then arouse the passions of listeners through their manner of performance. In order to do this, performers need to understand *elocutio*, that is, the beautification of the matter through the application of "apte wordes and picked sentences" (Wilson 1553: 32). Rhetoricians considered the figures of rhetoric ("apte words and picked sentences")—and those in music—to be important tools for inflaming the mind of the listener as no orator could "by the waight of his wordes . . . perswade his hearers, having no helpe of them [i.e., the figures]" (Peacham the Elder 1577: fol. A3r). With figures,

> the Oratour may leade his hearers which way he list, and draw them to what affection he will: he may make them to be angry, to be pleased, to laugh, to weepe, and lament: to love, to abhorre, and loath: to hope, to feare, to covet, to be satisfyed, to envye, to have pittye and compassion: to mervaile, to beleeve, to repent: and briefely to be moved with any affection that shall serve best for his purpose. . . . [Furthermore, the Oratour may] paynt out any person, deede, or thing, so cunninglye with these couloures, that it shall seeme rather a lyvely Image paynted in tables, then a reporte expressed with the tongue. Fynally, the force of figures is so great, that the strength of apt and eloquent pleading and speaking, consisteth (sayeth Fabius) in these kinde of exornations.
>
> (Peacham the Elder 1577: fol. A3r)

Anyone who had received a typical grammar-school education in Elizabethan or Jacobean England would have been highly skilled in recognizing rhetorical devices, and rhetoricians particularly valued a knowledge of figures as an aid in reading and writing poetry. Henry Peacham the Elder (1577: fols. A2v–A3r) insisted that the utility of "Fyguratyve Flowers, both of Grammar and Rhetorick . . . is so great, that I cannot sufficiently prayse them, and the knowledge of them so necessary, that no man can reade profytably, or understand perfectlye, eyther Poets, Oratours, or the holy Scriptures, without them."

Quintilian (IX, 352–55) defined the term *figure* as a form of speech artfully varied from common usage, and George Puttenham (1589: 133) maintained that the

> figure it selfe is a certaine lively or good grace set upon wordes, speaches and sentences to some purpose and not in vaine, giving them ornament or efficacie by many maner of alterations in shape, in sounde, and also in sence, sometime by way of surplusage, sometime by defect, sometime by disorder, or mutation, and also by putting into our speaches more pithe and substance, subtilitie, quicknesse, efficacie or moderation, in this or that sort tuning and tempring them, by amplification, abridgement, opening, closing, enforcing, meekening or otherwise disposing them to the best purpose.

Figurative speech, then, lifted language from "the ordinarie habite and manner of our dayly talke and writing" (Puttenham 1589: 132) to a loftier style. Analogously, composers employed figures in music to grace a text and to elevate it from the ordinary to the sublime in order to enhance its style and thus its persuasiveness. Henry Peacham the Younger and Francis Bacon, quoted earlier, make this last point clear, and Henry Peacham the Elder (1577: fol. A3r) compared the colors of elocution, that is, the figures of grammar and rhetoric, to "flowers of sundry coullors, a gallant Garland: such as garnish it, as precious pearles, a gorgious Garment: suche as delight the eares, as pleasant reports, repetions, and running poyntes in Musick." The amount of figurative language orators employed depended on the style in which they chose to speak: the "great or mighty" style, the "smal" style, or the "lowe" style (Wilson 1553: 339). In the high style, orators used great words and vehement figures, whereas in the small or middle style speakers moderated their "heat," using fewer figures. But in the low style, orators went plainly to work, speaking only in common words (Wilson 1553: 339).

Peacham the Elder, in following the traditional teaching of English rhetoricians such as Richard Sherry (1550) and Thomas Wilson (1553), classified figures as either tropes or schemes. Tropes served to alter the signification of a word or words from the normal meaning to something not proper but quite close (for example, metaphor). Schemes, on the other hand, removed language from the common custom by creating highly artificial patterns of speech, as with repetitions of all sorts (Peacham the Elder 1577: fols. B1v, E1v; see also Lanham 1968: 101–3). The traditional view of figures was, however, not the only one current in England, for Peacham's contemporary George Puttenham (1589: 119) had devised his own system for classifying figures. In discussing exornation (the adorning or beautifying of language), Puttenham wrote about two sorts of "ornament Poeticall." One, called *enargia,* functioned to "satisfie & delight th'eare onely by a goodly outward shew set upon the matter with wordes, and speaches smothly and tunably running." The second, called *energia,* worked inwardly to stir the mind "by certaine intendments or sence of such wordes & speaches." Some figures, then, simply delighted the ear. Through these *auricular* devices, the exclusive property of poets, "not onely the whole body of a tale in poeme or historie may be made in such sort pleasant and agreable to the eare, but also every clause by it selfe, and every single word carried in a clause, may have their pleasant sweetnesse apart" (134). One way writers made clauses "pleasant and agreable to the eare" was to adorn them with the figure *zeugma,* or *adjunctio,* or its opposite *hypozeuxis,* or *disjunctio* (Puttenham 1589: 136–39). *Zeugma* involves making a single word serve more than one clause. If the common servitor appears in the first clause of the series, the figure *prozeugma* results:

> Her beautie perst mine eye, her speach mine wofull hart:
> Her presence all the powers of my discourse.

Here the verb "perst" "satisfieth both in sence & congruitie all those other clauses that followe him." Conversely, with *hypozeuxis* poets adorn the language by supplying the same word in more than one clause:

> Unto the king she went, and to the king she said,
> Mine owne liege Lord behold thy poore handmaid.

In this example, the words "to the king" supply both of the first two clauses, beautifying the language with much "pleasant sweetnesse."

Other figures, called *sensable*, functioned to stir the mind, and these devices belonged to both poets and orators. They gave language efficacy; that is, by altering conceit or sense, they gave language the power to move listeners (Puttenham 1589: 133, 148). Puttenham (1589: 153) provides a particularly potent example in his description of *emphasis*, the figure that enforces "the sence of any thing by a word of more than ordinary efficacie." A much more powerful way of stating "O gratious, courteous and beautifull woman," he suggests, would be to say "O rare beautie, ô grace, and curtesie." Still other figures serve both purposes, delighting the ear while stirring the mind, and these Puttenham called *sententious* or rhetorical. Puttenham reserved such devices for the orator alone, because once speakers made words and clauses "as well tunable to the eare, as stirring to the minde," they needed to apply figures designed "all at once to beautifie and geve sence and sententiousnes to the whole language at large." These, the most powerful figures, enlarged the entire matter with all sorts of amplifications and allowed orators to utter and persuade both copiously and vehemently (119, 133, 163). Puttenham, of course, did not really state anything new here, for earlier writers, such as Henry Peacham the Elder, also recognized the greater persuasiveness of certain types of figures over others. This especially applies to Peacham's "Schemates Rhetoricall" (1577: fol. H4v) which "doe fashion a pleasant, sharpe, evident and gallant kinde of speaking, giving unto matters great strength, perspecuitie and grace." Moreover, embodied in the "Schemates Rhetoricall" were the techniques of amplification, which Peacham particularly valued (1577: fols. N2v–N3r), because with them the orator "may easily draw the mindes of his hearers whether he will, and wynde them into what affection he list. . . . The Oratoure with helpe thereof, eyther breaketh all in peeces, like a thunderbolt, or else by little and little, like the flowing water, creepeth into the mindes of his hearers, and so by a soft and gentle meanes, at last winneth their consent . . . the whole strength of apte and eloquent pleading, sayeth Fabius, consisteth in this kinde of exornation."

Striking examples of *sententious* language can be found in the figures of repetition. *Symploche (complexio)*, one of the many different forms of word repetition, occurs "when one and the selfe [same] word doth begin and end many verses in sute" (Puttenham 1589: 166–67). This figure, typical of its class, moves and delights the listener with language both sweet and pithy. Puttenham's illustration of a man who sportingly complains about his untrustworthy mistress demonstrates the effect:

> Who made me shent for her loves sake?
>> Myne owne mistresse.
> Who would not seeme my part to take,
>> Myne owne mistresse.
> What made me first so well content
>> Her curtesie.
> What makes me now so sore repent
>> Her crueltie.

Thus spoken discourse achieved its greatest persuasiveness, and hence its highest style, when adorned with *sententious* figures that at once both delight the ear and stir the mind.

Similarly, musical discourse reached its loftiest and most passionate state when composers copiously decorated the texts of their songs with *sententious* figures. It should come as no surprise, of course, that songs received the same treatment as poems and orations, for composers were expected to have a knowledge of poetry. In fact, Charles Butler (1636: 95–96) clearly thought that musicians should understand poetry: "For hee that knoweth bothe [Poesi and Musik], can best fit his Poesi to his own Musik, and his Musik to his own Poesi. And morover hee is enabled to judg of such verses as ar browght unto him, and, for a neede, soomwhat to alter them; that the woords may bee the more consonant to his present vein." According to Butler, a knowledge of poetry not only would allow composers to write their own poems but also would allow them to alter the poems of others to suit their purposes. The type of alteration normally made by English composers in the early seventeenth century involved the amplification of the basic structure of the poetry through the addition of figures not present in the poem. Because singing had long been considered the musical equivalent of spoken oration, composers embellished texts in order to turn the written poem, which frequently did not contain the style of amplification needed for successful oral persuasion, into a vehicle through which singers, with the help of figures, could move their listeners to specific passions. And, naturally, Elizabethan and Jacobean composers never would have expected poems to contain these kinds of devices, because rhetoricians reserved the *sententious* figures Puttenham lists for orators (Sherry 1550: 25;

Puttenham 1589: 133). Thomas Hobbes (1637: 118), in his translation of Aristotle's *Rhetoric*, explains the different characteristics of writing and speaking. Written orations, Hobbes maintains, appear flat when spoken. They lack the types of verbal devices, specifically figures of repetition, so necessary for orators to move listeners. One could, however, make writing more persuasive simply by adding these figures—repetitions that become amplification in the spoken realm, inflaming and capturing the listeners' minds. Composers added these and other figures to poems to enhance the persuasive quality of the affections expressed in the poems, and singers skilled in recognizing the purpose of these devices based their style of delivery on them. Hence, a knowledge of rhetorical structure was prerequisite to eloquent delivery.

The lute songs of the early seventeenth century represent some of the loftiest and most affective musical orations of the late Renaissance and frequently take the form of the lover's complaint. Many of them belong either to the great or mighty style, using many vehement exornations (*sententious* figures) of both language and music to inflame the passions, or to the middle style, distinguishing the song with fewer ornaments. Lute songs contain an enormous number of figures, but I will limit my discussion of *elocutio*, for the most part, to those rhetorical and musical figures that singers actually need to make manifest through their style of delivery. Commonly, the amplifications involve reiterations of words or phrases that emphasize the importance of the repeated material. These figures of repetition, the same ones to which Hobbes referred, include not only some of the basic devices with which lute-song composers amplified poems but also the kinds of *sententious* figures Puttenham (1589: 165–68) describes as the most important ones for altering and affecting the ear and the mind of the listener. Puttenham explains why orators employ these devices: "And first of all others your figure that worketh by iteration or repetition of one word or clause doth much alter and affect the eare and also the mynde of the hearer, and therefore is counted a very brave figure both with the Poets and rhetoriciens." The frequent use of *epizeuxis* (*subjunctio*), the immediate restatement of a word or two for greater vehemence (Peacham the Elder 1577: fol. J3r), embodies a compositional decision to stress and thus elicit in the listener the state of mind associated with that word. Hoskins (1599: 126) maintains that orators should not use this figure except in passion, and Peacham (1593: 47–48) further notes that it "may serve aptly to expresse the vehemencie of any affection, whether it be of joy, sorrow, love, hatred, admiration or any such like, in respect of pleasant affections it may be compared to the quaver [eighth note] in Musicke, in respect of sorrow, to a double sigh of the heart, & in respect of anger, to a double stabbe with a weapons point."

Various passages exemplify the procedure. At the opening of John Danyel's song "Griefe keepe within" (1609: no. 9), subtitled "M^rs. M.E. her Funerall teares for the death her husband," the repetition of the word *griefe* draws attention to and establishes the character of the ruling passion. In the unadorned poem, printed at the end of the song, the first line reads "Greefe keep within and scorne to shew but teares." Danyel, however, reiterates the initial word three times, transforming the line from the poetical realm to the world of oration: "Griefe, Griefe, Griefe, Griefe, keepe within and scorn, to shew but teares." If the composer had not intended this new line to have been sung, it would have, to borrow the words of Thomas Hobbes (1637: 118), been "justly condemned" in writing. Nevertheless, rhetoricians permitted this type of repetition in the spoken realm because in discourse repetition becomes amplification. Playwrights often make effective use of the figure. Particularly germane to Danyel's song is a passage from William Shakespeare's *The Tragedie of King Lear* (1623: V, iii, p. 309) in which Lear mourns for the dead Cordelia, heightening the expression of his grief through *epizeuxis*: "Thou'lt come no more, Never, never, never, never, never."

Songwriters frequently expand the notion of *epizeuxis* to include not just one or two words but lengthier phrases. Examples of this type of repetition frequently occur in the songs of many English composers of the early seventeenth century, Dowland using the repetition of the phrases "that nowe lies sleeping" (line 7) of the first verse of "Weepe you no more sad fountaines" (1603: no. 15) and "while she lies sleeping" (line 7) of the second verse to emphasize the reconciling effect that sleep has on a troubled mind:

> Weepe you no more sad fountaines,
>   What need you flowe so fast,
> Looke how the snowie mountaines,
>   Heav'ns sunne doth gently waste.
> But my sunnes heav'nly eyes
>   View not your weeping,
>   That nowe lies sleeping
>   That nowe lies sleeping
> Softly[,] softly[,] now softly lies sleeping.

> Sleepe is a reconciling,
>   A rest that peace begets:
> Doth not the sunne rise smiling,
>   When faire at ev'n he sets,
> Rest you, then rest sad eyes,
>   Melt not in weeping,
>   While she lies sleeping
>   While she lies sleeping
> Softly[,] softly[,] now softly lies sleeping.

Similarly, to continue with the theme of sleep, Thomas Morley repeats the phrase "sleepe then my eyes" in the first two verses of "Sleepe slumbringe eyes give rest unto my cares" (1600: no. 18, line 5) to underscore the importance of sleep for banishing sorrow from one's breast. But in the third verse, the poet suddenly reverses this sentiment when the protagonist realizes that the eyes have become the true partners of unrest. Morley's repetition of "wake then my eyes" (line 5) heightens the contrast between the verses and emphasizes the poet's conclusion:

Sleepe slumbringe eyes give rest unto my cares,
My cares the Infants of my troubled braine,
My cares surprisde, surprisde with Blacke dispaire
Doth the assention of my hopes restraine.
Sleepe then my eyes, sleepe then my eyes O sleepe & take your Reste
To banishe sorrow, to banishe sorrow from a free borne Breste.

My freborne brest borne Free to sorrowes Smarte
Brought in subjection to my wandringe Eye
Whose traytrus sighte conceavd that to my harte,
For which I waile, I sob, I sighe, I Dye.
Sleepe then my eyes, sleepe then my eyes disturbed of quiet reste,
To banishe sorrow, to banish sorrow from my captive breste.

My captive brest stounge by these glistringe starres:
These glistringe starres: the bewty of the skye:
That bright blacke skye which doth the soone beames baine:
From Her sweete comforte on my harts sad eye:
Wake then my eyes, wake then my eyes trewe partners of unreste:
For Sorrow still, for Sorrow still must harboure in my breste.
(1600: no. 18; although listed in the table of contents, the piece is actually missing in this source; the text is reproduced here from Oxford, Christ Church Library, MS. 439, p. 1)

In addition to the pervasive use of *epizeuxis*, the song composers add two other figures of repetition to the poetry they adapt, *anadiplosis* (*reduplicatio*) and *epanalepsis* (*resumptio*). John Dowland employs both of these figures in his setting of the poem "In darknesse let mee dwell" (in his son's volume, R. Dowland 1610: no. 10). Through *anadiplosis*, that is, the repetition of the last word or words of one phrase at the beginning of the next (Peacham the Elder 1577: fol. J3r), the line

The roofe Dispaire to barre all cheerfull light from mee
(see Coprario 1606 no. 4 for the unadorned poem)

becomes

The roofe Dispaire to barre all, all cheerfull light from mee.

In connection with *anadiplosis*, Peacham the Elder (1593: 47) states: "this exornation doth not onely serve to the pleasantnesse of sound, but also to adde a certaine increase in the second member," and John Hoskins (1599: 126) comments: "and as noe man is sicke in thought upon one thinge, but for some vehemency or distresse, Soe in speech there is noe repeticion without importance." Rhetoricians called the device Dowland used to conclude the song *epanalepsis* and defined this figure as a sentence that begins and ends with the same word (Peacham the Elder 1593: 46). Although Peacham warns writers not to place too many members or words between the beginning and the end, Dowland expands this traditional notion of *epanalepsis* and applies the figure to an entire verse. The words "In darknesse let mee dwell" open and close the song, and Peacham (1593: 46) clarifies the intent of this figure: "place a word of importance in the beginning of a sentence to be considered, and in the end to be remembered."

Composers did not always have to add figures of repetition to the poetry to turn it into musical discourse, however, for some of the *sententious* figures discussed above, such as *anadiplosis*, as well as other figures, such as *anaphora* (*repetitio*), were part of the poem's original structure. Although English songwriters rarely used *anaphora*, the same word iterated at the beginning of successive sentences (Fraunce 1588: I, ch. 19), John Dowland did employ the figure in the first verse of "Al ye, whom love or fortune hath betraid" (1597: no. 14):

> Al ye, whom love or fortune hath betraid;
> All ye, that dream of blisse but live in griefe;
> All ye, whose hopes are evermore delaid;
> All ye, whose sighes or sicknesse wants reliefe;
> Lend eares and teares to mee most haplesse man,
> That sings my sorrowes like the dying Swanne.

This figure serves to delight the ear as well as the mind of the listener. The property of both poets and orators, its use becomes at once both *auricular* and *sententious*. Hoskins (1599: 127) comments on the efficacy of *anaphora*: "this figure beates uppon one thing to cause the quicker feeling in the audience, & to awake a sleepie or dull person." The same duality of function occurs in *anadiplosis*, and this figure can be found in a number of poems, where composers frequently employ it as a link to establish the logical connection between two ideas. Morley includes the figure in the first verse of "Sleepe slumbringe eyes" to draw attention to the ideas associated with the word "surprisde" (line 3):

> Sleepe slumbringe eyes give rest unto my cares,
> My cares the Infants of my troubled braine
> My cares surprisde, surprisde with Blacke dispaire.
> (for similar examples from the works of Shakespeare, see Joseph 1947: 82–83)

Other types of rhetorical figures woven into the fabric of poems by the poets themselves served to amplify the vehemence of the sentiments expressed. Two figures in particular present themselves in the songs, *auxesis* (*incrementum* or *progressio*) and *synathroismos* (*congeries* or *accumulatio*). *Auxesis* involves ascending by degrees to the top of some matter as "when we make our saying grow and increase by an orderly placing of our words, making the latter word always exceede the former, in force of signifycation. . . . In this fygure, order must be dilligently observed, that stronger may follow the weaker, and the worthyer the lesse worthy" (Peacham the Elder 1577: fol. Q2v). In other words, the poet amplifies the subject through a continuous and unbroken series of steps in which each new word is stronger than the last. It becomes, in short, the "Orators scaling ladder, by which he climeth to the top of high comparison" (Peacham the Elder 1593: 169). Perhaps Dowland's "Come again: sweet love doth now invite" (1597: no. 17) contains the most famous example of this device from the song repertoire:

> Come again: sweet love doth now invite,
> Thy graces that refraine,
> To do me due delight,
> To see, to heare, to touch, to kisse, to die,
> With thee againe in sweetest sympathy.

> Come againe that I may cease to mourne,
> Through thy unkind disdaine:
> For now left and forlorne,
> I sit, I sigh, I weepe, I faint, I die,
> In deadly paine and endlesse miserie.

The fourth line of each verse ascends by degrees to the top of the ladder, both verses using the same structural device to intensify the contrasting sentiments of the poem.

The first verse itemizes the ideal chain of events and the second the painful reality of the situation. The beauty of Dowland's figurative language is that both ladders reach their climax on the word "die," the first verse using the word euphemistically and the second verse using it metaphorically. Dowland further reinforces the antithetical nature of the poem by summarizing the contrasting sentiments of the two verses in the last words of each stanza: "sweetest sympathy" versus "endlesse miserie."[1]

Similar passages occur in other songs. Thomas Morley, for example, employs the same sort of ladder in the second verse of "Sleepe slumbringe eyes" (1600: no. 18, line 4):

> My freborne brest borne Free to sorrowes Smarte
> Brought in subjection by my wandringe Eye
> Whose traytrus sighte conceaved that to my harte,
> For which I waile, I sob, I sighe, I Dye.
> Sleepe then my eyes, disturbed of quiet reste,
> To banishe sorrow From my captive breste.

And Philip Rosseter uses the device to lead the anguish of the speaker's torments from the earthly realm to the celestial in the last line of the first verse of "No grave for woe" (1601: no. 3, line 4):

> No grave for woe, yet earth my watrie teares devoures,
> Sighes want ayre, and burnt desires kind pitties showres,
> Stars hold their fatal course my joyes preventing,
> The earth, the sea, and aire, the fire, the heav'ns vow my tormenting.

Danyel, however, increases the complexity of his figurative language by coupling *auxesis* with *epimone* (*versus intercalaris*), the regular repetition of one phrase at equal distance because that phrase "beareth the whole burden of the song" (Puttenham 1589: 188), to continuously reemphasize the depths of sorrow Mrs. M. E. shows with her "Funerall teares for the death of her husband" (1606: no. 9, last line of each verse):

The first part.

> Greefe keep within and scorne to shew but teares,
> Since Joy can weepe as well as thou:
> Disdaine to sigh for so can slender cares,
> Which but from Idle causes grow.
> Doe not looke forth unlesse thou didst know how

> To looke with thine owne face, and as thou art,
> And onely let my hart,
> That knowes more reason why,
> Pyne, fret, consume, swell, burst and dye.

The second part.

> Drop not myne eyes nor Trickle downe so fast,
> For so you could doe oft before,
> In our sad farewells and sweet meetings past,
> And shall his death now have no more?
> Can niggard sorrow yeld no other store:
> To shew the plentie of afflictions smart,
> Then onely thou poore hart,
> That knowst more reason why,
> Pyne, Fret, Consume, Swell, Burst and Dye.

The third part.

> Have all our passions certaine proper vents,
> And sorow none that is her owne?
> But she must borow others complements,
> To make her inward feelings knowne?
> Are Joyes delights and deathes compassion showne,
> With one lyke face and one lamenting part?
> Then onely thou poore hart
> That know'st more reason why,
> Pyne, Fret, Consume, Swell, Burst, and Dye.

Synathroismos, on the other hand, entails a different type of amplification, one involving "a multiplication or heaping togeather of manye wordes, sygnifyinge dyvers thinges of like nature" (Peacham the Elder 1577: fol. Q2r). John Dowland accumulates many words of the same meaning in "If fluds of teares" (1600: no. 11; lines 5 and 6) in order to reach the same sort of climax that one could achieve through *auxesis*, the main difference being that in *synathroismos* writers attain the effect not through a series of graduated steps but by piling up words (Peacham the Elder 1593: 169):

> If fluds of teares could cleanse my follies past,
> And smoakes of sighes might sacrifice for sinne,

> If groning cries might salve my fault at last,
> Or endles mone, for error pardon win,
> Then would I cry, weepe, sigh, and ever mone,
> Mine errors, fault[s], sins, follies past and gone.

And Robert Jones (1600: no. 2, line 3) heaps together various words to emphasize the folly of youths who make love a god only to be bound by marriage:

> Fond wanton youths make love a God,
> Which after proveth ages rod,
> Their youth, their time, their wit, their arte,
> They spend in seeking of their smarte,
>   And which of follies is the chiefe,
>   They wooe their woe, they wedde their griefe.

Composers were not content, however, merely to decorate the poetry with figures, for although the adornments they added to the texts of songs enhanced the persuasiveness of the poetry, they heightened the passionate appeal of that *sententious* language even more by introducing musical figures to parallel poetic devices. In fact, the ability to combine words and music in this way lies at the heart of song composition, and Thomas Campion (1614: no. 5) captured the essence of the composer's task so perfectly in the passage quoted at the beginning of this section:

> Happy is hee whose words can move,
> Yet sweet Notes help perswasion.
> Mix your words with Musicke then,
> That they the more may enter.

Throughout the entire corpus of early seventeenth-century English lute song, figures of melodic repetition frequently coincide with textual figures, and composers clearly favored *palillogia, synonymia, climax,* and *gradatio,* as well as *articulus,* for setting textual *epizeuxis* and *auxesis.*[2]

Palillogia, the repetition of a melodic fragment at the same pitch (Bartel 1997: 342–44), occurs in John Dowland's "Farewell too faire" (1603: no. 1) for the immediate reiteration of single words (Example 2.1a) and in his setting of Fulke Greville's "Who ever thinks or hopes of love" (1597: no. 2) for the repetition of short phrases (Example 2.1b).

EXAMPLE 2.1 *(a) "Farewell too faire" (Dowland 1603: no. 1); (b) "Who ever thinks or hopes of love" (Dowland 1597: no. 2)*

The rhetorical parallel of this musical device explains its effect. In the language arts, the figure serves to add weight to the idea expressed in the text by emphasizing a particular aspect of its meaning, as "when the word repeated hath another significa-tion" (Peacham the Elder 1577: fol. J2v, Diaphora). Peacham (1577: fol. J2v) supplies an example: "What man is there living, that would not have pitied that case if he had bene a man. In the latter place man signifieth humanitie, or the pittifull affection that is in man." The notion of repetition drawing attention to another meaning associated with the repeated word lies at the heart of the musical device, for an exact repetition of a melodic fragment gives new significance to the repeated material. And when composers couple musical devices with rhetorical figures, they enhance the vehemence of persuasion in a way that would have been impossible for either music or language to achieve on its own. Charles Butler (1636: 97), in discussing the repetition of points ("a Point is a certain number and order of observable Notes in any one Parte, iterated in the same or in divers Partes"; 1636: 71), stresses that melodic repetition increases the listener's understanding of the subject matter of the poem: "If the Points Ditti [words] bee not apprehended at the first; yet, in the iterating thereof, it [the Ditti] may. Such Repetes shoolde bee Emphatical [that is, should be delivered emphatically], importing soom special matter: and which, in Divine uses, may help bothe to excite and to expres due zele and Devotion." By pairing musical *palillogia* with textual *epizeuxis* in "Farewell too faire" and "Who ever thinks or hopes of love," Dowland makes the passages both *auricular* and *sententious*, and this simultaneously delights the ear and affects the mind of the listener.

At other times, composers set the restatement of short phrases and single words by means of *synonymia*, the repetition of a melodic fragment at a different pitch level (but not single steps higher or lower).[3] The rhetorical connotations of this term also help to illuminate the musical function of the figure. In the language arts, *synonymia* specifies a figure designed to make the sense stronger and more obvious by using words that differ from the preceding ones in form or sound but mean the same (Sherry 1550: 49; Peacham the Elder 1577: fol. P4r; Puttenham 1589: 179). George Puttenham (1589: 223) provides an example:

> What is become of that beautifull face,
> Those lovely lookes, that favour amiable,
> Those sweete features, and visage full of grace,
> That countenance which is alonly able
> To kill and cure?

Ye see that all these words, face, lookes, favour, features, visage, countenance, are in sence but all one. Which store, neverthelesse, doeth much beautifie and inlarge the matter.

The parallel between the musical figure and its rhetorical antecedent is obvious. In music, we can view the repetition of a melodic fragment at another pitch level as a composer using notes that mean the same (because the songwriter maintains the intervallic integrity of the fragment) but sound different (because the fragment actually appears on new notes).

In the first verse of "Behold a wonder here" (1603: no. 3, line 3), John Dowland reiterates the word *hundred* to stress the length of time that love had been blind. His decision to use the musical figure *synonymia* at this point draws further attention to the word, and his melodic design duplicates the type of inflection that one might have employed when speaking the line (Example 2.2):

> Behold a wonder here
> Love hath receiv'd his sight
> Which manie hundred yeares,
> Hath not beheld the light.

EXAMPLE 2.2 *"Behold a wonder here" (Dowland 1603: no. 3)*

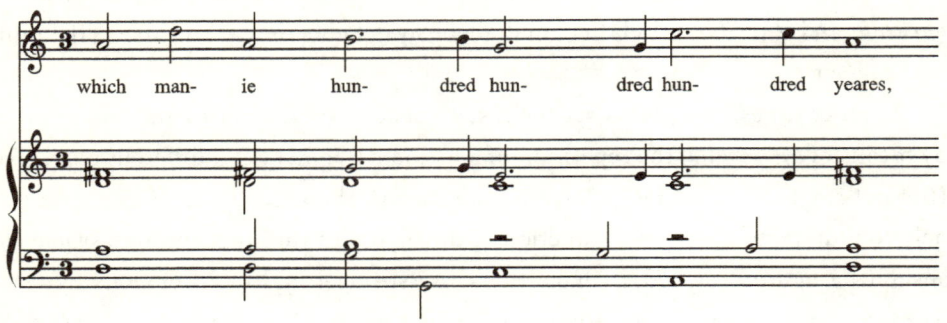

Composers similarly set repeated phrases to *synonymia*, and this frequently provides the *auricular* pleasure that became so much a part of *sententious* language. Such is the case with Francis Pilkington's treatment of Thomas Watson's poem "With fragrant flowers we strew the way" (1605: no. 20). The refrain of this song reads "O gracious King, of second Troy, accept of our unfained joy," and Pilkington chose to highlight the most important words in the refrain, "O gracious King," the words praising James I, through *synonymia* (Example 2.3).

Interestingly, Pilkington arranges his restatements of the melodic figure in a manner similar to John Hoskins' description of another device discussed earlier, the rhetorical figure *auxesis*. In fact, Hoskins' comments (1599: 140) exactly parallel Pilkington's use of musical *synonymia*: "[To] make the matter seem the higher advaunced, sometimes [the figure] descends the lower; it is a bad grace in dancing either to shrinke much in, or sincke farr downe, that you may rise the higher caper, But it is an ornament in speech, to begin att the lowest that you the better aspire to the height of amplyficacion." Pilkington states the melodic idea and then descends "the lower" so that the textual *epizeuxis* may rise to the height of amplification. Once again, a songwriter has made

EXAMPLE 2.3 *"With fragrant flowers we strew the way"* (Pilkington 1605: no. 20)

the figurative language even more persuasive through a combination of musical and rhetorical devices.

When composers arrange the quasi-ladder effect Pilkington created for this passage in a stepwise progression, musical *climax* (*gradatio*) results (Bartel 1997: 220–25). Thomas Wilson (1553: 405–6) defines the figure in rhetoric as one in which "the worde, whiche endeth the sentence goyng before, doeth begin the nexte." His example demonstrates the structure of the device: "Labour getteth learnyng, learnyng getteth fame, fame getteth honour, honour getteth blesse for ever." George Puttenham (1589: 173) expands the notion of this figure, characterizing it as one in which "after the first steppe all the rest proceede by double the space, and so in our speach one word proceedes double to the first that was spoken, and goeth as it were by strides or paces." John Hoskins (1599: 126) also comments on the vehement effect of this figure and states that with *climax* we lead listeners by degrees in which the last word becomes a step to further meaning, and Peacham the Elder (1593: 133–34) reminds the orator that the figure usually consists of three or four degrees and should end with a clause of importance. Indeed, rhetoricians regularly compare the figure to stairs (Wilson 1553: 405), degrees (Peacham the Elder 1577: fol. Q3r), steps (Hoskins 1599: 126), or ladders (Puttenham 1589: 173), and through these carefully graduated increments, the device increases the vehemence of the passions

EXAMPLE 2.4 *(a) "I saw my Ladye weeping" (Morley 1600: no. 5); (b) "Faire, sweet, cruell"
(Ford 1607: no. 7)*

expressed in the text. Musical *climax/gradatio*, then, just like Pilkington's use of *synonymia* in "With fragrant flowers we strew the way," usually begins at the lowest
point and ascends to the top, creating in music the same effect that Hoskins attributes to rhetorical *auxesis*.

But in the lute-song repertoire, composers often reduce the ladder to a single step,
and in order to adapt contemporary terminology to their practices, I employ the term
climax for single repetitions and *gradatio* for extensions of the figure beyond one restatement. Thomas Morley employs single repetitions (*climax*) in "I saw my Ladye weeping"
(1600: no. 5) to emphasize the fairness and perfection of his lady's eyes into which sorrow crept so proudly (Example 2.4a, line 3):

I saw my Ladye weeping,

And sorrowe proud to bee advaunced so,

In those fayre eyes, in those fayre eyes, Where all perfection kept

Her face was full of woe, But such a woe, but such a woe,

Beeleeve mee as winnes mennes heartes,

Then myrth can doo, then mirth can doo with her intising partes.

And Thomas Ford takes full advantage of the technique to heighten the desperation of the speaker in "Faire, sweet, cruell" (1607: no. 7). The repetition of the words "tarrie then" (line 5) leads to the exclamation "Oh tarrie," and the use of *climax* to set "tarrie then, tarrie then" allows the speaker to ascend through a single degree to the emotional outburst that precedes his insistence that his lady take him with her (Example 2.4b):

Faire, sweet cruell, why doest thou flie mee, why dost thou flie me,

Go not, goe not, oh goe not from thy deerest,

Though thou doest hasten I am nie thee

When thou see'mst farre then and I neerest,

 Tarrie then Tarrie then Oh tarrie,

 Oh tarrie then and take me with you.

EXAMPLE 2.5 *(a) "No grave for woe" (Rosseter 1601: no. 3); (b) "Flow my teares" (Dowland 1600: no. 2)*

With musical *gradatio*, however, composers form a true ladder. The purest arrangement of this figure, that is, the one paralleling the rhetorical definition the most closely, can be found in the song repertoire in settings of both textual *epizeuxis* and *auxesis*. Rosseter links the steps together during the graduated climb from earth to heaven (*auxesis*) in "No grave for woe" (1601: no. 3; Example 2.5a), with the last note of one step becoming the first note of the next, and John Dowland employs the same type of ladder to heighten the torturous ascent from tears to sighs and groans and from fear to grief and pain in the third and fourth verses of "Flow my teares" (1600: no. 2; Example 2.5b).

But Thomas Campion uses this pure form of musical *gradatio* to set textual *epizeuxis* in "Mistris since you so much desire" (Rosseter 1601: no. 16; Example 2.6). He chooses obvious words to depict through *gradatio* and musically portrays each step of the ladder as the speaker's lady looks "but a little higher" for the place of Cupid's fire:

> Mistris since you so much desire,
> To know the place of Cupids fire,
> In your faire shrine that flame doth rest,
> Yet never harbourd in your brest,
> It bides not in your lips so sweete

EXAMPLE 2.6 *"Mistris since you so much desire" (Rosseter 1601: no. 16)*

Nor where the rose and lillies meete,

But a little higher,

There there, O there lies Cupids fire.

However, another form of musical *gradatio*, one in which composers did not link the steps of the ladder together but began every new rung on the next scale degree, can be found in the repertoire. Campion, once again, chooses the most obvious words to set to this latter form of rising ladder. In "Sweet exclude mee not" (1613/2: no. 11; Example 2.7), the phrase "yet a little more" receives the same sort of literal treatment as "but a little higher."

EXAMPLE 2.7 *"Sweet exclude mee not" (Campion 1613/2: no. 11)*

One can, of course, traverse a ladder in two directions, and composers did not miss the opportunity to use descending ladders to depict the sense of the poetry. Francis Pilkington's setting of Campion's poem "Now let her change and spare not" (1605: no. 8; Example 2.8) employs downward *gradatio* for the words "but she is gon" (line 5), Pilkington imposing an interpretation on the poem that reflects, perhaps, the sinking realization that the woman who has proved so false is actually gone:

Now let her change and spare not,

Since she proves false I care not,

Fained love so bewitched my delight,

That still I doated on her sight,

But she is gon, New desires imbracing,

And my deserts disgracing.

EXAMPLE 2.8 *"Now let her change and spare not"* (Pilkington 1605: no. 8)

Composers also use *gradatio* to set another sort of repetition, not the repetition of the same word as in *epizeuxis*, but the kind Abraham Fraunce describes as the repetition of like sounds. Fraunce (1588: I, ch. 24) defines this rhetorical figure, *paronomasia* (*allusio*), as one in which "a word is changed in signification by changing of a letter or sillable." Through it, poets juxtapose words similar in sound but different in meaning, and this helps them create the utmost grace in poetry, especially if writers did not use it too often (Peacham the Elder 1593: 56). Robert Jones adorns all three verses of "Whither runneth my sweet hart" (1601: no. 12; Example 2.9) with this device and embeds the figure within either musical *gradatio* or *climax*.

On numerous occasions, composers made the figurative language just discussed even more *sententious* by combining textual *epizeuxis* with *articulus* (*brachylogia*). In rhetoric, *articulus* refers to the separation of "words & clauses one from another, either by distinguishing the sound [with commas], or by separating the sense" (Peacham the Elder 1593: 56). It serves to express any vehement affection, and Peacham the Elder (57) states that "in peaceable and quiet causes it may be compared to a sembreefe [whole note] in Musicke, but in causes of perturbation and hast, it may be likened to thicke & violent strokes." Peacham's equation of *articulus* to the semibreve suggests that semibreves, at least in "peaceable and quiet causes," should be separated from one another by some sort of an articulation. Indeed, certain composers seem to concur with Peacham's observation, for both John Danyel and Robert Jones compose rests into their vocal lines to separate semibreves from other notes when their songs begin with repetitions of the word grief (Example 2.10).

EXAMPLE 2.9 *"Whither runneth my sweet hart"* (Jones 1601: no. 12)

not too	fast,	to much haste	mak-eth	waste,
Daie and	night	I de-	light	in thy	sight,
Now can	I	wil-ling-	ly	wish to	die,

thy	minde	doth binde	so	doth	thy	truth
my	strength	at	length	hath	not	for-	got
come	prove	my	love,	love showne	and	knowne

EXAMPLE 2.10 *(a) "Griefe keepe within"* (Danyel 1606: no. 9); *(b) "Griefe of my best loves absenting"* (Jones 1609: no. 14)

(a)

Griefe,	Griefe,	Griefe,	Griefe,	keep with-in

(b)

Griefe,	griefe	of my	best

At other times, composers combine *articulus* with musical *gradatio* in order to further strengthen the affective power of textual *epizeuxis*. By separating the restatements of a melodic fragment, thereby paralleling commas in the text, a composer can draw further attention to the passion associated with the repeated word. Jones achieves this effect most persuasively in "My love bound me with a kisse" (1601: no. 2; Example 2.11). He momentarily suspends the frivolous nature of the text with a mock-serious exclamatory

outburst of "alas" (line 5) set to a rising *gradatio* of falling thirds, the increasing vehemence of each step of the ladder being accentuated by rests:

> My love bound me with a kisse
> That I should no longer stay
> When I felt so sweete a blisse,
> I had lesse power to part away,
> Alas that women doth not know
> Kisses makes men loath to goe.

EXAMPLE 2.11 *"My love bound me with a kisse" (Jones 1601: no. 2)*

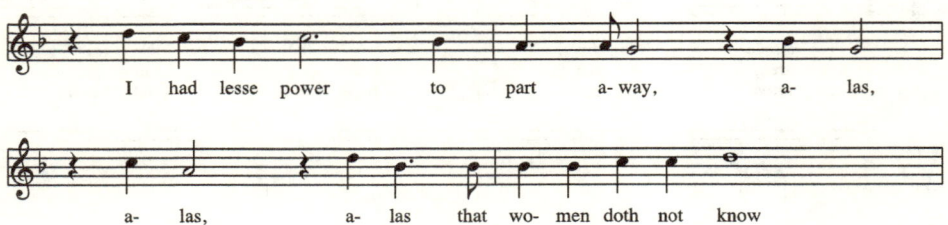

In addition to heightening the passionate appeal of textual *epizeuxis, articulus* plays an
important role in *synathroismos,* and composers sometimes set the accumulated words to
the longer note values of the semibreve (whole note) or minim (half note). This approach
parallels Peacham the Elder's description of the device and affords performers an opportunity to detach each word quite clearly from the rest of the series, thus enabling the listener to reflect momentarily on every idea in the figure. Dowland makes full use of the
rhetorical connotations of semibreves, and by extension minims (half notes) in slower
tempos, to increase the climactic effect of the words "but thinks sighes, teares, vowes,
praiers, and sacrifices" in "Times eldest sonne" (1600: no. 6; Example 2.12a) and the
words "deare, sweet, faire, wise" in "Deare, if you change" (1597: no. 7; Example 2.12b).

   The rhetorical artifice present in the songs of the early seventeenth century does more
than control much of the melodic structure, however, for it influences the very character of
the *concentus,* that is, the vertical combination of notes sounding together. In many songs,
especially those dealing with sorrow, grief, sadness, etc., musical figures involving dissonant elements help establish the ruling passion, thereby enhancing the impact of the text.
In particular, certain composers exploit nonharmonic relations (the *mi-fa* clash of the false
relation or other dissonances between parts; Bartel 1997: 352–56), or in musical-rhetorical
terms *parrhesia* (*licentia*) to express the passions of sorrow and grief. The rhetorical definition of the figure clarifies the parallel between music and the language arts: the use

EXAMPLE 2.12 *(a) "Times eldest sonne" (Dowland 1600: no. 6); (b) "Deare, if you change"* *(Dowland 1597: no. 7)*

(a)

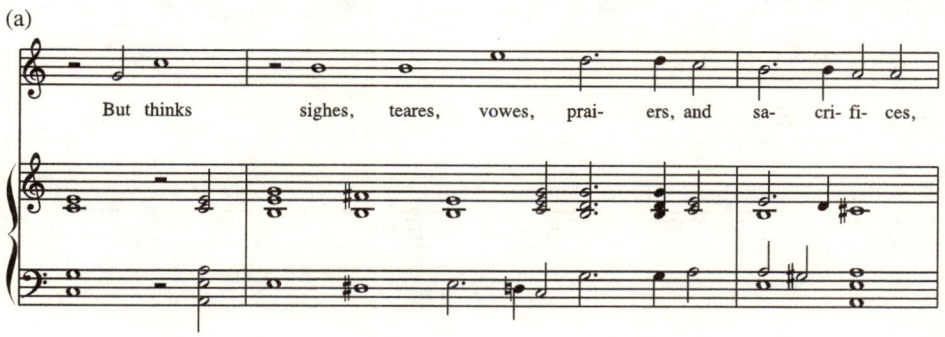

But thinks sighes, teares, vowes, prai- ers, and sa- cri- fi- ces,

(b)

Deare, sweet, faire, wise, change, shrink, nor be not weake:
Earth, heaven, fire, ayre, the world trans- form'd shall view,

of pungent language to reprehend the hearers for some fault (*Rhetorica*: IV, 348–55). Fraunce adds the idea that this figure represents a type of exclamation in which one speaks boldly and confidently (1588: I, ch. 27; similar descriptions appear in Wilson 1553: 396 and Peacham the Elder 1577: fol. M2v). Danyel's three-part song "Griefe keepe within" (1606: no. 9) presents a virtual thesaurus of figures of dissonance both within the lute accompaniment itself and between the lute and voice parts. The highly dissonant nature of the music constantly reminds us of the grief and sorrow Mrs. M. E. feels after the death of her husband. In many passages of the song, Danyel combines musical figures to gener- ate a web of devices that pervade the entire texture. The music for the words "since Joy can weepe as well as thou" (Example 2.13) not only incorporates *gradatio* in the voice part but also includes *parrhesia* (false relations within the voice part itself between C♯ and C, as well as direct dissonance between the voice and the lute, C♯/F). In addition to these two figures, the excerpt contains an unprepared dissonance created by the leap from a consonant note (B in the voice part) to a dissonant one (D), or *heterolepsis* (Bartel 1997: 293–94).

Other passages intensify the rhetorical persuasion using various techniques. For the words "griefe keepe within," Danyel chose to couple *syncope* (a suspension; Bartel 1997: 399–401) with *syncopatio catachrestica* (an irregular resolution of a suspension;

EXAMPLE 2.13 *"Griefe keepe within" (Danyel 1606: no. 9)*

EXAMPLE 2.14 *"Griefe keepe within" (Danyel 1606: no. 9)*

401). The suspended A in the voice part of Example 2.14 resolves not to a consonant note but to a dissonant one, and this helps maintain tension in the vertical sonority. In the second part of the song, Danyel employs *mutatio toni*, an abrupt change in *concentus* for expressive purposes (Bartel 1997: 334–39), to characterize through modal instability the distress that continued suffering causes (Example 2.15, especially the latter portion).

Similar in effect to these rhetorical figures is *pathopoeia (imaginatio)*, a generic term also adopted by *musica poetica* theorists to designate chromaticism (Bartel 1997: 359–62), for two categories of devices that move the minds of listeners to indignation, anger, fear, envy, hatred, hope, gladness, mirth, laughter, sorrow, or sadness. Rhetoricians called the first type imagination, and this category embraced "sharp figures" that stir the sorts of vehement affections found in tragedy, that is, matters considered great, cruel, horrible, marvelous, pleasant, etc. The second type, commiseration, helped orators bring their listeners to tears or move them to pity or forgiveness (Sherry 1550: 68; Peacham the Elder 1577: fol. P3r). In music, composers often set certain of these vehement affections to rising or falling chromatic lines, chromaticism that underlined the torment of words such as woe, bitter grief, sorrow, mists and darkness, and tears[4] (see Example 2.16 for one such setting by Thomas Ford).

EXAMPLE 2.15 *"Griefe keepe within" (Danyel 1606: no. 9)*

EXAMPLE 2.16 *"Goe passions to the cruell faire" (Ford 1607: no. 5)*

The rhetoricians' discussions of *pathopoeia* not only alert us to the rhetorical nature of chromaticism in the song repertoire but also enable us to discover those figures Peacham the Elder considered the most suitable for stirring the vehement affections he describes. He placed *ecphonesis* (*exclamatio*), a device regularly employed in song poetry, at the head of his list of "sharp figures" and characterized it as follows: "when through affection either of anger, sorrow, gladnesse, marveyling, feare, or any such lyke, we break out in voyce with an exclamation, & outcry to express the passions of our minde, after this manner. O lamentable estate, O cursed misery, O wicked impudency,

O joy incomparable, O rare and singuler bewty" (1577: fol. K4r). George Puttenham (1589: 177) reinforces Peacham's description of the figure, advising that all words showing extreme passion embody such outcries, and Abraham Fraunce (1588: I, ch. 27) gives us a list of the range of affections the figure covers: wonder and admiration, despair, wishing, indignation, derision, protestation or obtestation, grief and misery, pity and commiseration, and cursing. Peacham (1593: 63) cautions, however, that speakers should not use *ecphonesis* too often lest it becomes odious. Most of the sentences containing these emotional outbursts, as illustrated by Peacham's examples given above, begin with an exclamatory "O!" or "Alas!" Composers usually set this opening interjection to the longer notes of the semibreve (whole note), the dotted minim (half note), or the minim, Dowland favoring the dotted minim or semibreve and other composers preferring the minim. These longer notes, particularly dotted minims and semibreves, draw attention to the exclamatory interjection and allow singers time to color the note dynamically (Example 2.17).

EXAMPLE 2.17 *"Sweet stay a while" (Dowland 1612: no. 2)*

Related to *pathopoeia* and *ecphonesis*, with their vivid depiction of vehement affections, is another figure, the music theorist's *hypotyposis* (*demonstratio*), which acts as a generic term for any musical device that illustrates the text in a literal fashion (Bartel 1997: 307–11). Composers often use this sort of pictorial representation in the song repertoire, setting words referring to rising and height or sinking and lowness to melodies moving either up (*anabasis*) or down (*catabasis*; Bartel 1997: 179–80, 214–15). In addition, they depict sighs through rests and occasionally set words such as relish, words that also designate musical ornaments, to written-out forms of the embellishments.[5] Robert Jones' setting of "now up now downe" typifies the approach (Example 2.18).

EXAMPLE 2.18 *"When love on time"* (*Jones 1600: no. 9*)

But composers can, of course, vividly portray poetry in much subtler ways, and John Dowland perfectly blends music and rhetoric at the close of "In darknesse let mee dwell" (in his son's volume, R. Dowland 1610: no. 10). In rhetorical delivery, orators can demonstrate their emotional state most vehemently if they terminate a speech without a word of explanation, as if their sorrow had become too great to continue (Peacham the Elder 1577: fol. N1v). Dowland brilliantly constructs "In darknesse let mee dwell" to produce this effect (Example 2.19). Textual and musical *epanalepsis* conclude the song, and the melody Dowland fashions for this purpose ends unexpectedly with a remarkably short resolution of the prolonged *syncope* (music theorists called the extension of a dissonance beyond the normal expectation *prolongatio*; see Bartel 1997: 371–72). This hasty abandonment of the last note of the song creates the musical counterpart of *aposiopesis*, the rhetorical figure denoting abrupt terminations.

EXAMPLE 2.19 *"In darknesse let mee dwell"* (*R. Dowland 1610: no. 10*)

Up to this point, I have concentrated on passages from the songs in which composers chose to augment the persuasive qualities of a text's rhetorical language with
musical devices. But songwriters did not always further the effect of textual figures
through compositional procedures, particularly when a figure, such as *auxesis*, appears
in a second or third verse but not in the first. Thomas Morley's "Sleepe slumberinge
eyes" (1600: no. 18), for example, contains the textual *auxesis* discussed earlier only in
the second verse, and undoubtedly few composers would have missed the opportunity
for setting this figure to musical *gradatio*. But since Morley seems to have conceived
his music in terms of the first verse, he could not provide special musical treatment for
figures appearing in later verses. His song, then, lends support to my belief that many
composers wrote their music to suit the first verse and rarely worried about the appropriateness of that music for subsequent verses. And one certainly observes this same
phenomenon in many other strophic songs. Textual figures in first verses frequently
receive detailed musical figuration, so detailed in fact that later verses often fit the music
most imperfectly. In John Dowland's "O sweet woods" (1600: no. 10; Example 2.20),
the seventh line of the first verse reads "to birds, to trees, to earth, impart I this," and
Dowland appropriately parallels the textual *articulus* with rests in the melody. This melody is, however, most unsuitable for the remaining three verses, for in conceiving the
corresponding lines of these verses as longer continuous phrases, the halting effect of
the rests in his melody interrupts the forward motion.[6]

EXAMPLE 2.20   *"O sweet woods" (Dowland 1600: no. 10)*

Thomas Campion's work presents a notable exception to this practice, for in
some of his songs he conceived the poetry and music in such a way that in all verses,
to borrow his frequently quoted phrase, the words and notes have been coupled
lovingly together (1613/1: "To the reader"). In "Author of light" (1613/1: no. 1;
Example 2.21), for example, the music works as well for the second verse as it does
for the first.

EXAMPLE 2.21 *"Author of light" (Campion 1613/1: no. 1)*

For blinde, for blinde with world- ly vaine
the faint, the faint and fad- ing hart
are mists and dark- nesse being com- par'd to thee.
and their sharp paines and griefe in time as- suage.

But, of course, Campion set his own poetry to music, which might explain the difference between his songs and those of his compatriots, whereas other composers, especially if Robert Jones' statement regarding his willingness "to embrace the conceits of such gentlemen as were earnest to have me apparell these [i.e., their] ditties for them" (1600: "To the reader") represents the norm, often set poems written by anonymous courtiers and did not have the luxury of conceiving their poetry and music simultaneously.

Interestingly, the songbooks also contain works in which the music seems to have been composed with the second verse in mind instead of the first—exactly the opposite situation to that found in "O sweet woods." In Dowland's setting of the poem "The lowest trees have tops" (1603: no. 19; Example 2.22), ascribed to Sir Edward Dyer (on the various ascriptions for this poem, see Doughtie 1970: 520–21), the second verse and not the first clearly inspired the music for the final line of each stanza. The rising *gradatio* perfectly suits the words "they heare, and see, and sigh," but the corresponding words in the first verse "and love is love in beggers" would not have suggested to early seventeenth-century composers, I believe, the *gradatio* figure punctuated by *articulus*.

However, the songs do contain a number of musical figures for which no parallel textual devices exist, and although rhetoric and music were sister arts in the late

EXAMPLE 2.22 *"The lowest trees have tops" (Dowland 1603: no. 19)*

Renaissance, the presence of these figures reminds us that composers considered some musical devices as *auricular* rather than *sententious*. In other words, songwriters did not always couple musical and rhetorical figures every time the opportunity arose. John Dowland, for instance, occasionally employed musical *climax* not to underscore textual *epizeuxis*, one of the most common uses of *climax*, but simply to set the first two lines of "When others sings Venite exultemus" (1600: no. 8; Example 2.23) to the same musical phrase repeated one step higher.

EXAMPLE 2.23 *"When others sings Venite exultemus" (Dowland 1600: no. 8)*

And just as composers use musical figures for their own sake, as in Example 2.23, textual devices do not always receive support from their musical counterparts. *Epizeuxis*, for example, finds no further help in Dowland's "I saw my Lady weepe" (1600: no. 1; Example 2.24), and he also overlooked *anaphora*, an obvious choice for strengthening the persuasiveness of the reiterated words through the repetition of the same melodic fragment, in "Al ye, whom love or fortune hath betraid" (1597: no. 14; see the song text given above).

EXAMPLE 2.24 *"I saw my Lady weepe" (Dowland 1600: no. 1)*

Nonetheless, to a greater or lesser degree (perhaps corresponding to higher or lower styles), the vast majority of songs from this era do "fit the Note to the Word" (Jones 1600: "To the Reader"), enjoying a coupling of music and rhetoric worthy of Campion's remarks, quoted at the outset, which act as a proposition for this whole section. Peacham the Elder (1577: fol. S2v) asserts that with *propositio* (*prolepsis*) we state in a "few wordes the summe of that matter, whereof we presently intend to speake":

> Happy is hee whose words can move,
> Yet sweet Notes help perswasion.
> Mixe your words with Musicke then,
> That they the more may enter.
>
> (1614: no. 5)

The discussion of these songs through rhetorical concepts and terminology—the precepts most relevant to the vocal music of this era—helps modern musicians not accustomed to the principles of rhetoric acquire the necessary tools for identifying the significance of musical procedures they might otherwise pass over. Moreover, the knowledge of the musical-rhetorical structure of the song repertoire provides singers today with the same skills sixteenth- and seventeenth-century vocalists would have possessed, and the ability to recognize technical devices enables performers to construct an appropriate framework within which to place their intuitive emotional responses to the songs. Once singers understand the purpose of figures, they can then generate in listeners the passions present in the text. In this regard, performers might wish to bear in mind the words of Henry Peacham the Elder (1577: fol. A3r) that I quoted earlier: "the force of figures is so great, that the strength of apt and eloquent pleading and speaking, consisteth (sayeth Fabius) in these kinde of exornations." Thus, we probably should use our knowledge of rhetorical devices to help us inflame and capture the minds and hearts of our listeners. The following discussion of the methods for delivering figurative language will familiarize singers with the techniques that form the basis of singing with a passionate voice.

NOTES

1. Dowland appears to have supplied two separate poems for the song, one with two verses and the other with four. All the printed editions of *The First Booke of Songes or Ayres* (1597, 1600, 1603, 1606, and 1613) number the verses 1, 2 and 1, 2, 3, 4 (note, however, that the Giles Earle Songbook [British Library, MS Add. 24665, p. 22] numbers the verses from 1 to 6). The two poems are complete within themselves and express distinct but related sentiments. In the first poem (given above), the speaker dies metaphorically in the second verse. It makes little sense, therefore, for the poem to continue. The other poem, however, presents a new story, Dowland contrasting the first two verses "all the day" and "all the night." Structurally, the last two lines of each verse in this second poem differ considerably from the equivalent lines in the first poem. *Auxesis* is not present in the penultimate lines, and the ultimate lines contain eight syllables instead of ten. Dowland's reason for including two poems remains obscure, unless of course he simply wanted to supply a longer, alternate poem for those who wished more verses to sing. The second poem appears below.

> All the day the sun that lends me shine,
> By frownes doth cause me pine,
> And feeds mee with delay:
> Her smiles, my springs, that makes my joyes to grow,
> Her frownes the winters of my woe:
>
> All the night my sleepes are full of dreames,
> My eyes are full of streames.
> My heart takes no delight,
> To see the fruits and joyes that some do find,
> And marke the stormes are mee assignde.
>
> Out alas, my faith is ever true,
> Yet will she never rue,
> Nor yeeld me any grace:
> Her eyes of fire, her heart of flint is made,
> Whom teares, nor truth may once invade.
>
> Gentle love draw forth thy wounding dart,
> Thou canst not peerce her heart.
> For I that doe approve,
> By sighs and teares more hot then are thy shafts,
> Did tempt while she for triumph laughs.

2. Various *musica poetica* theorists assign rhetorical terms to somewhat divergent musical procedures, and no standardized definitions of either rhetorical or rhetorical-musical figures appear to have existed in the sixteenth and seventeenth centuries. On the surface, then, some of the connections between rhetorical and musical definitions can seem tenuous (see Vickers 1984 for a discussion of what he considers, too harshly in my view, as several problems). But if one searches carefully, useful rhetorical parallels do emerge, and in those cases where close connections exist, the rhetorical background of the musical procedure often helps to clarify the intent of the musical device. I will cite, therefore, those musical and rhetorical definitions that seem to be the most closely related. Unfortunately, we do not know which rhetorical definitions music theorists might have been acquainted with, and this forces me to supply a suitable definition without being able to prove that the music theorist in question actually was aware of that definition. Moreover, I derive many of the explanations of musical figures from treatises written in Germany. Nevertheless, my study proceeds on an empirical basis, for even though a fairly large number of musical-rhetorical devices were defined in late sixteenth- and early seventeenth-century English treatises (nineteen are listed in Butler 1980), the definitions of certain figures present in English lute songs are found only in foreign treatises, particularly those from Germany. The authors of some of these documents, such as Joachim Burmeister and Johannes Nucius, were contemporary with the lute-song repertoire, whereas others, such as Christoph Bernhard, were not.

3. Walther (1708: II, 6, 158) mentions *synonymia* but does not define it, referring the reader to Johann G. Ahle's *Musikalisches Sommer-Gespräche* (1697) for elaboration. Ahle, however, gives only a rhetorical definition of the term (see Bartel 1997: 405–8), but the musical equivalent is encountered frequently in the early seventeenth-century lute-song repertoire. Therefore, in following the practices of contemporary theorists, I apply the rhetorical term to an analogous compositional technique, bringing my use of the term into line with that established in Bartel 1997.

4. For woe, see Dowland (1612: nos. 10, 15); for bitter grief, see Campion (1613/2: no. 21); for sorrow, see Ford (1607: no. 5; Example 2.16); for mists and darkness, see Campion (1613/1: no. 1); and for tears, see Dowland (1597: no. 14).

5. For depictions of rising, see Danyel (1606: no. 19); Jones (1600: no. 9; and 1601: nos. 1, 18, 21). For representations of falling, see Danyel (1606: no. 10); Dowland (1600: nos. 2, 3; and 1612: no. 19); and Jones (1600: no. 21). For depictions of sighs, see Dowland (1612: no. 10); Jones (1605: no. 7; and 1609: no. 17). Danyel imitates the relish in 1606 no. 4.

6. For another example of the inappropriateness of the music for later verses of strophic songs, see the discussion of Dowland's "His golden locks" (1597: no. 18) in the section "All the Senses Satisfied" in Part 3 of this book.

PRONUNCIATIO: SINGING ELOQUENTLY AND ACTING APTLY

The Art of Vocal Delivery

So sweet is thy discourse:
please the Eye, charm the Ear, and move the Passions

(Campion 1618/4: no. 6/Le Faucheur 1657: 37)

FOUR HUNDRED YEARS AGO, COMPOSERS DID NOT NOTATE SUBTLETIES OF rhythm, phrasing, dynamics, pauses, accents, emphases, tempo changes, or ornamentation. Clearly, they had no desire (or need) to capture on paper the elements of performance that moved listeners in the ways described by Castiglione, Poliziano, Praetorius, and Vicentino (see the Introduction for the appropriate passages). But if we wish to inflame the hearts and minds of our listeners in a similar fashion, we probably should approach their music along the lines period writers suggested. We can then use the knowledge of sixteenth-century performing style we acquire from the wide range of documents that transmit Renaissance musical culture to us as the basis for our own personalizations of both solo and part songs.

Sixteenth-century performers persuaded their auditors through a style of delivery comprising two principal parts—singing eloquently and acting aptly (adapted from Wright 1604: 172). Using both voice and gesture, the external signs of internal affections, singers made their passions manifest by appealing to the ears and the eyes of listeners, the two sensory organs through which affections penetrated the soul (Quintilian: XI, 248–51). But to capture the minds of others successfully, performers had to discover what passions the song contained and use the textual and musical figures with which the music had already been adorned to help them make the imaginary person in the poem actually seem to appear before the listener. Their style of performing, then, had to suit the emotions of the poem perfectly, for they considered persuasive delivery the fundamental goal of both spoken and musical oration.[1]

Thomas Wilson (1553: 431) defined *pronunciatio* (delivery or utterance) as "an apte orderinge bothe of the voyce, countenaunce, and all the whole bodye, accordynge to the worthines of suche woordes and mater as by speache are declared." The mastery of utterance had become one of the primary functions of sixteenth-century education in the language arts, and training in delivery, educators maintained, should begin early, John Brinsley (1622: 55) insisting that in grammar schools pronunciation be taught in the lowest forms. Brinsley (1612: 213) also recommended that students apply the same principles of delivery to poetry and prose: "so in all Poetry, for the pronuntiation, it is to be uttered as prose; observing distinctions and the nature of the matter; not to bee tuned foolishly or childishly after the manner of scanning a Verse as the use of some is." Moreover, prospective orators needed to practice, for both nature and art required regular exercise to transform students into potent persuaders (Wright 1604: 183). Pupils should select good masters with whom to study and bear in mind that the "*Rules of this Art... are far more magnificent in Practice than in Praecept*" (Le Faucheur 1657: 207–8).[2]

The road to excellence, then as now, must have been arduous, for one of the basic methods of perfecting delivery was to repeat a sentence over and over until the speaker could pronounce it "according to *Art*" (Le Faucheur 1657: 214). In fact, teachers in England encouraged Elizabethan and Jacobean schoolchildren to study *prosopopoeias*, exclamations, and the like when practicing the imitation of affections (Brinsley 1612: 213–14), for these texts demanded a passionate manner of declamation, Thomas Wright (1604: 175) underscoring the importance of employing voice and gesture to bring forth the emotions of the text:

> Furthermore, the passion passeth not only thorow the eyes, but also pierceth the eare, and thereby the heart; for a flexible and plyable voyce, accommodated in manner correspondent to the matter whereof a person intreateth, conveyeth the passion most aptly, pathetically, & almost harmonically, & every accent, exclamation, admiration, increpation, indignation, commiseration, abhomination, exanimation, exultation, fitly (that is, distinctly, at time and place, with gesture correspondent, and flexibilitie of voice proportionate) delivered, is either a flash of fire to incense a passion, or a bason of water to quench a passion incensed.

Thus, communicators moved the affections of listeners through two closely related channels, the subject matter itself, perceived by the ears, and the action of the person concerned, seen with the eyes (Wilson 1553: 266).

But, of course, these channels worked effectively to stir the minds of others only when the orator/singer first became moved by the passions in the text, for as Thomas Wright (1604: 172) commented, "it is almost impossible for an Orator to stirre up a

Passion in his auditors, except he bee first affected with the same passion himselfe." In the same vein, Thomas Wilson (1553: 273), writing under the heading "Heate, causeth heate," believed that "nothyng kyndeleth soner then fire. And therefore a fierie stomack, causeth evermore a fierie tongue. And he that is heated with zeale and godlinesse, shall set other on fire with like affeccion." He even suggested that in representing grief the orator actually should weep: "Again, nothyng moysteth soner then water. Therefore a wepyng iye causeth muche moysture, and provoketh teares. Neither is it any mervaile: for suche men bothe in their countenaunce, tongue, iyes, gesture, and in all their body els, declare an outwarde grief, and with wordes so vehemently and unfeinedly, settes it forward, that thei will force a man to be sory with them, and take part with their teares, even against his will" (273–74). Wilson did not advocate anything new, for in the first century A.D. Quintilian admitted that he often was moved to tears when speaking: "I have frequently been so much moved while speaking, that I have not merely been wrought upon to tears, but have turned pale and shown all the symptoms of genuine grief"/"Frequenter motus sum, ut me non lacrimae solum deprehenderent, sed pallor et veri similis dolor" (trans. in VI, 439). But one should not dwell too long in such affections, for "though a vehement talke maie move teares, yet no arte can long hold theim. For as Cicero doth saie, nothyng drieth soner, then teares, especially when we lament another mans cause, and be sory with him for his sake" (Wilson 1553: 274).

Given these remarks, we can easily understand what later writers, such as Wright (1604: 179), meant when they suggested prospective orators observe people "appassionate," taking note of "how they demeane themselves in passions, and observe what and how they speake in mirth, sadnesse, ire, feare, hope, &c, what motions are stirring in the eyes, hands, bodie, &c." Orators, it would seem, should imitate real life, but in doing so Wright also recommended tempering excessive behavior with prudence. Wright's attitude finds precedence in Quintilian (XI, 276–77), who said that true emotion, such as grief, anger, and indignation, lacks art and needs to be formed by methodical training. Both William Shakespeare and Michel Le Faucheur confirm Wright's contention. Shakespeare describes moderation in acting in *The Tragedie of Hamlet* (1623: III, ii, 266):

> For in the verie Torrent, Tempest, and (as I may say) the Whirle-winde of Passion, you must acquire and beget a Temperance that may give it Smoothnesse. . . . Sute the Action to the Word, the Word to the Action, with this speciall observance: That you ore-step not the modestie of Nature; for any thing so over-done, is from the purpose of Playing, whose end both at the first and now, was and is, to hold as 'twer the Mirrour up to Nature; to shew Vertue her owne Feature, Scorne her owne Image, and the verie Age and Bodie of the Time, his forme and pressure.

Similarly, Le Faucheur (1657: 31, 76) maintained that one should use *"plausible Pronunciation and Gesture"* because *"pronunciation* ought to be *natural,* and we must do as *Nature* dictates: For the nearer it comes up to *Nature,* the more *perfect* it is; and the further off from it, the more *vicious."*

In other words, orators, and singers for that matter, imagined themselves to be in the situation of the person they represented, uttering the very same words the person would have said. Moreover, speakers and singers learned to model their external actions on people "appassionate" so that voice and gesture could unite to portray the thoughts and emotions of their texts convincingly. John Brinsley (1612: 212) encapsulates the approach as follows: "cause them to utter every dialogue lively, as if they themselves were the persons which did speake in that dialogue, & so in every other speech, to imagine themselves to have occasion to utter the very same things." But as no one could imitate real life truly effectively by reading aloud from a book, orators spoke from memory, freeing themselves from the written page in order to concentrate on matching the style of delivery to the affections contained in their texts.[3] By the middle of the sixteenth century, the connection between oratory and singing in this regard had been made explicit: "when music is sung from memory, it will be much more pleasing than when it is sung from the leaves of books. Take the example of preachers and orators, for if they recited their sermons and orations from the written page, they would have neither the favor nor the appreciation of the audience"/"quando la Musica sarà cantata alla mente sarà molto più gratiata, che quando sarà cantata sopra le carte, & si piglierà l'essempio dalli predicatori, & da gli Oratori, che si recitassero quella predica, et quella oratione, sopra una carta scritta quelli non havriano ne gratia, ne audienza grata" (Vicentino 1555: IV, 42, fol. 94v; see also the quotation from Vicentino given in the Introduction, "An Age of Rhetorical Persuasion").

ALL THE SENSES SATISFIED

Within the two subdivisions of *pronunciatio,* speaking eloquently (voice) and acting aptly (gesture), orators considered the voice the more important intermediary between speaker and listener, for as Quintilian states (XI, 250–51, 276–79) orators even adapted their gesture to it. Because of this preeminence, treatises on rhetoric often devoted a great deal of space to the voice, and in keeping with traditional teaching in both rhetoric and music, the first aspect of the voice that deserves our attention concerns the techniques by which orators, as well as singers, articulated the structure of their discourses so that listeners could easily comprehend the thoughts and emotions of the texts.

Orators considered distinctions or points (punctuation) vital to an effective delivery, and writers throughout the period regularly referred to the important role distinctions played in both speaking and singing. Johannes Galliculus (1538: fol. Bviii), for instance, commented on the necessity of punctuation for ensuring comprehension of both written and sung texts:

> Since in constructing a discourse, it is necessary to make certain silent distinctions [pauses], in order for the listener to comprehend the diverse closes, and likewise he who speaks, takes breath, greatly sharpening his delivery, it is also necessary to do the same in singing.

> Etenim, ut in sermonis ductu, necesse est fieri quasdam silentij distinctiones, cum ut auditor intelligat clausularum diversitatem, tum etiam ut is qui loquitur, captato spiritu, maiori acrimonia pronunciet. Idem quoque faciamus oportet in cantionibus.

Giovanni del Lago (1540: 40) concurred, linking spoken and sung distinctions:

> Cadences truly are necessary and not arbitrary (as some people inadvisedly say), especially in song composed on words. And through them the parts of the oration are distinguished; that is, one makes the pause of the comma, colon, and period so that the sense of the parts of the oration can be understood perfectly, whether in verse or in prose. The cadence is like a stop, or rather a certain distinction and rest in the melody, or to be more precise, the cadence is a termination of a [particular] part of the melody, as is the middle distinction and full stop in the context of an oration. . . . And take heed, then, to make cadences where a part of the oration, that is, a member, finishes, and not always in the same place, for the proper location of the cadences is where the sense, in the context of the words, ends, because it is a convenient thing for the words and the notes to reach, and likewise, to finish together at a pause.

> La cadentie veramente sono necessarie, et non arbitrarie, come alcuni inconsideratamente dicono, massimamente nel canto composto sopra le parole. Et questo per distinguere le parti di la oratione, cioe far la distintione del comma, et cola, et del periodo accio che sia intesa la sententia delle parti della oratione perfetta, si nel verso, come nella prosa, perche la cadentia e come il punto, overo una certa distintione et riposo nel canto, overo la cadentia e una terminatione di essa parte del canto come e nel contesto dell'oratione, la media distintione et la finale . . . et avertite di far le cadentie, dove la parte dell'oratione, overo il membro finisce, et non sempre in un medesimo luoco, perche il luoco proprio delle cadentie e, dove finisce la sententia del contesto delle parole, perche glie cosa conveniente tendere et parimente insieme finire la distintione, et delle parole, et delle notule.

Somewhat later, Francis Clement (1587: 24–25) used the words "the breath is relieved, the meaning conceived, the eye directed, the eare delited, and all the senses satisfied" to characterize the importance of pointing, while other writers, such as Thomas Heywood, echoed Galliculus and Lago. Heywood (1612: fol. c3v) felt that if orators wished to speak well and with judgment, they needed to heed, among other things, commas, colons, full points, parentheses, breathing spaces, and distinctions. The proper pronunciation of pauses, then, eloquently organized and paced the delivery of ideas and emotions, and when orators modeled their style of articulation on people "appassionate," that is, on the speech of someone in an appropriate state of mind, they could move the affections of listeners through the "good delivery of words" (Greene 1615: 18). Eloquent singing also relied on a skillful application of pauses to satisfy the senses, for according to Johann Vogelsang (1542: fol. Ev), the "artistic omission of sound" had been "invented both for the rest and breathing of singers and for the sweetness of song"/"Pausa, Est artificiosa vocis omissio. Inventa, tum ad cantantium quietem, respirationemque, tum ad cantus suavitatem."

The term *distinction* encompassed a number of symbols and usually consisted of these elements[4]:

1. *Comma/subdistinctio/*subdistinction or the rest [,]
2. *Semicolon/semi-media distinctio/*imperfect colon [;]
3. *Colon/media distinctio/*middle distinction or the joint [:]
4. *Periodus/plena ac perfecta distinctio* or *comprehentio/*full and perfect distinction or the point [.]
5. *Interrogatio/*interrogation or the asker [?]
6. *Admiratio/*admiration or exclamation or the wonderer [!]
7. *Parenthesis/interpositio/*interlocution or the closer [()]

Speakers pronounced the comma, the shortest rest in reading (Clement 1587: 25; Hart 1569: fol. 40v), with a little pause, taken with or without breath (Granger 1616: fol. 03v), that lasted about the time of a crotchet (quarter note; Hart 1551: 157). This pause allowed listeners a brief moment to reflect on what had just been said, for it signified that the sentence was unfinished, momentarily suspending the sense in a such a way that the ideas which follow ought presently to succeed. The *colon*, a longer pause than the comma, gave the expectation that much more remained to be spoken and divided the sentence into equal or nearly equal principal parts (Clement 1587: 25). Grammarians compared its value, roughly double that of the *subdistinctio*, to the minim (half note; Hart 1551: 160). Charles Butler (1633: 58, 59) suggested that unlike the comma, which required no change in tone of voice (that is, pitch inflection and volume), the colon called for the speaker to deliver the last word just before the colon with a tone of voice that falls below its ordinary level (Butler's discussion of *ecphonesis* makes it clear that the phrase "tone of voice" includes both pitch and volume; see below for a discussion of *ecphonesis*). Grammarians described the semicolon, on the other hand, as an imperfect colon indicating a pause somewhat longer than a comma but shorter than the colon itself, and like the comma it did not require a change in the tone of voice (Butler 1633: 59). Speakers used the *periodus* when sentences were fully and perfectly finished (Clement 1587: 25–26), and such a pause gave listeners enough time to "resolve in minde [that is, reflect on] the summe of the whole period [sentence]" (Granger 1616: fol. 04r). Moreover, John Smith (1657: postscript) cautions that this pause should not be shorter than the ear expects, and Butler (1633: 58) advises that the tone of voice should fall on the last word and be followed by a long pause.

Speakers considered interrogation and exclamation as additions to the period, interrogation denoting a question and exclamation being used when a sentence, to borrow the words of John Hart (1551: 160), "cometh by a sodein and great moving, of the vital and lively powers: by wondring or fearing, by myrth, sorow or anger, which are interjections: as O! phi! alas! and ho!" To this list of affections suitable for exclamatory delivery may be added admiration, indignation, exoptation, desperation, exultation, lamentation, terror, and commiseration (Butler 1633: 61). Hart (1551: 160) maintains that both interrogations and exclamations begin sharply (loudly) and end in a lower tune (pitch and volume), according to the length of the sentence. And even when these types of sentences contain only one word, they still should be delivered sharply. In contrast, sentences ending with a normal full point must not have had their opening words uttered sharply, for Hart (1569: 200) contends "their tunes [that is, the pitch and volume of interrogations and exclamations] doe differ from our other maner of pronunciation at the beginning of the sentence." Butler (1633: 61) concurs:

> Ecphonesis [exclamation] falleth as a period, and raiseth the tone in the particle of Exclamation, [o, oh, ah, alas, fie upon, out upon:] or, for want of such, in soom Emphatical woord: and always requireth a louder sound; and, when it maketh perfect sens, pauseth as a Period: ... Erotesis [interrogation], ... if it begin with a woord interrogative; as, [who, what, how, where, when, why, &c;] it falleth as a Period, and raiseth the tone in the Interrogative: as *Luk* 17, 17. Were there not ten clensed: but where are the nine?

He also maintains (1633: 60–61) that when interrogation is "urging" or "earnest Avouching the contrari," such as in the phrases "Ar yee so without understanding also?" ("urging") and "Can the blinde lead the blinde: shall they not bothe fall into the ditch?" ("earnest Avouching the contrari"), the speaker strains the sound of the voice throughout the whole interrogation. Parenthesis, on the other hand, enabled writers to insert some other matter into a sentence, almost as an aside, so short that its omission would not harm the sense of the rest of the sentence. Speakers would differentiate the bracketed words from the other parts of the sentence through their tone of pronunciation, Richard Mulcaster (1582: 167) suggesting that one deliver parenthetical phrases with a lower (pitch and volume) and quicker voice. Butler (1633: 32) corroborates Mulcaster's observation, commenting that "parenthesis is wholly sounded with a lower voice."

Undoubtedly, educated classes in Renaissance society valued a good knowledge of punctuation (pointing being fundamentally important to speaking and writing well), and as we have seen, numerous writers disclose the parallels between grammatical and musical punctuation. In a discussion of distinctions for both ditti (words) and harmony, Charles Butler (1636: 97), like earlier continental writers, equated rests and cadences in music to the punctuation used in writing and oratory. For just as poets distinguish the ditti with points (period, colon, semicolon, and comma), he begins, so do composers distinguish the harmony with pauses and cadences. Semibreve (whole note) rests, one or more, correspond to a period or colon, whereas minim (half note) and crotchet (quarter note) rests equate to semicolons, commas, breathings, and sighs. Thomas Morley (1597: 178) confirms this notion and states that "you may set a crotchet or minime rest above a coma or colon, but a longer rest then that of a minime you may not make till the sentence bee perfect, and then at a full point you may set what number of rests you will. Also when you would expresse sighes, you may use the crotchet or minime rest at the most, but a longer then a minime rest you may not use, because it will rather seeme a breth taking then a sigh." In other words, Butler and Morley recommend not only paralleling points in sentences with appropriate rests in music but also expressing sighs with rests. When pronouncing a sigh, one must take an audible breath at the rest, for a sigh seems to have meant inhalation rather than exhalation. In reference to sighing, William Shakespeare wrote in *The First Part of King Henry the Fourth* (1623: II, iv, 58) "a plague of sighing and griefe, it blowes a man up like a Bladder." But in addition to using rests as an opportunity for either sighing or replenishing the breath, singers regularly divided breves (double whole notes), semibreves (whole notes), and minims (half notes) in half for the purposes of respiration and frequently took breath on the dots of dotted notes, unless these notes occurred at the start of the composition or directly after a rest (Vicentino 1555: II, 3, fol. 28v; IV, 13, fol. 78).

Similarly, Butler continues, perfect primary cadences, which close the harmony, equal the periods of the ditti (poem), both within it and at the end. Secondary perfect cadences, on the other hand, correspond to colons or interrogations, but improper and imperfect cadences equate to the points of imperfect sense, that is, commas and semi-colons.[5] These directions, he concludes, once observed (but with discretion) will help a great deal in making the sense of the ditti obvious and comprehensible. Again, Thomas Morley concurs (1597: 178):

> you must not make a close (especiallie a full close) till the full sence of the words be perfect: so that keeping these rules you shall have a perfect agreement, and as it were a harmonicall concent [state of accordance] betwixt the matter and the musicke, and likewise you shall bee perfectly understoode of the auditor what you sing, which is one of the highest degrees of praise which a musicion in dittying can attaine unto or wish for.

As Butler, Morley, and their continental counterparts clearly demonstrate, cadences were the punctuation of music, and through them performers made the structure of musical sentences evident to listeners. By observing these distinctions, the meaning could be conceived and the senses could be satisfied. It follows, then, even though Renaissance authors did not state so directly, that punctuation in the poem implied inserting pauses of various lengths in musical sentences: a short pause (perhaps the value of a crotchet or quarter note) for a comma, a somewhat longer pause (possibly a minim or half note) for a colon, and an even longer pause (maybe a semibreve or whole note) for a period/full stop.

Several principles emerge from the theories surrounding grammatical and musical punctuation that pertain to a reconstruction of the practices associated with eloquent singing. First, and most important, singers should observe the punctuation of the text, articulating their musical discourses in the same way that orators pointed sentences. Of course, in the real world of musical composition, as opposed to the theoretical models propounded in treatises, musical cadences and rests do not always coincide with punctuation in the text, especially in the subsequent verses of strophic song (see below for further discussion of this problem). Nonetheless, wherever possible performers should insert pauses of varying lengths into the musical fabric to correspond to the points in the text. In the solo songs of John Dowland, for example, either he already has added punctuation to the voice part by incorporating rests at the time of composition, or he has provided enough leeway in the song for the singer to insert pauses during performance. This last observation includes certain types of punctuation now unfashionable in certain quarters, notably the comma just before the penultimate word in a series, that is, just before the "and" or the "or." The pronunciation of this final comma contributes greatly to the vehement effect of figures such as *auxesis*, because it detaches and draws attention to the last and most important word of the figure. But this comma is present, and probably should be pronounced, in other sorts of sentences that list things as well. For instance, Dowland uses it in "Times eldest sonne" (1600: no. 6) to separate each element in the lines "olde age the heyre of ease, Strengths foe, loves woe, and foster to devotion," "but thinks sighes, teares, vowes, praiers, and sacrifices," and "as good as showes, maskes, justes, or tilt devises."

Second, this approach usually requires us to abandon many recent "scholarly" editions in favor of original manuscripts or prints, for present-day editors sometimes "modernize" and "regularize" punctuation. This unfortunate practice distorts one of the most potent tools singers possess for impressing the meaning of sentences on listeners, and when editors quite arbitrarily choose to update certain aspects of Renaissance sources but not others, a most unsatisfactory mix of the old and the new can result. Third, seamless delivery within musical sentences and paragraphs seems foreign to an era that organized and paced the presentation of ideas and emotions so that listeners could easily comprehend a song's meaning. Fourth, pointing sentences helps eliminate one of the main problems in performing strophic song, that is, moving the affections of listeners in second or third verses when each new strophe is sung to the same short, simple tune. Because the punctuation in most songs differs for each verse and follows the dramatic unfolding of the poem's story, singers can create interest simply by adhering to the points marked in the sources, and nowhere is this more evident than in the strophic songs from Dowland's *The First Booke of Songes*, especially in "Awake, sweet love" and "His golden locks."

The First Booke of Songes initially appeared in 1597 and enjoyed four reprints over the next sixteen years (1600, 1603, 1606, and 1613). The 1606 issue contained important revisions, repeated in the 1613 printing, in which someone, perhaps Dowland himself, significantly altered the punctuation in certain songs to strengthen the hierarchical relationship between the points. By doing this, the structure of the sentences became easily discernible, and singers had a more detailed guide to follow. The editor added new commas and converted many of the commas in the earlier prints to the longer pauses of the colon or period. These changes provide better satisfaction for the ear, to borrow Francis Clement's words (1587: 24–25), and clearly distinguish the parts of the sentences from one another, making the meaning readily apparent. Without this "tunable uttering of our words and sentences" (Mulcaster 1582: 166), performers would find it almost impossible to move the affections of others, for a good command of punctuation has always been one of the main components in the art of speaking and singing well.

In "Awake, sweet love," for example, the emended punctuation orders the parts of the sentences into their proper relationship and indicates the prominence singers might assign the various members. Commas separate what John Hart (1551: 159) refers to as "short saings" in which "the matter hangeth loking for more to be said," and semicolons,

colons, and periods further articulate the unfolding sense of the sentences. A comparison of the 1597 and 1613 versions of the first verse demonstrates how the later punctuation aids delivery (Example 3.1).

EXAMPLE 3.1 *"Awake, sweet love"*

1597

Awake sweet love thou art returnd,
My hart which long in absence mournd
Lives nowe in perfect joy,
Let love which never absent dies,
Now live for ever in her eyes
When came my first anoy,

Only herselfe hath seemed faire,
She only I could love,
She onely drave me to dispaire
When she unkind did prove.
Dispayer did make me wish to die
That I my joyes might end,
She onely which did make me flie
My state may now amend.

1613

Awake, sweet love, thou art returnd:
My hart, which long in absence mournd,
Lives now in perfect joy.
Let love, which never absent dies,
Now live for ever in her eyes,
Whence came my first annoy.

Only herselfe hath seemed faire:
She only I could love,
She only drave me to despaire,
When she unkind did prove.
Despaire did make me wish to die;
That I my joyes might end:
She only, which did make me flie,
My state may now amend.

If we observe the punctuation in the ways described by Hart, Mulcaster, Smith, and others and use the tone of voice (volume) they suggest for differentiating the various members of a sentence, we can begin to re-create the style of delivery common in Dowland's lifetime. The first two periods of "Awake, sweet love" might be read/sung as follows (larger type represents the main sense of the sentence and smaller type indicates what the editor must have considered "short saings," uttered with a lower [quieter] voice, which interrupt yet expand the overall meaning):

> Awake, sweet love, thou art returnd:
> My hart, which long in absence mournd,
> Lives now in perfect joy.
> Let love, which never absent dies,
> Now live for ever in her eyes,
> Whence came my first annoy.

In uttering these sentences, singers not only would distinguish the parts by means of dynamic shading but also would incorporate the textual articulations into the musical line. In Example 3.2, I have followed the advice of Hart and Butler and equated commas with crotchet or quarter note rests (in one case, I have retained Dowland's minim or half note rest), colons with minim rests, and periods with semibreve or whole note rests. But, of course, singers should not interpret these rests too literally, either in duration or in placement, for the pauses should reflect the flexibility writers from the era prized. This approach enables performers to enliven their delivery even when, as

EXAMPLE 3.2 *"Awake, sweet love," first and second periods*

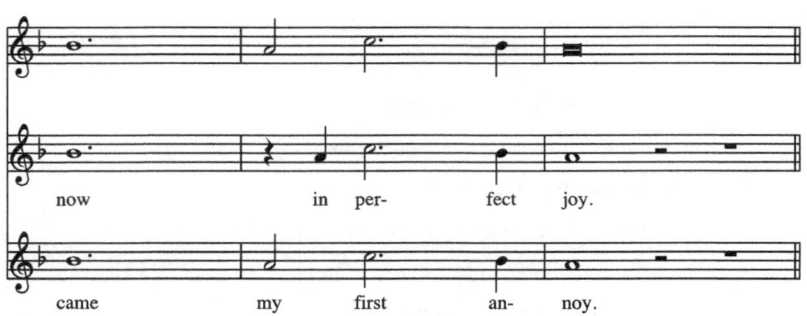

the example demonstrates, the poem progresses to new words and thoughts while the music repeats. Careful observance of points, then, coupled with a change in the tone of voice (volume) to suit the hierarchical importance of each member within those points, coherently arranges the ideas in the poem and creates variety; this helps singers project the story and the affections it contains to the listener.**O**

In other strophic songs, such as "His golden locks," the punctuation in the 1613 edition demonstrates that, even though the points provide a remarkably clear plan for pacing the projection of the story, Dowland conceived the vocal line in terms of the punctuation in the first verse alone (Example 3.3). This, of course, presents obstacles for singers to overcome in delivering the second and third verses, particularly in the last two lines of each verse, and highlights the inherent difficulty performers face in making strophic songs dramatically convincing.

The poem recounts the plight of an aging knight, who after a life of dedicated service seeks a position more suited to his advanced years, and as in "Awake, sweet love,"

EXAMPLE 3.3 *"His golden locks," 1613 (variants in punctuation from 1597 are shown in brackets)*[6]

His golden locks time hath to silver turnde. [,]
O time too swift, O swiftnesse never ceasing! [,]
His youth gainst time & age hath ever spurnd,
But spurnd in vain, youth waneth by increasing. [:]
    Beautie, strength, youth are flowers but fading seene: [,]
    Dutie, Faith, Love are roots and ever greene.

His helmet now shall make a hive for Bees,
And lovers Sonets turne to holy Psalmes:
A man at armes must now serve on his knees,
And feed on prayers which are ages almes: [,]
    But though from Court to cotage he depart, [no punctuation]
    His Saint is sure of his unspotted heart.

And when he saddest sits in homely Cell,
Hee'l teach his swaines this Caroll for a song,
Blest be the hearts that wish my Soveraigne well,
Curst be the soule that thinks her any wrong. [:]
    Goddes allow this aged man his right,
    To be your Beadsman now that was your Knight.

someone strengthened the punctuation, substituting periods for commas and colons and appropriately turning the second line of the first verse into an exclamation. Yet only in the first verse do the points suit the vocal line perfectly, and this confirms my contention that Dowland conceived the music in terms of the first verse alone (Example 3.4). The music Dowland composed for the exclamation "O time too swift, O swiftnesse never ceasing!" is the melodic equivalent of John Hart's sharp beginning followed by a lower ending, and the vocal line easily accommodates the comma, as it helps the singer (and listener) prepare for the repetition of the exclamatory "O!" However, this musical period works imperfectly for the second and third verses, the corresponding lines of these verses being single, longer units of thought without emotional outburst:

> *Verse 1*: O time too swift, O swiftnesse never ceasing!
> *Verse 2*: And lovers Sonets turne to holy Psalmes:
> *Verse 3*: Hee'l teach his swaines this Caroll for a song.

A similar problem occurs with the melody Dowland composed for the fourth line of the first verse. The two members from verse 1 "but spurnd in vain, youth waneth by increasing," fit the music well (Example 3.4), the antithetical nature of the melody, the first part rising and the second falling, paralleling the sense of these members (that is, their cause-and-effect relationship) and the comma providing the natural break both text and music require. But once again, the second and third verses do not suit a melody conceived as a bipartite structure:

> *Verse 1*: But spurnd in vain, youth waneth by increasing.
> *Verse 2*: And feed on prayers which are ages almes:
> *Verse 3*: Curst be the soule that thinks her any wrong.

Yet the greatest problem for the singer in subsequent verses lies in the music written for the last two lines of the first stanza, music so perfectly suited to the text that one can hardly imagine other words adapted to it. Dowland's melodic setting certainly reflects the contrast between the two members of this period, the first one detailing what once was and the second listing those unwavering qualities that are ever present. The first part begins with a repetition of the final of the mode and comes to rest on the transitory cadence note A, which, like the colon it represents, gives the expectation that much more remains to be spoken. The second part fulfills this anticipation, as it begins a fifth above the final and maintains a somewhat higher tessitura, gradually bringing the musical thought to a full and perfect close with a cadence on G, the structural foundation of the mode. Singers can achieve a most persuasive delivery of this period if they observe the rhetorical figure *articulus* and separate the words from one another by pronouncing the commas (see the discussion of this figure in Part 2, "Every Trope, Every Figure"). This approach draws attention to and emphasizes each quality in the list, and Dowland seems to have designed his melody with this form of delivery in mind, for he employs the longer note values of semibreve (whole note) and minim (half note) to set the words, notes which by their very nature, especially when delivered slowly, should receive emphasis and be separated.

In the second and third verses, however, Dowland constructed the corresponding lines quite differently:

> *Verse 1*: Beautie, strength, youth are flowers but fading seene:
> Dutie, Faith, Love are roots and ever greene.
> *Verse 2*: But though from Court to cotage he depart,
> His Saint is sure of his unspotted heart.
> *Verse 3*: Goddes allow this aged man his right,
> To be your Beadsman now that was your Knight.

These lines contain continuous thoughts and lack the accumulation of like words (*synathroismos*) that characterizes the first verse. The succeeding pairs of lines drive forward, requiring only one articulation at the midpoint, but unfortunately Dowland's melody does not seem appropriate for these sentences. The semibreves (whole notes) and minims (half notes) that suited the first verse so well halt the forward motion and produce an unnatural declamation of the text (Example 3.4).

Nonetheless, Dowland shows his brilliance as a songwriter in his highly imaginative and thoroughly convincing setting of the first verse, and the problems identified in subsequent verses are by no means insurmountable. The second lines of stanzas 2 and 3 require singers to perceive the melody as one long unit rather than as two separate members of a period, and the fourth lines of these verses present even fewer problems, because the dividing point in Dowland's melody occurs in each case just before a relative pronoun (*which* or *that*), a natural location for the introduction of the brief articulation the melody implies. But the final periods of stanzas 2 and 3 cannot be remedied so easily, for singers generally find it difficult to completely reverse the halting effect of the semibreves (whole notes). However, small changes to the melody's rhythm can alleviate much of the awkwardness, and in Example 3.4, I have reorganized the note values not only to eliminate the emphasis on unaccented syllables and less important words but also to separate "Goddes" from the following words in order to draw attention to the singer's direct plea to the sovereign. This noble neglect of rhythm, a procedure similar to the interpretive freedom implied in the Italian concept of *sprezzatura*, allows performers to correct deficiencies in a way similar to that suggested by both Caccini (1614: "Alcuni avvertimenti") and Zenobi (c. 1600: 101):

> Sprezzatura is that elegance which is given to song through the transgression of several quavers [eighth notes] or semiquavers [sixteenth notes] on various strings [i.e., pitches], like those [transgressions] made in tempo. It removes from song a certain confining rigidity and dryness; thus it renders [song] pleasing, free, and airy, just as in common speech, eloquence and fecundity [abundant variety] make the matters on which one speaks easy and pleasant.

> La sprezzatura è quella leggiadria la quale si da canto co'l trascorso di più crome, e simicrome sopra diverse corde co'l quale fatto à tempo, togliendosi al canto una certa terminata angustia, e secchezza, si rende piacevole, licenzioso, e arioso, si come nel parlar comune la eloquenza, e la fecondia rende agevoli, e dolci le cose di cui si favella. (Caccini 1614: preface)

> [Singers] should at times carry their voices with disregard, at times with a dragging manner, at times with a gallantness of motion.

> Deve tall'hora portar le voci con disprezzo, tall'hora con modo strascinarle, tall'hora con galanteria di motivo. (Zenobi c. 1600: 101)**O**

Persuasive delivery in the sixteenth and early seventeenth centuries presupposed a knowledge of punctuation, and singers needed to be thoroughly familiar with the purpose and pronunciation of distinctions. The emendations to punctuation in the later printings of *The First Booke of Songes* demonstrate how points could control compositional style by suggesting melodic figures that would enhance, at least in first verses, the projection of the affections contained in the poem. Punctuation made musical discourse intelligible, and through its observance the meaning could be conceived, the ear delighted, and all the senses satisfied. Without correct utterance of punctuation, to paraphrase Quintilian (XI, 262–63), all the other merits of oratory are worth nothing.

EXAMPLE 3.4 *"His golden locks," suggestions for pointing*

Melody as written:

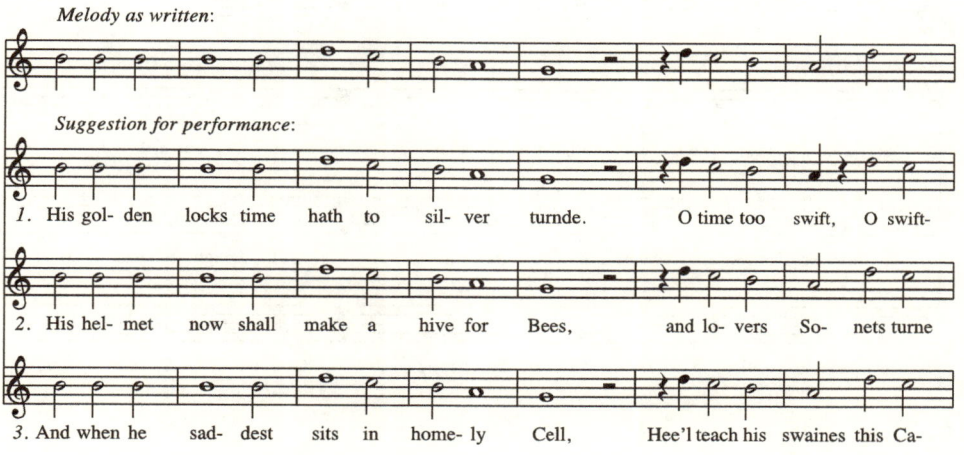

Suggestion for performance:

1. His gol- den locks time hath to sil- ver turnde. O time too swift, O swift-

2. His hel- met now shall make a hive for Bees, and lo- vers So- nets turne

3. And when he sad- dest sits in home- ly Cell, Hee'l teach his swaines this Ca-

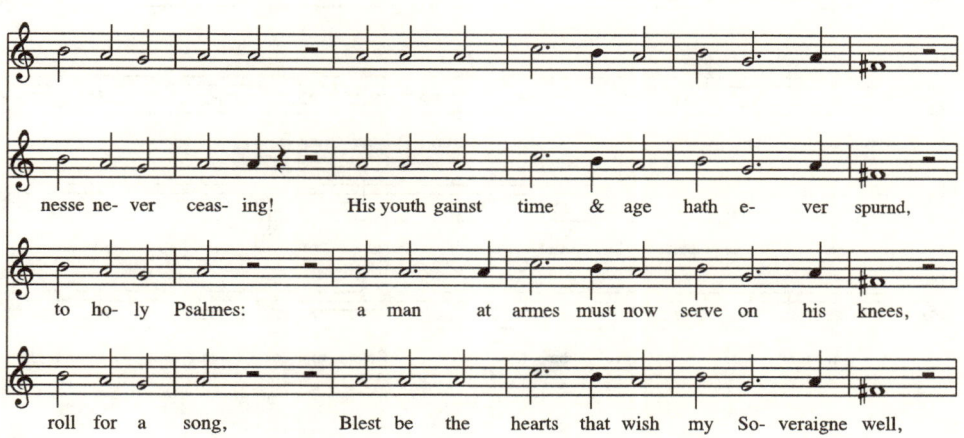

nesse ne- ver ceas- ing! His youth gainst time & age hath e- ver spurnd,

to ho- ly Psalmes: a man at armes must now serve on his knees,

roll for a song, Blest be the hearts that wish my So- veraigne well,

(Continued)

EXAMPLE 3.5 (*Continued*)

but spurnd in vain, youth wa- neth by in- creas-ing. Beau- tie, strength, youth are

and feed on prayers which are a- ges almes: But though from Court to

curst be the soule that thinks her a- ny wrong. God-des al- low this

flowers but fa- ding seene: Du- tie, Faith, Love are roots and e- ver greene.

co- tage he de- part, his Saint is sure of his un- spot- ted heart.

a- ged man his right, to be your Beads- man now that was your Knight.

ACCENT AND EMPHASIS

In the previous section, Dowland's false accent and emphasis required the adjustment of specific rhythmic values in "His golden locks" so that singers would not inadvertently elevate unaccented syllables and less important words to positions of prominence. This method of correcting compositional defects corresponds to advice given by a number of sixteenth-century writers, who often referred to such offenses as barbarisms. Giovanni del Lago (1540: 40–41), for instance, in offering guidance to composers, suggested that they should

> not commit barbarisms in composing notes to words; that is, do not place a long accent on short syllables or a short accent on long syllables, which is contrary to the rules of the grammatical arts, without which [that is, without these rules] no

one can be a good musician, which [grammatical rules also] teach how to utter and write correctly.

non far barbarismi nel comporre le notule sopra le parole, cioe non ponete lo accento lungo sopra le sillabe brevi, over l'accento breve sopra le sillabe lunghe, quia est contra regulam artis grammitices, senza la quale niuno puo esser buono musico, la quale insegna pronunciare et scrivere drittamente.

Barbarisms of this nature forced singers to perform long syllables as short ones and short syllables as long ones (Vanneo 1533: 93r–93v), and since these errors violated basic principles of grammar, singers corrected any problems they encountered by altering the lengths of the offending notes, or at least so suggested Biagio Rossetti in 1529 (fol. cii[v]):

in hymns and proses or sequences, and in psalms and antiphons, one can make a master of the maidservant grammar, for when one delivers a short syllable, one should shorten the melody's note, even if there are two notes set to one short spoken syllable.

in hymnis et prosis vel sequentiis et in psalmis et antiphonis possumus de ancilla grammatica facere dominam, ut quando pronunciamus syllabam brevem debemus abreviare notulam cantus etiam si fuerint duae notulae supra unam syllabam dictionis brevem.

Along these lines, Andreas Ornithoparchus, writing in 1517 (p. 89 in John Dowland's translation), praised singers in the Church of Prague for making "the Notes sometimes longer, sometime[s] shorter, than they should," and at the end of the sixteenth century, Luigi Zenobi (c. 1600: 80, 97) expected vocalists to improvise solutions to compositional errors: "the eighth [quality . . . for singing with assurance] would be that he [the singer], on finding an error, either by the composer or the copyist, would know how to improvise a remedy to the mistake"/"la Ottava [conditioni . . . per cantar securo] sarebbe, ch'egli, ritrovando errore, o di compositore, o di copia, sapesse rimediare improvisamente all'errato." Moreover, if vocalists did not correct the problems they encountered, Gioseffo Zarlino (1558: 341) felt they would fail to achieve a beautiful and elegant manner of singing ("viene a mancare il bello; & lo elegante modo di cantare"). In fact, the mispronunciation of words, especially when singing in another language, would, as Nicola Vicentino suggested in 1555 (IV, 29, fol. 85v), reduce native speakers to laughter "if, . . . for example, in the French, the Spanish, and the German language, they [singers] would pronounce long syllables short and short [ones] long, that nation would laugh at such a pronunciation"/"si . . . (in essempio) come se nella lingua Franzese, & Spagnuola, et Tedesca, le sillabe loro lunghe fussero pronuntiate brevi, & le breve lunghe, la natione loro riderebbe di tal pronuntia."

But beyond correctly accenting syllables within words, orators also drew attention to important words and ideas through emphasis. Schoolchildren in England received instruction in this aspect of delivery: "let them also be taught carefully, in what word the Emphasis lyeth; and therefore which is to be elevated in the pronuntiation" (Brinsley 1612: 213–14). By emphasis and elevation, the author, John Brinsley, meant the extra stress placed on a word so that it would, according to Abraham Fraunce (1588: II, ch. 1), "plainly appeare." In general, speakers and singers pronounced emphasized words louder and stronger than those around them, and by varying emphasis performers could alter their expression so that listeners could differentiate one idea from another.

The sensitive application of both emphasis and accent allowed singers not only to adapt their voices to the changing emotional content of the words but also to alleviate the tedium of multiple verses sung to short, repetitive tunes. A number of Italian *frottole* from the early sixteenth century certainly could benefit from this manner of delivery, and the eight stanzas of the anonymous setting of the spiritual *capitolo*, "Se mai per maraveglia," published by Petrucci in 1511 (Example 3.5 a, b), provide a useful case study for demonstrating how we today might observe the natural accentuation of the Italian language, as well as emphasis, to shape and continuously vary the rhythmic profile of a simple melody.

EXAMPLE 3.5a *"Se mai per maraveglia," Bossinensis 1511: Jacopo Sannazaro's text, with an English translation (b) as arranged for voice and lute by Franciscus Bossinensis*

Se mai per maraveglia alzando'l viso	If ever in marvel, lifting up your face
Al chiaro ciel pensate o cieca gente	to the bright heavens, think, O blind people,
A quel vero signor d'il paradiso	of that true Lord of Paradise.
Volgeti gli occhi in qua che ve presente	Turn your eyes this way that I may show you
Non quella forma (ahime) non quel dolore	not that body (alas) not that grief,
Che contemplaron gli occhi de la mente	which you may contemplate with your mind's eye.
Piangete il grave universal dolore	Weep for the grievous universal sorrow.
Piangeti l'aspra morte e'l crudo affanno	Weep for the bitter death and cruel suffering,
Se spirto di pieta vi punge il core	if the spirit of pity touches your heart.

Per liberarci da l'antico inganno

Pende come vedete al duro legno

E per salvarci dal perpetuo damno

Dolce caro soave: altero pegno

Se perder la propria vita: offrir il
sangue

Per cui sol di vederlo non fu degno

Ecco che hor vi dimostra il volto
exangue

Le chiome lacerate: el capo basso

Come rosa dismessa in terra langue

Qual huom esser porria di pianger
lasso

Pensando a tal suplitio et a tal morte

Se ben havesse il cor d'un duro sasso

Gia la ferrate e inexpugnabil porte

De l'infernal reame ha rotte e prese

Per far il mondo piu costante e forte

Et aspetarci con le braccia tese

To free us from original sin,

he hangs, as you see, upon the hard wood,

and to save us from eternal damnation.

Sweet, precious, gentle: a lofty pledge,

to lose his own life: to offer blood,

so alone against those not worthy to look
on him.

Behold that now he shows you his
bloodless face,

the hair matted, the head drooped,

like a discarded rose withering upon the
ground.

What man is there who could tire of
weeping,

thinking of such suffering and such a
death,

even if he had a heart as hard as stone.

Already the locked and indestructible
gates

of the infernal realm have been broken and
conquered,

to make the world more constant and
strong,

and he waits with arms outstretched.

(Continued)

EXAMPLE 3.5b *"Se mai per maraveglia," as arranged for voice and lute by Franciscus Bossinensis*

Se mai per mara- ve- glia al zan-

do'l vi- so

al chia- ro ciel pen- sa- te o cie- ca gen-

(Continued)

EXAMPLE 3.5b (*Continued*)

te   a quel   ve-   ro   si-   gnor   d'il

pa- ra- di-   so

The individual strophes of this song consist of three text lines, the first two of which the composer set in recitation style, and just as in "His golden locks" the music fits the first verse better than it does subsequent stanzas. In Example 3.6, I have underlain the words taking into account, as much as possible, accents, text structure, and word placement in Petrucci's publication. In the first line of each verse, for example, structural considerations suggest an underlay for the second musical phrase, which begins at an appropriate moment on a gerund ("alzando," verse 1), relative pronoun ("che," verse 2), preposition ("da," verse 4, "di," verse 7), conjunction ("e," verse 8), the first word of an objective completion ("il volto exangue," verse 6), or after a colon ("soave:" verse 5). However, the skeletal nature of the notated rhythm makes it impossible to avoid the sorts of accentual barbarisms writers warned singers to correct. Yet if we follow Biagio Rossetti's advice (1529: cii^v) and match note length with the spoken accentuation of language and adhere to Zenobi's expectation (c. 1600: 80, 97) that singers remedy problems at the time of performance, then a natural manner of delivery, reminiscent of the sixteenth century, can result.

Since the basis of a natural delivery centered on accentuation, I have marked the stressed syllable in every word of the text (Example 3.7) and then have suggested a rhythmic profile for the first three verses based on principles discussed by Rossetti and others. In Example 3.8, strong syllables receive longer note values than weak syllables, and rhythmic displacement further promotes a speechlike flow in the melodic line. Moreover, I have shortened the final note at the ends of text phrases, particularly when the member concludes with an unaccented syllable or an unimportant word, and at

EXAMPLE 3.6 *Possible text underlay (for ease of viewing, the verses have been spread across two staves, each staff containing the singer's melody; the two measures of lute interlude between the first and second lines of the stanzas have been omitted)*

every pause singers might wish to let the voice fall in Charles Butler's sense of decrescendo (1633: 58, 59). In addition, the parenthetical expression "(ahime)" in the middle of the second verse could be uttered in the usual sixteenth-century manner as an aside with a quieter voice (Mulcaster 1582: 167). The application of these principles helps the story line move forward, because even though the basic melodic outline repeats, the subsequent verses furnish singers with an opportunity to re-create, that is, to shape and individualize, the tune anew.

EXAMPLE 3.7 *Text with accents marked*

Se mai per maravèglia alzàndo'l vìso
Al chiàro ciel pensàte o cièca gènte
A quel vèro signòr d'il paradìso

Volgèti gli òcchi in qua che ve presènte
Non quèlla fòrma (ahimè) non quel dolòre
Che contemplàron gli òcchi de la mènte

Piangète il gràve universàl dolòre
Piangèti l'àspra mòrte e'l crùdo affànno
Se spìrto di pietà vi pùnge il còre

Per liberàrci da l'antìco ingànno
Pènde còme vedète al dùro lègno
E per salvàrci dal perpètuo dàmno

Dòlce càro soàve: altèro pègno
Se pèrder la pròpria vìta: offrìr il sàngue
Per cui sol di vedèrlo non fu dègno

Ècco che hor vi dìmostra il vòlto exàngue
Le chiòme laceràte: el càpo bàsso
Còme ròsa dismèssa in tèrra làngue

Qual huom èsser porrìa di piànger làsso
Pensàndo a tal suplìtio et a tal mòrte
Se ben havèsse il cor d'un dùro sàsso

Già la ferràte e inexpugnàbil pòrte
De l'infernàl reàme ha ròtte e prèse
Per far il mòndo più costànte e fòrte
Et aspetàrci con le bràccia tèse

EXAMPLE 3.8 *Possible rhythmic profile (the first three verses based on principles of accent)*

Melody as written:

1. Se mai per mara- ve- glia al- zan- do'l vi- so
2. Vol- ge- ti gli oc- chi in qua che ve pre- sen- te
3. Pian- ge- te il gra- ve u- ni- ver- sal do- lo- re

Suggestion for performance:

1. Se mai per ma-ra-ve- glia al- zan- do'l vi- so

2. Vol- ge- ti gli oc- chi in qua che ve pre- sen- te

3. Pian- ge- te il gra- ve u- ni- ver- sal do- lo- re

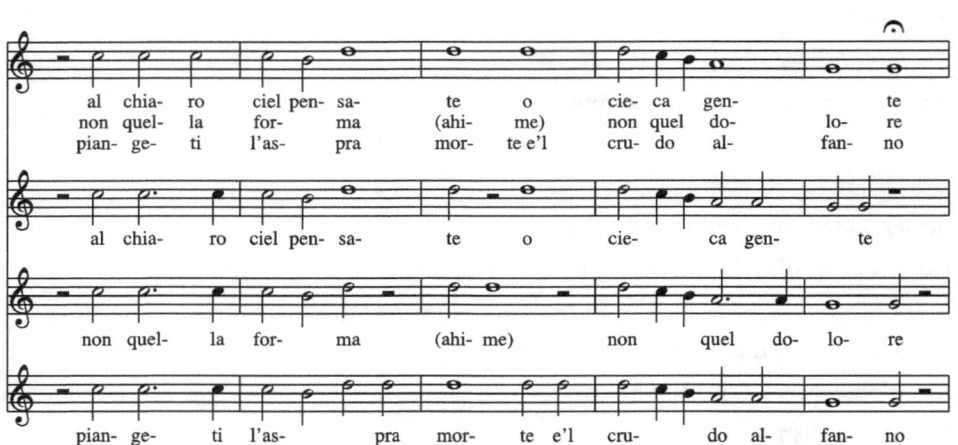

al chia- ro ciel pen-sa- te o cie- ca gen- te
non quel- la for- ma (ahi- me) non quel do- lo- re
pian- ge- ti l'as- pra mor- te e'l cru- do al- fan- no

al chia- ro ciel pen-sa- te o cie- ca gen- te

non quel- la for- ma (ahi- me) non quel do- lo- re

pian- ge- ti l'as- pra mor- te e'l cru- do al- fan- no

a quel ve- ro si- gnor d'il pa- ra- di- so
che con- tem- pla- ron gli oc- chi de la men- te
se spir- to di pie- ta vi pun- ge il co- re

a quel ve- ro si- gnor d'il pa- ra- di- so

che con-tem- pla- ron gli oc- chi de la men- te

se spir- to di pie- ta vi pun- ge il co- re

PRONOUNCING DISTINCTLY

Clarity of delivery depended on two things: punctuation, as we have just seen, and another equally important factor, enunciation (Quintilian XI, 260–61). From at least Quintilian's time, rhetoricians stressed the necessity of uttering words distinctly, later English writers repeating anecdotes about the methods of correcting poor enunciation that were centuries old. In 1553, Thomas Wilson (433) told the story of Demosthenes, who, being unable to pronounce the letter "r," practiced speaking with little stones under his tongue until he spoke as plainly as any other man. Musicians in England, Wilson continued, used to resort to a similar custom; that is, they placed gags in the mouths of children "that they might pronounce distinctely." But, alas, he bemoaned the loss of this tradition in his own time (433).

Writers recognized improper enunciation as a common fault in speaking, and Wilson (1553: 434) provides us with two examples of typical problems. He tells of a priest, as nice as a "Nonnes Henne," who had such bad diction that he would say *Dominus vobicum* for *Dominus vobiscum*, while others say "blacke vellet" instead of "blacke velvet." Similar anecdotes had been in circulation from at least 1500, for Rutgerus (c. 1500: 41) mentions "Daminos vabiscom" as an example of mispronounced vowels. The confusion this indistinct speech would cause in listeners is obvious, and the dangers of poor enunciation probably led Zarlino (1558: 204) and Lodovico Zacconi (1592: fol. 57) to caution singers to deliver words, especially vowels, clearly and without errors. Moreover, in early seventeenth-century England, Charles Butler (1636: 98) advised vocalists "to sing as plainly as they woolde speak: pronouncing every Syllable and letter (specially the Vouels) distinctly and treatably ... [so that] ... the Ditti (which is half the grace of the Song) may bee known and understood." The foundation of persuasive discourse, then, in both speaking and singing consisted of clarity in delivery, that is, words uttered distinctly and sentences articulated carefully, to enable listeners to assimilate the sense of the text easily. John Brinsley (1612: 17) recommends that schoolchildren learn to utter every syllable "truly, plainly, fully, and distinctly" so that "others who heare may understand," and in analyzing sentences (Brinsley's term), students should observe all the points in order to "see and consider both the beginning, middest, and end of the sentence together; and also each clause in it" (1612: 95). Once orators and singers had mastered these basic principles of eloquent delivery, they could then explore the many techniques for enlivening discourse.

FIGURES AND PASSIONATE ORNAMENTS
MADE MANIFEST

The voice possesses an infinite variety of expression (Quintilian: XI, 252–53), and orators and singers adjusted the nature and quality of the voice to suit the affections they needed to portray (Wright 1604: 179–81). Writers and speakers constructed poetry, discourses, orations, etc. from many smaller parts, each with its own affection, and every part required individual treatment in delivery (180). Even when the overall effect of a text could be assigned to a single passion, orators often used elements of contrast within the text to help them persuade listeners (180). And in order to capture the minds of hearers with texts "woven with various periods, and compounded of sundry parts" (180), orators made their utterance conform to the structure of the text, following principles of delivery dating back to ancient times. In discussing the attributes of good reading, Quintilian (I, 146–47; XI, 266–67) listed the three main components of speaking that enabled orators to create the variety so necessary for persuasive utterance. One should avoid monotony, he suggested, by raising or lowering the voice (modulating it within each phrase), by increasing or slackening speed, and by speaking with greater or lesser energy. Without this approach to delivering the various members within sentences (even when a member consisted of just one word), every word in the discourse would appear to be of equal importance (XI, 268–71). In the middle of the sixteenth century, Nicola Vicentino (1555: IV, 42, fol. 94v) had recommended virtually the same manner of performance for singing in consort:

> sometimes [singers] use a certain method of proceeding in compositions that cannot be written down, such as uttering softly and loudly or quickly and slowly, and following the natural course of the words, to move the measure [that is, change the tempo] to demonstrate the effects of the passions of the words and harmony. It will not seem a strange thing to anyone, this method of changing the tempo all at once [that is, suddenly], for it is understood that while singing in consort, where one has this change of tempo, it is not an error. And a composition sung with a change of tempo is more pleasing by means of that variety than [a composition] continued to the end without being varied. And experience with such a manner [of singing] will make everyone secure [in it], for in vernacular works, one will find that this procedure will please listeners more than the tempo always continuing in one manner, [for] one should move the tempo according to the words, more slowly and more quickly.

> qualche volta si usa un certo ordine di procedere, nelle compositioni, che non si può scrivere, come sono, il dir piano, & forte, & il dir presto, & tardo, & secondo le parole, muovere la Misura, per dimostrare gli effetti delle passioni delle parole, & dell'armonia, ad alcuno non li parrà cosa strana tal modo di mutar misura, tutti à un tratto cantando mentre che nel concerto s'intendino, ove si habbi da mutar misura che non sarà errore alcuno, & la compositione cantata, con la mutatione della

misura è molto gratiata, con quella varieta, che senza variare, & seguire al fine, & l'esperienza di tal modo farà certo ognuno, però nelle cose volgari si ritroverà che tal procedere piacerà più à gl'oditori, che la misura continua sempre à un modo, & il moto della misura si dè muovere, secondo le parole, più tardo, & più presto.

In the Vicentinian world of performance, then, vocalists sang *piano e forte* and *presto e tardo* to conform to the ideas of the composer and to impress on listeners the passions of the words and harmony. This manner of delivery seems to have been the norm from the late fifteenth to the early seventeenth centuries, for Angelo Poliziano (1498), commenting on solo singing; Giangiorgio Trissino (1524), describing the performance of Isabella d'Este; Vincenzo Giustiniani (c. 1628), discussing vocalists in Mantua in the mid-1570s; and Michael Praetorius (1619), writing about the consort singing of his day, made similar observations. As noted earlier, Poliziano praised the young singer Fabio Orsini with the words:

> The voice itself was not entirely that of someone reading aloud nor entirely that of someone singing, but yet both could be discerned, neither separated from the other. Nevertheless, it was varied according to what the passage required, either even or modulated—now punctuated, now continuous, now raised, now restrained, now subdued, now vehement, now slow, now swift, always faultless, always clear, always delightful, the gesture neither indifferent nor sluggish but yet not affected or offensive. Anyone would have said that the young Roscius [the ancient Roman actor] was on the stage.

> Vox ipsa nec quasi legentis, nec quasi canentis, sed in qua tamen utrunque sentires, neutrum discerneres, varie tamen prout locus posceret, aut aequalis, aut inflexa, nunc distincta[,] nunc perpetua, nunc sublata, nunc deducta, nunc remissa, nunc contenta, nunc lenta, nunc incitata, semper emendata[,] semper clara, semper dulcis. Gestus non ociosus, non somniculosus, sed nec vultuosus tamen ac molestus. Rosciolum prorsus aliquem diceres in scaena versari. (Poliziano 1498: Bk. 12, fol. pviii; cited in Abramov-van Rijk 2009: 364)

Trissino (1524: fols. C3r–v) depicted the abilities of Isabella d'Este as a singer in this way:

> But when, then, this woman turns to sing a few [songs], especially to the lute, . . . [she] diligently preserves the harmony, in a manner that in not one way oversteps the boundaries of rhythmic propriety, but moderates the song with elevation and

suppression of the tempo, and maintains concordance with the lute, and at once
accords her language, and one and the other hand [in playing the lute], with the
inflections of the song. . . .

Ma quando poi questa alcuna volta canta, e specialmente nel liuto, . . . il serbare dili-
gentissimente l'harmonia, in guisa che in niuna cosa il rithmo si varchi, ma a tempo
con elevatione, e depressione misurare il canto, e tenerlo con lo liuto concorde, e ad
un tratto accordare la lingua, e l'una, e l'altra mano, con le inflexioni de i canti. . . .
(cited in Prizer 1999: 49)

Giustiniani (c. 1628: 108) gave a detailed description of the performing style the
"Ladies of Mantua" employed in the late sixteenth century:

by moderating and increasing their voices, forte or piano, diminishing or swelling,
according to what suited the piece, now with dragging, now stopping, accompanied
by a gentle broken sigh, now continuing with long passages, well joined or separated [that is, legato or detached], now groups, now leaps, now with long trills, now
with short, and again with sweet running passages sung softly, to which one unexpectedly heard an echo answer; and principally with facial expressions, glances,
and gestures that appropriately accompanied the music and sentiment; and above
all without disgraceful movements of the mouth, hands or body which would not
address the purpose of the song; and with [their] enunciation they made the words
clear in such a way that one could hear even the last syllable of every word, which
was never interrupted or suppressed by passages and other embellishments.

col moderare e crescere la voce forte o piano, assottigliandola o ingrossan-
dola, che secondo che veniva a' tagli, ora con strascinarla, ora smezzarla, con
l'accompagnamento d'un soave interrotto sospiro, ora tirando passaggi lunghi,
seguiti bene, spiccati, ora grupi, ora a salti, ora con trilli lunghi, ora con breve, et
or con passaggi soavi e cantati piano, dalli quali tal volta all'improvviso si sentiva
echi rispondere, e principalmente con azione del viso, e dei sguardi e de' gesti che
accompagnavano appropriatamente la musica e li concetti, e sopra tutto senza moto
della persona e della bocca e delle mani sconcioso, che non fusse indirizzato al fine
per il quale si cantava, e con far spiccar bene le parole in guisa tale che si sentisse
anche l'ultima sillaba di ciascuna parola, le quale dalli passaggi et altri ornamenti
non fusse interrotta o soppressa.

And Praetorius (1619: bk. III, ch. 1, 132 [112]), like Vicentino before him, recommended basing performing style directly on the attributes of the composition:

But so often the composition itself requires, as well as the text and meaning of the words, that one, now and then, but not too often or really too much, moves the tactus [beat] now quickly, now again slowly.

Es erfordert aber solches offtermahls die composition, so wol der Text und Verstand der Worter an ihm selbsten: das man bisweilen/nicht aber zu offt oder gar zu viel/ den Tact bald geschwind/bald wiederumb langsam fuhre.

To these basic tenets of good delivery, a number of writers added the notion of altering the tonal quality of the voice, as the time and cause required, to produce a delivery "now harshe and hard, now smoothe and sweete" (Mulcaster 1581: 58), and in the middle of the seventeenth century, Michel Le Faucheur (1657: 80), in discussing Quintilian's three components of speaking mentioned above, stated that the voice had three principal "differences"—highness or lowness, vehemence or softness, and swiftness or slowness. Speakers avoided monotony by varying these elements "according to the quality of the *Subjects* he [the orator] treats of, the nature of the *Passions* he would shew in *himself* or raise in *others*, the several parts of his *Discourse*, the different *Figures* he makes use of, and the *variety* of his *words* and his *Phrase*" (Le Faucheur 1657: 92–93). And just like orators, singers needed to match the tonal quality of their voices to the affections present in each section of a song or else their voices would also have been considered monotonous, incapable of inflaming the passions of listeners. Dowland (1609: 89) captured the essence of the singer's task with the advice "Let every Singer conforme his voyce to the words, that as much as he can make the *Concent* [the state of accordance between the words and voice] sad when the words are sad; & merry, when they are merry." This form of counsel seems to have been commonplace, for in 1588 Zarlino (319) suggested singers vary the tonal quality of their voices in the same way that orators did:

[Sometimes the orator speaks] with a loud and horrible voice, shouting and exclaiming, to express his thoughts. And this he does when he speaks of things with which he wishes to induce fear and terror, and at other times he uses a soft and low voice when he wishes to induce commiseration. Thus, it is not an unbecoming thing for a musician to use similar procedures [attioni—changes in volume and tonal quality of the voice] in the high and low [pitches], [to sing] now with a loud voice, now with a subdued voice, as he recites his compositions. . . . Thus, I do not say that the singer should either shout or roar in singing, because these things have neither proportion nor decorum. . . . Just as the reciter is permitted to do this [change volume and tonal quality] for the benefit of the listeners, so the singer also is permitted some [of these] procedures in singing.

Con alta voce & horribile, gridando & esclamando, esprimere il suo concetto; & questo quando parla di cose, con lequali egli voglia indur spavento & terrore; & tallor con voce sommessa & bassa; quando vuole indur commiseratione, cosi non è cosa disconvenevole al Musico, d'usar simili attioni, nell'acuto & nel grave, hora con voce alta, & hora con voce sommessa, recitando le sue Compositioni . . . onde non dico, che'l Cantore cantando debba ne gridare, ne far strepito: percioche non è cosa habbia ne proportione, ne decoro . . . cosi se questo si permette al Recitante per il commodo de gli Ascol tanti; si permetterà anco al Cantore alcune attione nel Cantare.

Somewhat later in the century, Cyriacus Snegasius [Schneegass] (1596: fol. Iv), like Dowland, expected singers to adapt tonal qualities to the subject matter at hand:

Each singer should strive to adapt his voice to the words in such a way that he produces agreement—the mournful [is] sad, the cheerful [is] truly pleasant—in order to move the soul of the listener delightfully and to exhibit a certain affection.

Vocem quisque canentium, Verbis conformare studeat, ita ut in re lamentabili tristem, hilari verò iucundum concentum promat, et auditorum animos suaviter afficiat, et ad affectum aliquem traducat.

The passions in a piece of music changed rapidly, just as in oration, for as Richard Hooker (1597: 75) states, "whether it [the passion embodied in the 'artificiall musick' to which psalms are set] resemble unto us the same state wherein our mindes alreadie are, or a cleane contrarie, we are not more contentedly by the one confirmed, then changed and led away by the other." Obviously, this required singers to alter their style of delivery quickly from one phrase to the next, ensuring that, lest the mind of the speaker appear "unnaturall and distracted," they portrayed one passion at a time. Only when the "*Words, Tone, Greatnesse* of the Voice [and] *Gesture* of the body and Countenance" proceeded from a single passion did orators consider the text to be well pronounced (Hobbes 1637: 108). Nonetheless, Le Faucheur (1657: 90–91) expected a degree of gracefulness when speakers projected rapid changes of affection, for one should not vary the voice "so very grosly *all on the sudden* like a *Thunder-Clap*" because it would surprise and displease the auditors. Le Faucheur's statement, however, must be qualified by other passages in his book where he advocates that orators should imitate real life in the same way actors do and come as close as possible to natural pronunciation by changing the voice "according to the different *quality* of *persons* and the *diversity* of *Subjects*" (76–77). Similarly, all these comments on variation in the tonal

qualities of the voice need to be tempered by Hermann Finck's remark that in singing "when any voice rises higher, it should adopt a softer and sweeter sound; when
descending lower, its sound should be fuller"/"quaelibet vox quo magis intenditur,
eo submissior & dulcior sonus usurpetur: quo magis descendit, eo sonus sit plenior"
(1556: V, fol. Ssiii).

Nonetheless, speakers and singers clearly considered a close link between voice
and passion to be one of the essential features of eloquent delivery, and writers such
as Abraham Fraunce (1588), Thomas Wright (1604), and Le Faucheur (1657) specified the appropriate tonal quality for particular affections. The list of passions these
writers discuss covers a wide range of emotions and includes pity, lamentation, anger,
fear, anguish, hatred, sadness, grief, joy, gladness, love, confidence, and compassion.
Moreover, Wright (1604: 181–82) warns orators not only to match the voice's tonal
quality to the desired affection but also to ensure the words spoken would actually
come from a person in such a state of mind. His advice reminds us that an understanding of the text on all levels, that is, from surface emotional content to deeper
structural elements (involving rhetorical devices that communicate passions to listeners), remains essential to effective persuasion. Wright gives a humorous anecdote to
underscore the importance of matching words and style of delivery to the affection
embodied in the subject. One would not, he asserts, advise a neighbor of a fire in his
house by saying to him: "O deare neighbour, although I am far unfit by eloquence, to
perswade you to looke to your house, and carefully to watch about it, lest fire fall upon
it, as now of late I perceive it hath done, therfore provide water & succour, for otherwise both all your goods and mine will bee consumed" (181–82). The absurdity of
this unnatural speech is obvious, for it does not portray fear and danger realistically;
instead the speech and style of delivery should represent someone in the state of mind
more accurately: "he would runne crying into the street, fire, fire, help, help, water,
water, succour, succour, alas, alas, we are undone, quickly, speedily, run for ladders,
pull downe this rafter, cut that beame, untile the house; what meane you, stirre hands,
armes, and legs, hie thee for water, run thou for yron crookes, and hookes: hast, hast,
wee are all undone" (182). Words such as these when uttered with an appropriate pacing, tonal quality of voice, and so on would succeed in moving the passions of others,
inciting them to action.

In general, speakers based the tonal quality for a given passage on an observation
of people "appassionate," Le Faucheur (1657: 97) emphasizing that the orator must
"first consider the thing he's to speak of, with care, and carry a deep impression of it
in his *mind*, before he be either sensibly touch'd with it *himself* or able to move *others*
upon it with a more effectual *Sympathy*." Le Faucheur (99) went on to summarize his
guiding principle: "If your *Speech* proceeds from a *violent Passion*, it produces a *violent*

TABLE 3.1 Passions and the tonal quality of the voice

Passion	Fraunce (1588)	Wright (1604)	Le Faucheur (1657)
pity and lamentation	full, sobbing, flexible, interrupted	—	—
anger	shrill, sharp, quick, short	—	sharp, impetuous, violent, taking breath often and speaking short upon the passion
fear	contracted, stammering trembling	small, trembling	trembling, stammering
bashfulness	contracted, stammering trembling	—	—
anguish	"a hollow voyce fetcht from the bottome of the throate, groaning"	—	—
hatred	—	loud, sharp	sharp, sullen, severe
ire	—	loud, sharp	—
sadness and commiseration	—	grave, doleful, plain, interrupted with woeful exclamations	—
grief	"a hollow voyce fetcht from the bottome of the throate, groaning"	—	dull, languishing and sad moan, sometimes breaking off abruptly with a sob and fetching up a sigh or groan from the heart
compassion	—	—	very soft, submissive, pitiful
joy	tender, mild, sweetly flowing	plain, pleasant, soft, mild, gentle	full, flowing, brisk

Passion	Fraunce (1588)	Wright (1604)	Le Faucheur (1657)
gladness and pleasure	tender, mild sweetly flowing	—	—
desiring	smoothing and submissive	plain, pleasant, soft, mild, gentle	—
soothing, flattering yielding, gratifying	smoothing and submissive	—	
love	—	plain, pleasant, soft, mild, gentle	soft, gay, charming
confidence	—	—	loud and strong

Pronunciation; if it comes from a *Peaceable* and *Gentle Thought*, the *Pronunciation* again is as *Peaceable, Gentle* and *Calm*: so that the *Orator* would do well to adjust every *Tone* and *Accent* of his *Voyce* to each *Passion* that afflicts or overjoys him, which he would raise in *others* to a degree of *Sympathy*." Table 3.1 contains the various recommendations of Fraunce, Wright, and Le Faucheur.

Yet in addition to describing the vocal tone quality that suits individual passions, one of these writers, Fraunce, provides specific examples from Sir Philip Sydney (and other authors) of the pronunciations appropriate for specific texts. A full, sobbing, flexible, and interrupted voice (suitable for pity and lamentation) would be employed in the sentence "Ah silly soule, that couldest please thy selfe with so impossible imagination" (1588: fol. 13r). But in anger, a shrill, sharp, quick, and short voice works well for words spoken by a man thought to have been incapable of controlling his wife: "What, shall my Wife bee my Mistresse? Thinke you not that thus much time hath taught mee to rule her? I will mewe the Gentlewoman till shee have cast all her feathers, if shee rowse her selfe against mee" (fol. 14r). Fear and bashfulness produced a contracted, stammering, and trembling voice, as in "Alas how painfull a thing it is to a divided minde to make a well joyned aunswere?" (fol. 14v). However, the opposite, that is a tender, mild, and sweetly flowing voice, suited passages dealing with joy, gladness, or pleasure:

> Lock up faire lidds, the treasures of my heart,
> Preserve those beames, this ages onlie light:
> To her sweet sence, sweet sleepe, some ease impart,
> Her sence too weake to beare her spirits might. &c. (fol. J1r).

Similarly, a smoothing submissive voice served passions concerned with desiring, soothing, flattering, yielding, and gratifying: "By the happie woman that bare thee, by all the joyes of thy heart, and successe of thy desire, I beseech thee, turne thy selfe into some consideration of me, and rather shewe pitie, in now helping me, than in too late repenting my death, which hourlie threatens me" (fol. J2v). But for some of the more pitiful utterances, born from anguish and grief, "a hollow voyce fetcht from the bottome of the throate, groaning" was appropriate, as in "O Deserts, Deserts, how fit a guest am I for you? since my heart is fuller of wild ravenous beasts, than ever you were" (fol. J1). These descriptions of the voice have a direct bearing on song performance, for lute songs certainly contain exclamatory outbursts (see Examples 2.4b and 2.17 in Part 2, "Every Trope, Every Figure," and Examples 4.1 and 4.2 in Part 4, "The *Prosopopoeia* in England") and composers designed some of their melodies so that singers could insert sighs, sobs, and groans (see Example 2.10 in Part 2, and Examples 4.1 and 4.2 in Part 4). In fact, Thomas Morley (1597: 178) recommends representing sighs with rests of either a crotchet (quarter note) or minim (half note) duration.

But beyond the specific suggestions given by Fraunce, Le Faucheur offers advice of a more general nature. In speaking of natural things, especially when one wishes only to make the listeners understand and no more, a clean and distinct voice will suffice, for orators do not need any "great *heat* or *motion* upon the matter" (1657: 93). But in speaking of the actions of men, the vocal tone quality must match the deed. Express the just and the honest through a noble accent and a tone of satisfaction, honor, and esteem, but utter the unjust and infamous with a strong, violent, and passionate voice, as well as through a tone of anger, disgrace, and detestation (94). Moreover, if one represents a brave hero, Le Faucheur suggests using a lofty and magnificent tone (107), but to show contempt for a man, he recommends a scornful tone without any passion, eagerness, or violence in the voice (110). And when orators need to complain of a barbarous injustice, an elevated tone, proportioning the vehemence and passion of the voice to the cruelty of the injury, is most appropriate (115). However, after one has spoken with this sort of violent passion, Le Faucheur suggests speakers cool the voice both by lowering the tone and making it more humble (117). If one does not rest the voice, it may suddenly fail, the voice being incapable of withstanding this violence for long periods of time (82).

Later in his treatise (166–68), Le Faucheur turns his attention from the general to the specific and comments on the vocal tone quality required for pronouncing individual words. He discusses six categories of words, describing their affective character and the utterance suitable for each category. Emphatic words, that is, very strong and positive words (certainly, assuredly, infallibly, undoubtedly, necessarily, absolutely, expressly, and manifestly), should be uttered with emphasis and distinction in order to separate them from the surrounding words. Speakers use terms of honor (admirable, incredible, incomparable, ineffable, inestimable, glorious, glittering, pompous, triumphant, illustrious, heroic, august, majestic, and adorable) to praise and extol, and these expressions should carry a magnificent tone. But words such as cruel, heinous, wicked, detestable, abominable, execrable, and monstrous are employed to dispraise and detest, and one should utter them with a most passionate and loud voice. In dealing with sorrow, orators might choose terms of complaint or lamentation (unfortunate, miserable, fatal, mournful, pitiful, deplorable, and lamentable), and they should pronounce them with a melancholy accent. Similarly, words of weak, imperfect, or languishing resentment should have a doleful, moaning accent, as well as a low and slow voice, as in the sentence "When I search'd into the Faith of my Heart, I found it so weak, so imperfect, so languishing, &c." (167–68). And in using terms of extenuation and slight (pitiful, insignificant, little, low, mean, despicable, and feeble), employ a very low, lessening, abject voice with an accent of the greatest scorn and disdain. But lay more stress on words of quantity (grand, high, sublime, profound, long, large, innumerable, and eternal) and universality (all the world, generally, everywhere, always, and never) and pronounce the latter with "a certain *gravity* and *height* of *Accent*" (167).

Other sorts of individual words, particularly those contained in rhetorical figures, should receive emphasis as well, and John Brinsley (1612: 213–14) advises: "Let them [schoolchildren] also be taught carefully, in what word the Emphasis lyeth; and therefore which is to be elevated in the pronuntiation. As namely those wordes in which the chiefe Trope or Figure is." What Brinsley means by emphasis and elevation should be clear from the preceding discussion of the techniques for varying the voice to suit specific passions and words. Emphasis means stress, and connected to this meaning is the figure of the same name with which one can "inforce the sence of any thing by a word of more than ordinary efficacie" (Puttenham 1589: 153). Elevation refers to the change of voice that causes a word or words to be highlighted, but also it simply may mean louder. One of Fraunce's comments (1588: II, ch. 1) on the art of eloquent speaking reinforces Brinsley's statement: "In the particular applying of the voyce to severall words, wee make tropes that bee most excellent plainly appeare. For without this change of voyce, neither anie *Ironia*, nor lively *Metaphore* can well bee discerned". Moreover, a later writer, John Barton (1634: 35), provides an example of the figure *epizeuxis* and suggests how speakers could make it "plainly appeare": "*Thou, thou* art worthy to be praised. As

in every word some syllable is pronounced more acutely; so in every clause some word
is uttered with more vehemencie then the rest, as the first 2 words in this clause must
be." Speech becomes even more stirring, he continues, when a number of emphases
occur in the same sentence: "Now when we put many Emphases together, the sentence
is very moving. Rom. 8.38. Neither *death*, nor *life*, nor *angels*, nor *principalities*, nor *powers*, nor *things present*, nor *things to come*, nor *height*, nor *depth*, &c. all these [words in
italics] must be pronounced Emphatically" (35).

Figures of rhetoric numbered among the most important vehicles orators and singers possessed for inflaming the passions of listeners, yet apart from the few scattered
remarks mentioned here, many writers do not discuss the precise techniques orators
used to emphasize and elevate these figures. In English treatises, for example, we must
content ourselves with the tantalizingly short statements of Brinsley, Fraunce, and
Barton, whereas the Frenchman Le Faucheur offers a profusion of detailed advice on
the techniques of delivering no less than thirteen separate figures, some of them being
the figures most frequently encountered in the late Renaissance lute-song repertoire.
Since Le Faucheur's discussion of the tonal quality of the voice appropriate for specific passions (and other similar comments on the art of delivery) is virtually identical
to those of earlier writers, particularly those from England, I feel I am on reasonably
safe ground in using his tenth chapter, "*How to* vary *the* Voyce *according to the* Figures
of Rhetorick" (1657: 128–50), to explain practices treated briefly by other writers. Le
Faucheur's remarks find reinforcement in Barton's discussion of *epizeuxis* cited above
and on two other occasions by Henry Peacham the Elder in his revised edition of *The
Garden of Eloquence* (1593). For my purposes, the most important figures Le Faucheur
treats are *ecphonesis (exclamatio), prosopopoeia (conformatio), apostrophe (aversio), parrhesia (licentia), climax (gradatio), aposiopesis (praecisio), epizeuxis (subjunctio), anaphora
(repetitio)*, and *epistrophe (conversio)*, but he also discusses subjection, dialogism (conference), *antithesis (contrarium)*, and *epimone* (insistence).

With regard to *ecphonesis*, Le Faucheur (128) recommends pronouncing exclamatory outbursts with a louder voice and a more passionate accent. Peacham the Elder
(1593: 63) probably would have agreed with this advice, for he states "the principall
end and use of this figure is by the vehemency of our voice and utterance to expresse
the greatnesse of our affections and passions, and thereby to move the like affections
in our hearers." Peacham also reminds us that so vehement a form of speech should not
be used without some "great cause" and not too often, lest it become odious. In uttering
prosopopoeias, the rhetorical equivalent of the passionate ayre in music, Le Faucheur
suggests varying the voice according to the "*Diversity, Character* and *Business*" of the
person the orator feigns (1657: 131). Related to *prosopopoeia* is *apostrophe*, a turning of
one's speech to some new person in order to feign their presence (Hoskins 1599: 162),

and this, Le Faucheur asserts, demands a louder voice, as on a sudden diversion of the speech to another person, then one can return with a lower voice as if it were a secret soliloquy or a private reflection (1657: 133). With *parrhesia*, one takes the liberty to say everything one has a mind to express, and consequently the voice must be full and loud (140). But in *climax* or gradation, "where the *Discourse* climbs up by several *clauses* of a Sentence to a *Period* or Full Point; 'tis manifest that the *Voyce* must be rais'd accordingly by the same degrees of *elevation* to answer every *step* of the *Figure*, till it is at the utmost *height* of it" (142). Similarly, *aposiopesis* requires the parts of the figure to be differentiated one from another. In this figure, orators pronounce the words introducing it with the "*highest Accent*" but hold their peace and conceal what might be said further in the matter by lowering their voices a "tone or two" for the remainder of the passage. Le Faucheur provides an example to demonstrate his point: "For I can say of my self [he follows the abrupt ending of these words of the '*highest Accent*' by words spoken a 'tone or two' lower].—But I will not say any thing *piquant* or *severe* at the beginning, though every body sees he is come to accuse me of *Alacrity* and *Lightness of Heart*" (143).

Other figures of a like nature that also need a perceptible differentiation between the parts include subjection, *antithesis*, and dialogism. In subjection, the orator asks several questions and answers are given to all of them. Speakers deliver the figure by varying their voices so that they give the question with "one *Tone*, and the *Answer, another*; either pronouncing the *demand* higher and the answer *lower*, or on the contrary" (144). Although Le Faucheur does not clarify whether he refers to changes in volume or changes in vehemence, his remarks on the delivery of antithesis specifically mention alterations in volume to distinguish the contrarieties: "He [the orator] must distinguish upon both the *contraries*, and pronounce the *first* of 'em with a different *Tone* from the *latter*; *this* with a *louder Accent* than *that*, to shew the opposition betwixt the *one* and the *other* and to adjust the *voyce* to the *Contrariety*" (145). And in dialogism or conference orators must change their voices in turns as if two people actually were talking together (135).

Le Faucheur discusses several figures of repetition, clearly indicating how the reiterated words should be uttered. In *epizeuxis*, an immediate repetition of the same word, the orator must give the restated word a "different sound" and pronounce it "far *louder* and *stronger*" than on its first statement (147). However, the opposite occurs in *anaphora* and *epistrophe*; that is, speakers utter the repeated words (in the former, at the beginning of successive sentences and in the latter, at the end) with the same accent and sound, "but in a different manner from the *Pronunciation* of all the *other parts* of the *Period*, to give the *Figure* its due *Emphasis* and *Distinction* in his Discourse" (147–49). Incidentally, Le Faucheur's explanation of *anaphora* parallels the description mentioned earlier for the delivery of the equivalent musical figure *fuga* (point of imitation in modern parlance): use a clearer and more distinct voice ("voce clariore & explanata magis") than usual for delivering the *thema* of a *fuga* (mimetic point); that is, each voice in a *fuga* should stand out from the others (Finck 1556: V, fol. Ss3v). The last of Le Faucheur's figures, *epimone*, involves driving the argument home in several ways, and orators must use a brisk, pressing, and insulting voice for this figure (1657: 137).

By consistently matching the voice to the various passions in the text, as dictated by specific words and figures, orators inflamed the minds of listeners, and the detailed statements on the subject by Fraunce, Wright, and Le Faucheur outlined here clarify precisely what Fraunce meant when he made his rather cryptic remark, "Nothing is either better for his voyce that speaketh, or more pleasant to the eares of them that heare, than often changing" (1588: II, ch. 1). And if speakers and singers wished to achieve this coveted goal, that is, if they gained the ability to make passions and figures manifest through changes to the voice, then they certainly would have had to possess an infinite variety of expression in their voices. But orators did not achieve this sort of eloquent delivery without assiduous practice. Fraunce (1588: fol. J3r) maintains that because "practise and exercise is all in all: learne therfore some such speach wherein are contained all, or most varieties of voyce, and oftentimes use to pronounce the same in such order and with as great heed as if thou were to utter it in some great assemblie." In this last regard, John Brinsley (1612: 214) specifically mentions practicing the orations of Tullie, for they contain many figures (especially "Exclamations, Prosopopeis, Apostrophees, and the like") that will acquaint speakers with a wide variety of pronunciation.

The importance of this approach to delivery in the late sixteenth and early seventeenth centuries cannot be overestimated, for passionate utterance had become the crowning glory in the training of actors, lawyers, preachers, singers, and others who sought to persuade. The techniques for capturing and inflaming the minds of listeners were well known at the time, and enough documentation survives to enable us to reconstruct with some accuracy the principles behind the art of eloquent delivery. As writings from the period demonstrate, many aspects of speaking transfer directly to singing, and although modern singers of Renaissance vocal music generally are not accustomed to changing the tonal quality of their voices (or style of delivery for that matter) to match the character they wish to portray, they can use the older methods of delivery to bring the music to life in exciting ways.

NOTES

1. An important aspect of historical delivery, namely regional accents in spoken English and Italian, will not be discussed here. I refer readers to the work of Eric J. Dobson (1968) for a lengthy discussion of this feature of pronunciation in England, and to the appropriate chapters in McGee (1996).

2. Michel Le Faucheur's treatise is a most useful source for documenting earlier techniques of delivery. His discussion, for example, parallels that of Renaissance treatises, both Le Faucheur and his sixteenth- and early seventeenth-century counterparts basing their work on classical authors. The value of Le Faucheur's treatise for this book lies in its detailed description of the techniques for varying the voice according to figures and passions, a subject dealt with by other writers in a much less developed fashion. I will quote from Le Faucheur when necessary to flesh out techniques to which earlier authors allude without fully explaining the desired effect.

3. On speaking from memory, see Quintilian (XI: 256–57) and Mulcaster (1581: 57); and on deriving the style of delivery from the affections in a text, see Fraunce (1588: II, ch. 2) and Wright (1604: 132, 178–83).

4. The list and succeeding definitions have been taken from Hart (1551 and 1569), Lily (1567), Mulcaster (1582), Clement (1587), Granger (1616), Butler (1633), Robinson (1641, based on Lily 1567), and Smith (1657). I cite English authors because they explain the concepts most fully and equate the length of pauses implied by punctuation to specific note values.

5. According to Butler (1636: 66, 82), perfect primary cadences are formed on the final of the mode and come to rest on an octave or unison. He considers perfect cadences to be secondary when formed on the fifth, third, or fourth (in order of importance) steps of the scale (1636: 83). Imperfect cadences signify that the harmony or ditti will rest very little, for both music and words proceed further. In these cadences, either the voice rising to the cadence note drops out or it forms a third, fifth, or sixth with the bass (1636: 67). Presumably, imperfect cadences also could be primary or secondary in function. Improper cadences, on the other hand, are formed on the sixth, second, or seventh steps of the scale and are used sparingly, as they are "strange and informal to the Air" (1636: 83). For more information on cadences, see the Appendix, "Understanding Learned Compositions."

6. Lines 4 and 5 of the third verse follow 1597, 1600, and 1603 in using "her" and "Goddes" instead of "him" and "Yee Gods" (note that 1603 has "Gods"). The song received its first performance before Queen Elizabeth at the accession tilt of November 17, 1590 (see Doughtie 1970: 466), but as Elizabeth died in 1603, subsequent editions were changed. I have restored this aspect of the poem to its original intention.

TWO

A Garden of Embellishment

S INGERS IN THE SIXTEENTH AND EARLY SEVENTEENTH CENTURIES NEEDED to master not only persuasive utterance but also, judging by the descriptions of performances that survive, the techniques of melodic ornamentation. In 1591, the "Dittie of *Come againe* was sung, with excellent division, by two, that were cunning" (Hertford 1591: fol. E2v), and in 1613, Thomas Campion described the singing of an unnamed countertenor with the words "[a] Song was sung by an excellent countertenor voice, with rare varietie of division" (1613/3: fol. B1v). Moreover, in the middle of the sixteenth century, Adrian Petit Coclico (1552: fol. Hiiiv) advised young boys who wanted to learn the art of singing well and elegantly to find a teacher "who . . . can make music beautiful by ornamenting the phrases"/"qui . . . clausularum lenociniis Musicam laetam reddit," and four years later Hermann Finck (1556: fol. Ssiv) gave the opinion that "all the voices [in part song] could and should be sprinkled with embellishments"/"omnibus vocibus & possunt & debent coloraturae aspergi." And toward the end of the century, Lodovico Zacconi (1592: fol. 58) noted that singers enhanced the beauty of music through the addition of ornaments: "with graces and ornaments it [music] is always made to appear more beautiful"/"con le gratie, & gl'accenti la si fa parer sempre piu bella." Fortunately for us today, the styles of embellishment these writers must have known were documented by a number of musicians who left written records of the customs in vogue from around 1530 to about 1625. In this section, I wish to explore the range of practices singers employed during this period.

Within the surviving sources, two distinct types of ornamentation are found, graces and divisions. Graces consist of small melodic figures, frequently of no more than a few notes, that embellish single notes of the original melody, copyists frequently representing these ornaments with stylized signs. Singers applied longer figural patterns to two or more notes of the original melody, and this form of embellishment divided longer notes into shorter ones. Numerous examples of the division style exist, and examination of these ornamented pieces reveals the various ways musicians added figural patterns to the music they sang. Yet beyond these fully notated improvisations, didactic material, in the form of short decorative patterns designed to connect one note to another, survive in a number of sources. Knowledge of these melodic formulas enables modern performers to acquire a ready-made repertory of individual decorative patterns they can apply to music from the period.

DIVISIONS

The material furnished in books and manuscripts by Silvestro Ganassi (1535), Adrian Petit Coclico (1552), Diego Ortiz (1553), Giovanni Camillo Maffei (1562), Girolamo dalla Casa (1584), Giovanni Bassano (1585), Richardo Rogniono (1592), Giovanni Luca Conforto (1593), Giovanni Battista Bovicelli (1594), Aurelio Virgiliano (c. 1600), and Francesco Rognoni (1620) contain figural patterns singers and instrumentalists could add to melodic lines to join successive notes elegantly. The authors provide a number of alternative suggestions for connecting common intervals, ascending and descending, as well as figuration for scalar passages and cadences. In Examples 3.9–3.12, I have selected a number of patterns from these authors, transposed them to the same pitch level, and organized them into a series of figures progressing from simpler formulas to more complex ones. A great deal of stylistic similarity exists across the patterns recorded by the musicians listed above (in fact, the tutors appear to catalogue most of the melodic possibilities for filling in leaps of thirds, fourths, fifths, etc.), and for this reason, an easily identifiable chronology of changes in division style cannot be teased out of the surviving documents. Nonetheless, the dotted figures of Bovicelli and Conforto, as well as some of Rognoni's divisions, seem to represent the musical sensibilities of the late sixteenth and early seventeenth centuries more than they reflect earlier tastes.

Renaissance singers probably memorized many of the patterns contained in division tutors so that they could insert them at the time of performance, and vocalists today can begin their own study of the division style by following a similar plan. I suggest starting with the simpler figures, memorizing and applying them as if improvising, and as skill and flexibility in division making increases, singers can add some of the more complex figures to the repertory of patterns stored in their memories.

In solo songs, one of the division styles that enjoyed favor throughout much of the sixteenth century involved adding embellishments to a vocal melody in the way the Spaniard Diego Ortiz (1553) had done in the middle of the century, and Robert Parsons' song "Poure downe you powers devyne" from the Turpyn songbook (copied in England c. 1610–1615) illustrates how singers applied the older technique in the early seventeenth century (Example 3.13). Parsons died in 1570, and we do not know whether the Turpyn reading was newly created at the time of its copying or whether it had been in existence for decades. Nevertheless, its inclusion in a manuscript copied at some point between 1610 and 1615 suggests that these sorts of divisions remained in use until the second decade of the seventeenth century. The singer who devised this ornamented version of the song added figures to the melody either identical to or similar to those given by Ortiz in his embellishment tables, and the performer simply superimposed figural patterns on the vocal line, a procedure that allowed listeners to discern Parsons' melody quite easily beneath the divisions, one of the hallmarks of the ornamentation style in vogue between c. 1530 and c. 1560 (for a more fully developed discussion of this style, see Brown 1973–74). Indeed, several of the patterns begin and end on the original note (mm. 5, 15, 18, and 42), while others fill in melodic leaps (mm. 17, 28, 42, 52–53, and 79) similarly to some of the figures given in Examples 3.9 and 3.10. Moreover, the singer added the embellishments toward the end of phrases, mainly at the cadences themselves, and this makes these divisions excellent examples of how one might ornament *clausulae* in a mid-sixteenth-century style. Performers today can use the divisions in this source as an illustration of how they might add less-complicated figures to a melody. Their elegant simplicity represents just one end of the spectrum, though, for during the period, embellishments could be much more complex and virtuosic than the Turpyn manuscript suggests.

One of the other styles of division making common in the early seventeenth century (the time of the Turpyn manuscript), as well as in the late sixteenth century, consisted of figures composed of semiquavers (sixteenth notes) applied intermittently to

EXAMPLE 3.9 *Connecting semibreves (whole notes): (a) moving by a second; (b) three semibreves (whole notes) moving by a second; (c) moving by a third; (d) moving by a fourth; (e) moving by a fifth*

(Continued)

EXAMPLE 3.9 (*Continued*)

(b)

(c)

(Continued)

EXAMPLE 3.9c *(Continued)*

(d)

(Continued)

EXAMPLE 3.9d (*Continued*)

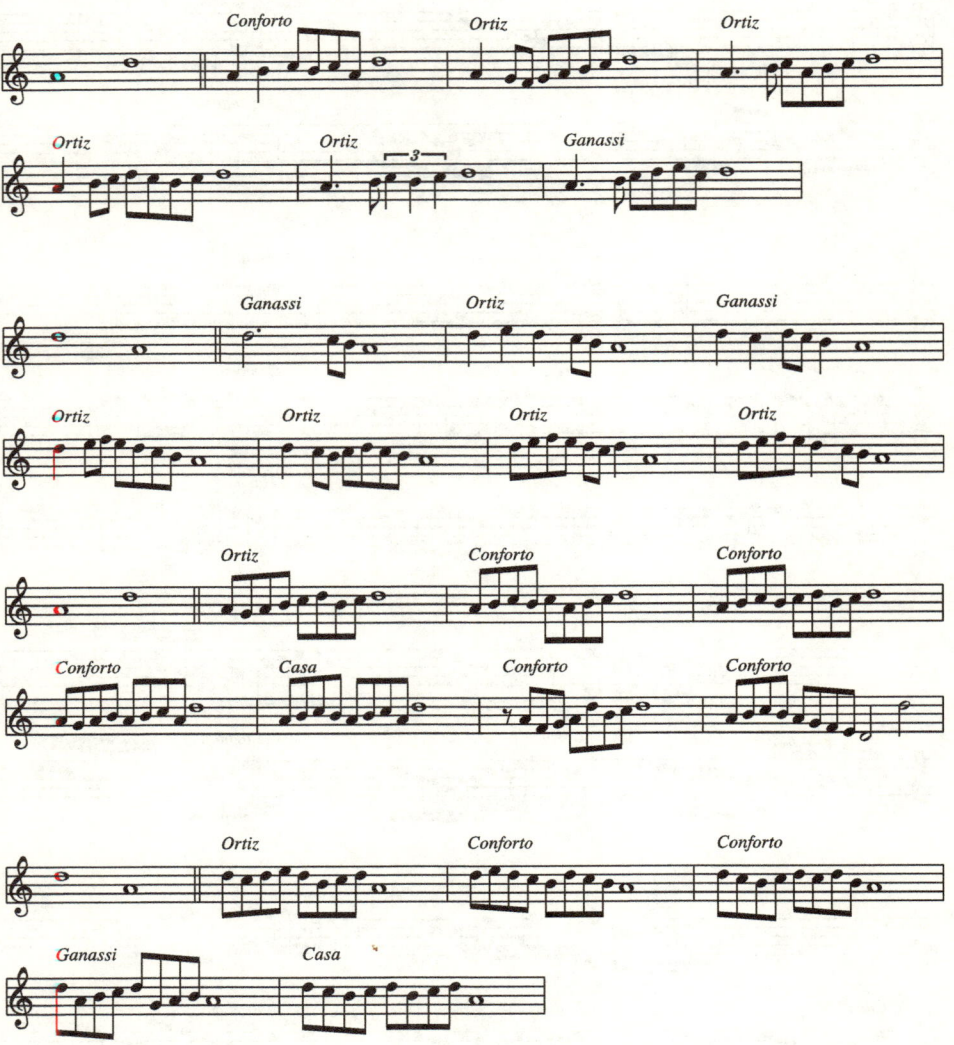

(Continued)

EXAMPLE 3.9d (*Continued*)

EXAMPLE 3.9e (*Continued*)

EXAMPLE 3.10 *Connecting minims (half notes): (a) moving by a second; (b) moving by a third; (c) moving by a fourth; (d) moving by a fifth*

(a)

(Continued)

EXAMPLE 3.10a (*Continued*)

(b)

(Continued)

EXAMPLE 3.10c

(d)

(Continued)

EXAMPLE 3.10d (*Continued*)

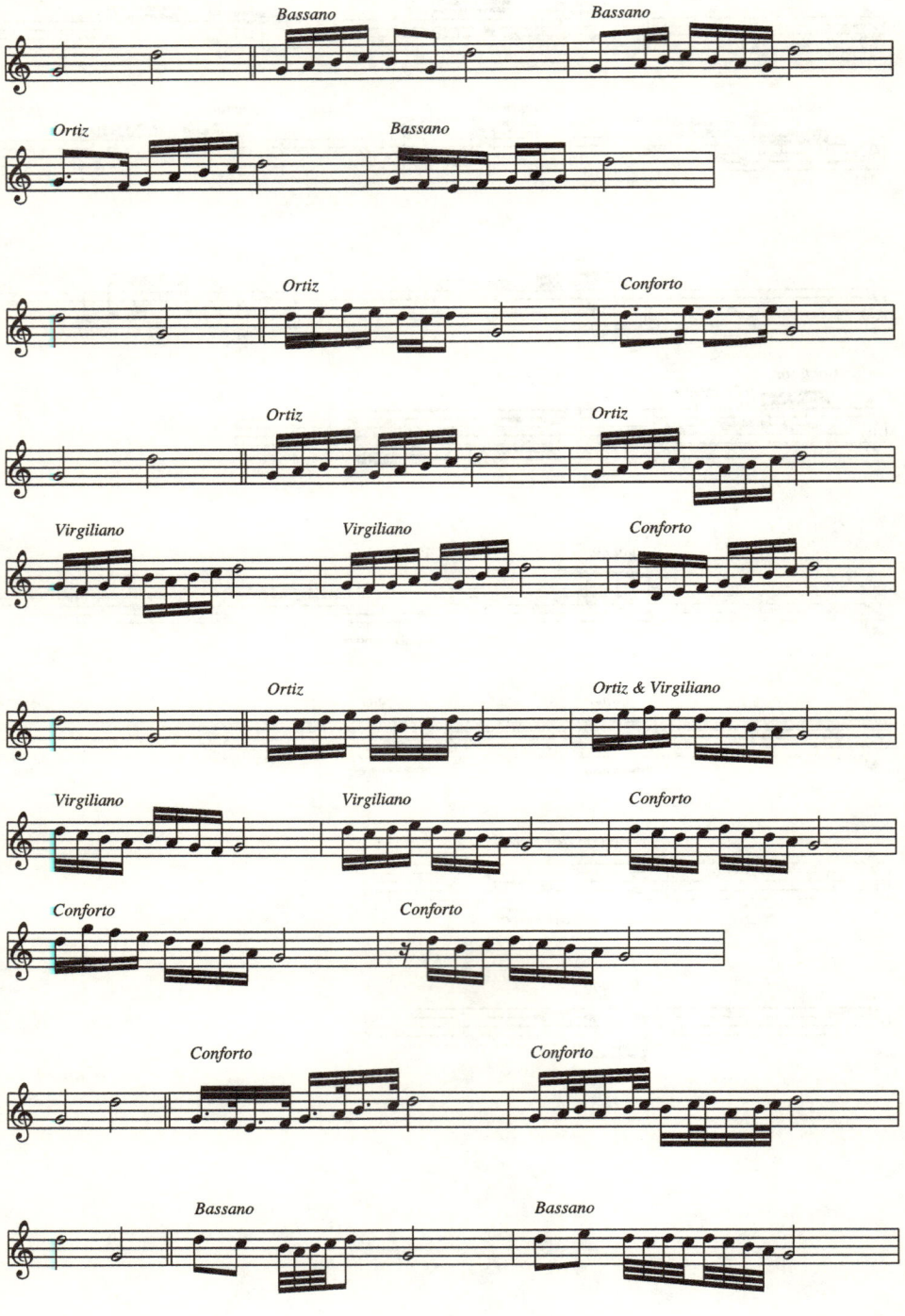

EXAMPLE 3.11 *Scale passages: (a) Ortiz 1553; (b) F. Rognoni 1620*

(a)

(b)

EXAMPLE 3.12 *Cadences: (a) Ganassi 1535; (b) Maffei 1562*

(a)

(b)

EXAMPLE 3.13 *Robert Parsons, "Poure downe you powers devyne"*

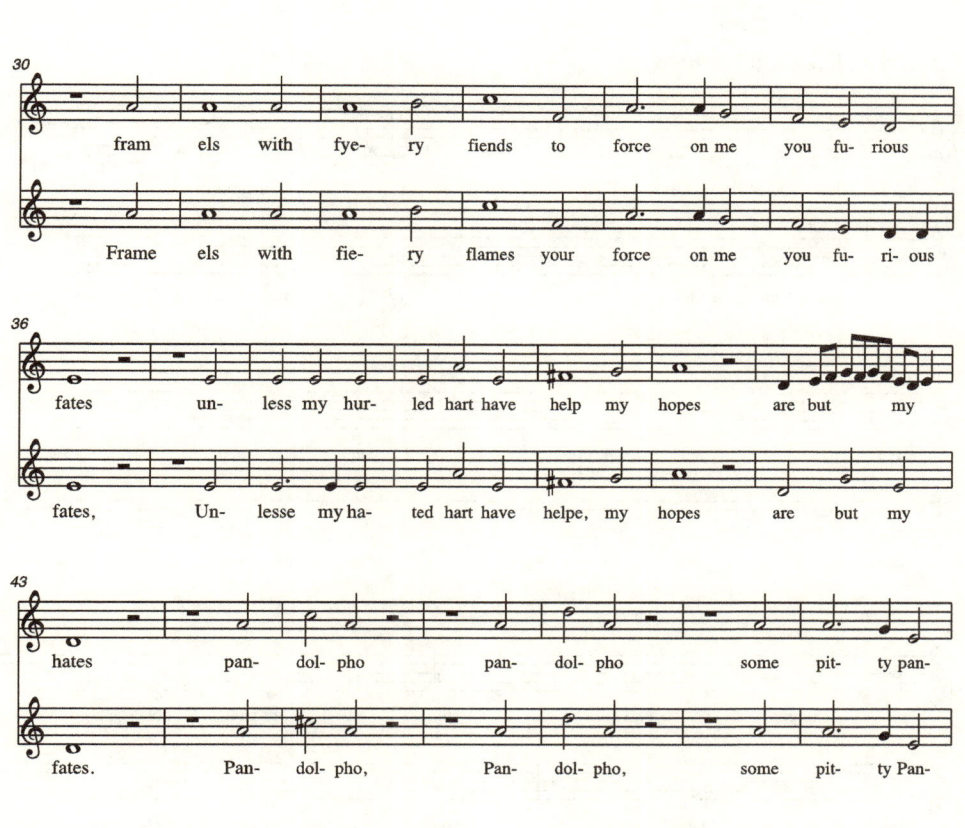

fram els with fye- ry fiends to force on me you fu- rious

Frame els with fie- ry flames your force on me you fu- ri- ous

fates un- less my hur- led hart have help my hopes are but my

fates, Un- lesse my ha- ted hart have helpe, my hopes are but my

hates pan- dol- pho pan- dol- pho some pit- ty pan-

fates. Pan- dol- pho, Pan- dol- pho, some pit- ty Pan-

dol- pho some pit- ty pan- dol- pho thus rest- less

dol- pho some pit- ty Pan- dol- pho Thus rest- lesse

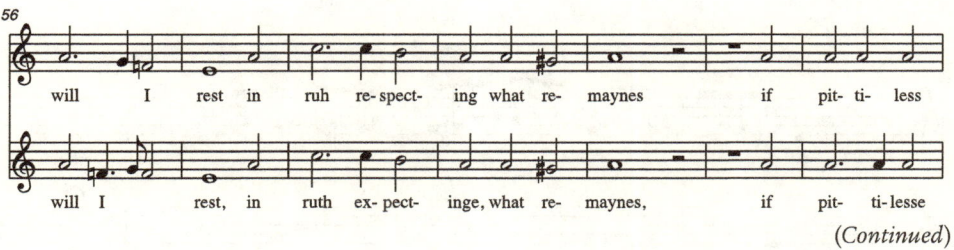

will I rest in ruh re- spect- ing what re- maynes if pit- ti- less

will I rest, in ruth ex- pect- inge, what re- maynes, if pit- ti- lesse

(Continued)

EXAMPLE 3.13 (*Continued*)

then plea- sure- less if pi- ti- full no

then plea- sure- lesse, if pit- ty feele noe

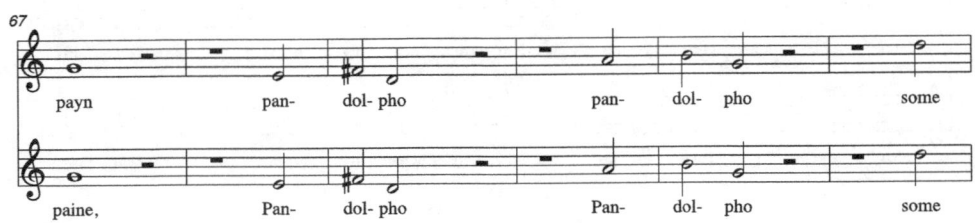

payn pan- dol- pho pan- dol- pho some

paine, Pan- dol- pho Pan- dol- pho some

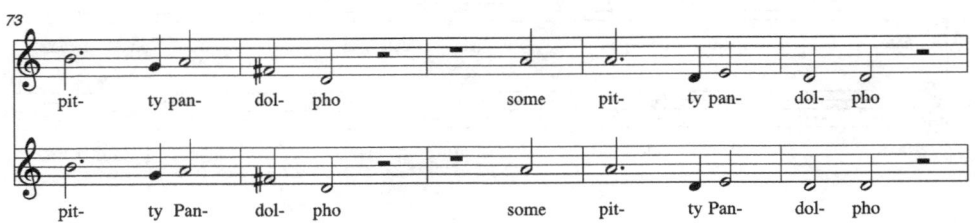

pit- ty pan- dol- pho some pit- ty pan- dol- pho

pit- ty Pan- dol- pho some pit- ty Pan- dol- pho

some pit- ty pan- dol- pho some

some pit- ty Pan- dol- pho some

pit- ty pan- dol- pho.

pit- ty Pan- dol- pho.

an entire song. A number of sources contain pieces ornamented in this way, and several manuscripts copied in England illustrate not only the procedures but also the degree to which the Italian manner, as exemplified by Casa (1584), Bassano (1585 and 1591), Rogniono (1592), Bovicelli (1594), and Rognoni (1620), had become popular in England. However, not surprisingly several embellishment styles existed within this general custom. A version of John Wilbye's "Weepe myne eyes" (Egerton 2971, second decade of the seventeenth century; Example 3.14) represents an approach in which the divisions replace longer notes with shorter ones in a way reminiscent of ornamentation found in Bassano (1585, 1591). The singer filled in leaps (mm. 3 and 7) and decorated repeated notes with figures that begin and end on the original note (mm. 4 and 10). But at other times, the divisions stray quite far from Wilbye's melody (m. 9), and at the end of the song the performer expanded the final cadence through divisions that doubled the length of the penultimate and antepenultimate notes. Although cadences receive a considerable amount of decoration throughout the song, the singer by no means restricted the ornamentation to *clausulae*, for divisions appear at both the beginning (m. 14) and the middle portions (mm. 5–7) of phrases. Furthermore, some figures employ musical *climax* as a method of increasing the forward drive and intensity of the figuration (mm. 7, 10, and 14). Interestingly, the singer seems to have conceived the ornamentation mainly for musical reasons, as unimportant words, such as "and" (m. 9), as well as rather more important words, such as "no" (m. 4) and "thousand" (m. 14), receive musical emphasis through divisions. All of these comments apply equally well to the three other ornamented songs in Egerton 2971, the anonymous "This merrie pleasant springe" (fol. 16v) and "Art thou that she" (fol. 9v), and Alfonso Ferrabosco's "Drowne not with teares" (fol. 13v). In fact, John Dowland may have had this nontextual approach in mind when he wrote of "simple Cantors, or vocall singers" and their "blinde Division-making" (1612: "To the Reader"). These types of divisions certainly would destroy any carefully constructed connection between verbal and musical rhetoric.

Undoubtedly, Dowland also would have scorned a singer like Giles Earle, owner of the manuscript British Library, Add. 24665, because the divisions in Earle's book easily would have earned the contemptuous remark that such "blinde Division-making" was the product of a singer "meerley ignorant, even in the first elements of Musicke" (Dowland 1612: "To the Reader"). However, in 1612 Dowland felt decidedly old-fashioned, and in reference to the "simple Cantors, or vocall singers," he laments "yet doe these fellowes give their verdict of me behinde my backe, and say, what I doe is after the old manner." Taste in "Division-making" obviously had changed for many musicians, and the version of Daniel Batchelar's "To plead my faith" in Earle's book (Example 3.15), in addition to illustrating another of the late sixteenth- and early seventeenth-century styles of ornamentation, may well contain the type of divisions Dowland's musical temperament could not abide. Nonetheless, on closer examination the divisions in "To plead my faith" really are not so blind; rather they exemplify the sophisticated liberty some singers took when incorporating divisions.

EXAMPLE 3.14 *John Wilbye, "Weepe myne eyes"*

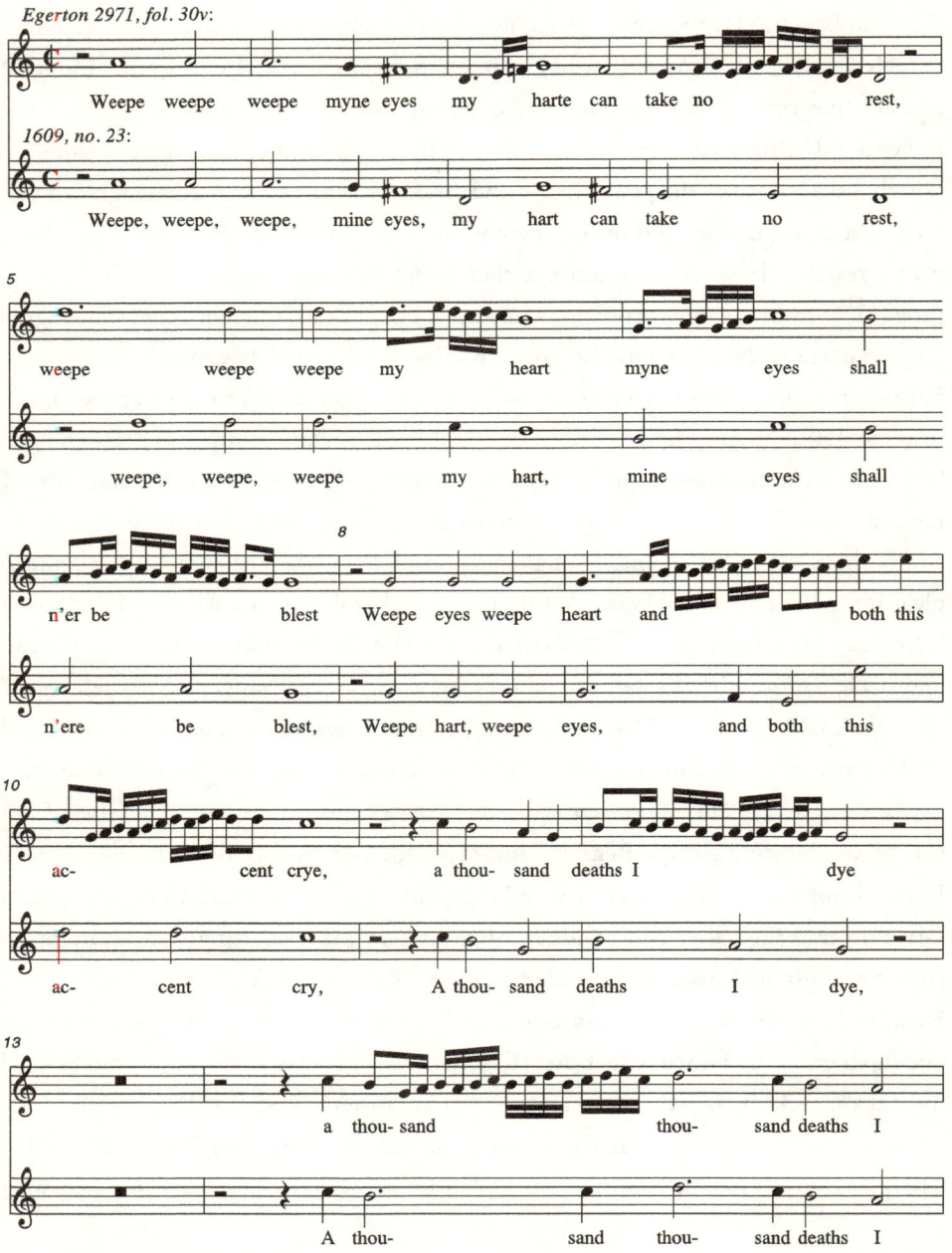

15

dye,   a thou- sand deaths I   dye, Aye

dye, I dye, a thou- sand thou- sand deaths I   dye, Aye

18

me! ah ah cru- ell For- tune Aye me! Nowe Le- an- der to dye I

me, ah, ah, cru- ell For- tune, Aye me, Now Le- an- der to dye I

21

feare not,   Death doe thie worst I care not, Death doe thie   worst I care

feare not,   Death doe thy worst I care not, Death doe   thy worst I care

24

not Death   doe thie worst I care not   I hope   I hope

not, Death   do thy worst I care not,   I hope,   I hope

28

when I am dead,   in E- li- zium playne   in E- li- zium   playne

when I am dead   in E- li- zian plaine,   in E- li-   zian plaine,

(Continued)

EXAMPLE 3.14 (*Continued*)

In contrast to singers represented in other sources from the period, Earle exhibited great rhythmic freedom in dividing longer notes into shorter ones. In fact, he showed little concern for replacing minims (half notes) with smaller notes that totaled the same rhythmic value as the original, for sometimes he substituted more notes than the time value strictly would allow (see m. 9, where he replaced the last minim with the equivalent of eleven semiquavers [sixteenth notes] instead of the usual eight, as well as mm. 31, 57, 59, and 63, where similar procedures occur on minims). Like other performers, however, he frequently expanded the penultimate and/or antepenultimate notes of the original to accommodate elaborate cadential figuration (mm. 11, 19, 23, 27, 31, and 39). But not all cadences received this expansive treatment (mm. 3–4, 7–8, 15–16, 35–36, 43–44, 47–48, 51–52, and 55–56), and he occasionally employed this sort of elaborate figuration at the beginning of a phrase as well (mm. 9 and 57). Nonetheless, the specific figural patterns he uses share many traits with those found in other sources, and similarly to "Weepe myne eyes" (Example 3.14), Earle's divisions seem to have been conceived for musical and not textual reasons. Earle, too, fills in leaps (m. 5) and strays from the original melody, even in the simplest ornamentation

EXAMPLE 3.15 *Daniel Batchelar, "To plead my faith"*

British Library, Add. 24,665, fol. 48v
(bar lines added editorially):

To plead my faith where faith hath noe re- ward,

1610, no. 6:

To plead my faith where faith hath no re- ward,

To move re- morce where fa- voure is not borne,

To move re- morse where fa- vour is not borne:

To heape com- plaintes which shee doth not re- gard

To heape com- plaints wher she doth

re- gard, were fruit- les, boot- les, vaine,

not re- gard, Were fruit- lesse, boote- lesse, vaine

and yeeld's but scorne. I lov- ed her whome all

and yeeld but scorne. I lov- ed her whom all

(Continued)

EXAMPLE 3.15 (*Continued*)

* One note has been added to make this cadential figure identical to that of bar 27.

† ms. = ♩.

34
name since she hath scorn'd my love, and woe- men-

name since you have scornde my Love, And wo- man-

38
like doe not too late la-

like doe not too late la-

40
ment, since for her sake I must all mis- cheife

ment: Since for your sake I doe all mis- chiefe

44
prove, I none ac- cuse, nor no- thing doe re-

prove. I none ac- cuse nor no- thing doe re-

48
pent. I was as fond as e- ver shee was

pent. I was as fonde as e- ver she was

* ms. = ♪

(*Continued*)

EXAMPLE 3.15 (*Continued*)

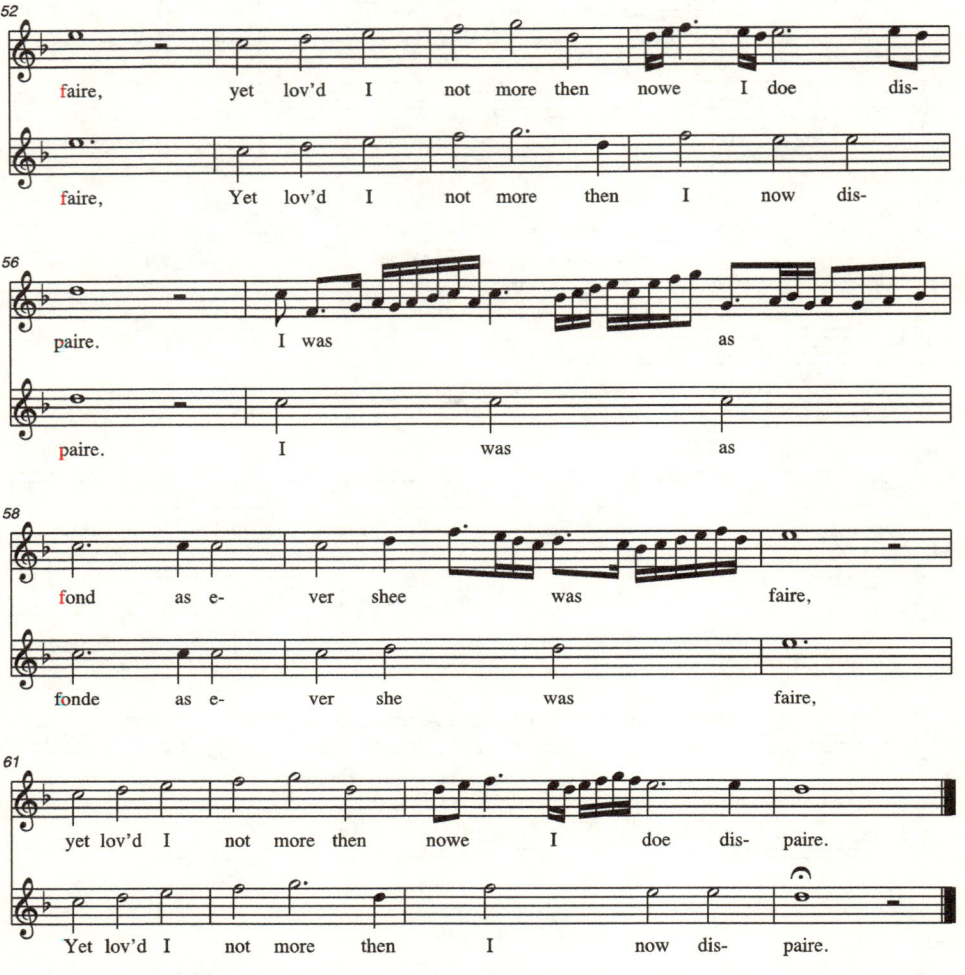

(mm. 14–15). He also creates, just like the singer in Egerton 2971 (Example 3.14), the musical figure *climax* through his embellishments, employing it to intensify the rising, stepwise motion of Batchelar's melody (m. 29). The use of *climax* and *gradatio* (the extension of the figure beyond one restatement) had become, of course, a common way of decorating scalar passages, and a number of examples can be found in both English and Italian sources (Example 3.16).

Four other manuscripts from about the same time period as Earle's songbook, Christ Church 439 (before 1620) and 87 (Elizabeth Davenant's songbook, c. 1624), Fitzwilliam Mu 782 (c. 1620), and British Library, Add. 29481 (1620s), show that the rhythmic freedom characteristic of some of the divisions in "To plead my faith" had

EXAMPLE 3.16 *Ascending and descending scalar passages (compare to the passages given in Example 3.11): (a) ascending; (b) descending*

(a)

1) *English*:

Anon., "This merry pleasant spring"

Eg. 2971, fol. 17r

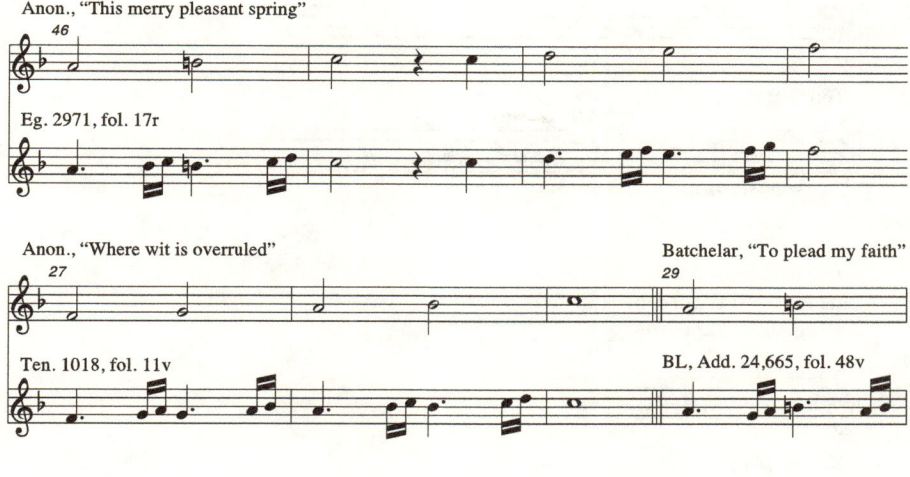

Anon., "Where wit is overruled"   Batchelar, "To plead my faith"

Ten. 1018, fol. 11v   BL, Add. 24,665, fol. 48v

Italian:

de Rore, "Ben qui si mostra"
(Erig 1979: 231)

Notari 1613

2) *English*:

Anon., "Nothinge ont earth remained"

Ten. 1019, fol. 6r

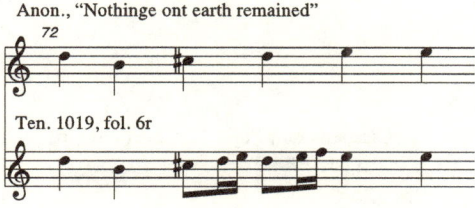

Italian:

de Rore, "Ben qui si mostra"   Crequillon, "Oncques amour"
(Erig 1979: 228)   (Erig 1979: 124)

Notari 1613   dalla Casa 1584

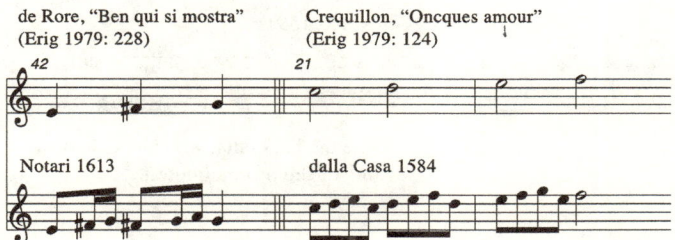

(Continued)

EXAMPLE 3.16 (*Continued*)

(b)

1)　*English*

Anon., "Nothinge ont earth remained"

2)　*English*

Batchelar, "To plead my faith"

Italian

de Rore, "Ben qui si mostra"
(Erig 1979: 225)

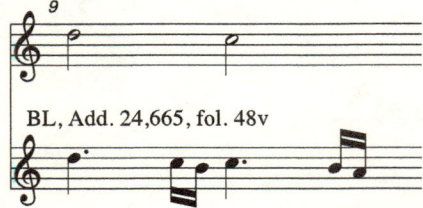

Clemens non Papa, "Frais et gaillard"　　　　Clemens non Papa, "Frais et gaillard"
(Erig 1979: 91)　　　　　　　　　　　　　　(Erig 1979: 99)

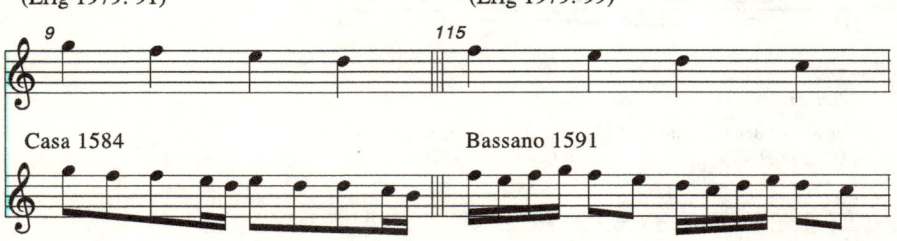

[Note the backfalls, which take half the
value of the original note.]

become a common feature of vocal ornamentation. In Ferrabosco's "Why stayes the bridegroome" (Christ Church 439; Example 3.17), the rhythmic freedom not only occurs near the beginning of the song (m. 3), but the singer also had expanded almost every cadence through elaborate ornamentation (mm. 5, 10, 15, and 23–24). Two songs by Campion illustrate the same principle, albeit to a lesser degree. Although "Come you pretty false-ey'd wanton" (Davenant's songbook; Example 3.18) receives rhythmic expansion in just one place (m. 7), the reading demonstrates how singers added divisions to an entire song more or less continuously. The second phrase is particularly instructive, for it shows a way of applying discrete figural patterns to about two-thirds of the notes while maintaining the contour of the original melody. "Shall I come sweet love to thee" (Add. 29481; Example 3.19) also contains rhythmic freedom in just one passage (mm. 10–11), and like the Turpyn songbook (Example 3.13), the vocalist confines the divisions to cadences. However, unlike the cadential treatment in Earle's songbook (Example 3.15) and Christ Church 439 (Example 3.17), the divisions remain within the context of the original melody, never increasing the overall length of cadential passages (Example 3.19; mm. 3, 15, 21, and 24).

The surviving sources, then, provide modern singers with a number of options for incorporating divisions in their performances. In mid-sixteenth-century music, one could either ornament cadences with divisions similar to those found in Ortiz 1553 and the Turpyn songbook (Example 3.13) or apply discrete figuration to entire musical phrases in the manner suggested by Christ Church 87 (Example 3.18). But for late sixteenth- and early seventeenth-century music, performers might prefer one of the highly elaborate embellishment styles. The rhythmic freedom and expansive treatment of cadences exhibited in Earle's songbook represent one alternative (Example 3.15), while the less flamboyant but still complex divisions of Egerton 2971 offer another possibility (Example 3.14). Of course, one could decide not to add any divisions at all, and this too follows historical precedent, for not every song in the manuscripts discussed here carries divisions.

Moreover, the placement of syllables in the embellishments shown in Examples 3.13–3.15 and 3.17–3.19 contravenes many of the principles of text underlay discussed above in Part 1, "Words Appropriately Fitted to the Notes," for these fully decorated versions illustrate the license copyists and/or singers took when making decisions about questions of text location. Divisions occur on both unimportant words (Example 3.13: "to"; Example 3.14: "and"; Example 3.15: "to," "and," "as"; Example 3.19: "the") and unaccented syllables (Example 3.17: "-bler" of "nobler"; 3.18: "-ir" of "craftir"; 3.19: "-ed" of "fained"), and undoubtedly someone like Giovanni Battista Bovicelli would have frowned on these practices, for in his discussion of word-note relations he listed virtually identical principles of text placement to those of earlier theorists (see 1594: 7–9,

EXAMPLE 3.17 *Alfonso Ferrabosco, "Why stayes the bridegroome"*

EXAMPLE 3.18 *Thomas Campion, "Come you pretty false-ey'd wanton"*

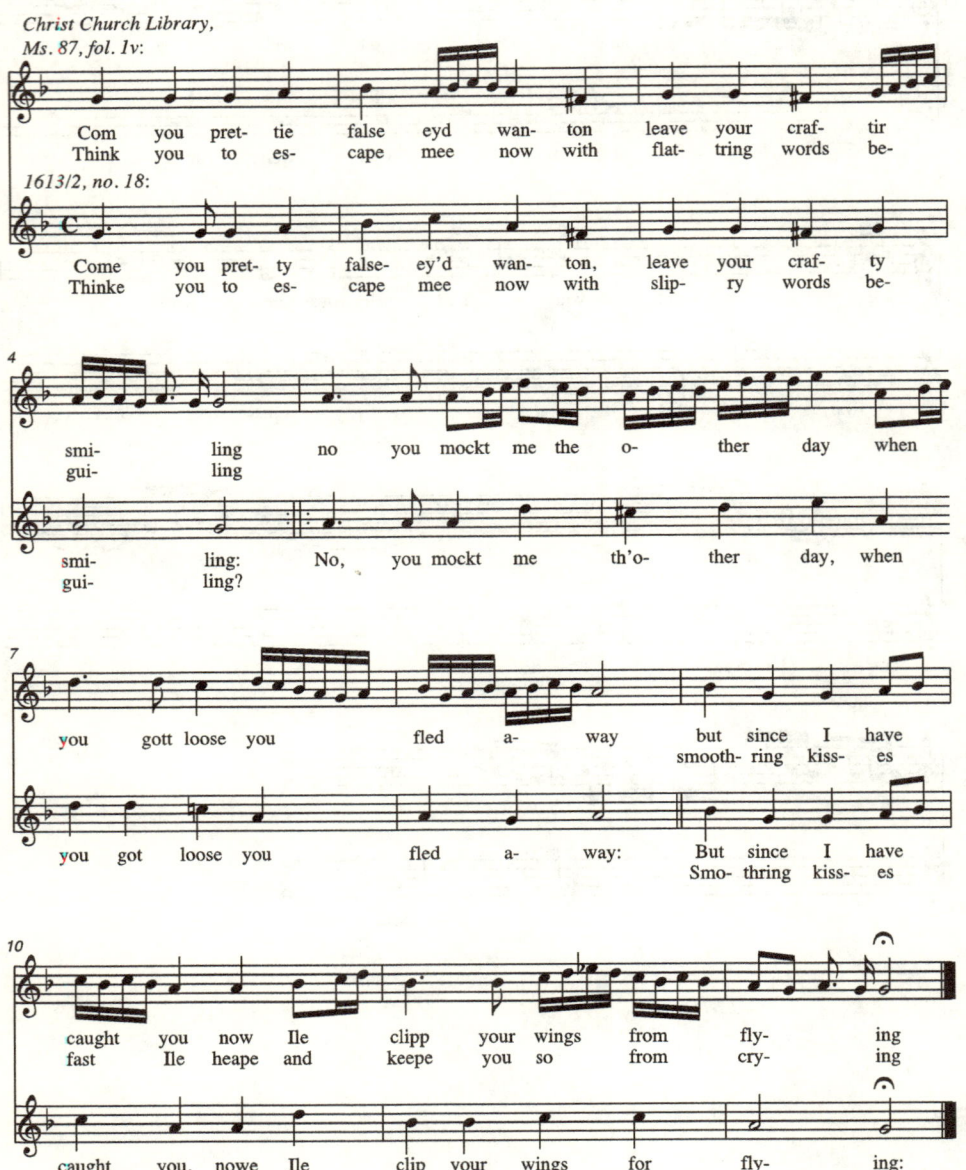

Christ Church Library,
Ms. 87, fol. 1v:

Com you pret- tie false eyd wan- ton leave your craf- tir
Think you to es- cape mee now with flat- tring words be-

1613/2, no. 18:

Come you pret- ty false- ey'd wan- ton, leave your craf- ty
Thinke you to es- cape mee now with slip- ry words be-

smi- ling no you mockt me the o- ther day when
gui- ling

smi- ling: No, you mockt me th'o- ther day, when
gui- ling?

you gott loose you fled a- way but since I have
smooth- ring kiss- es

you got loose you fled a- way: But since I have
Smo- thring kiss- es

caught you now Ile clipp your wings from fly- ing
fast Ile heape and keepe you so from cry- ing

caught you, nowe Ile clip your wings for fly- ing:
fast Ile heape, and keepe you so from cry- ing.

EXAMPLE 3.19 *Thomas Campion, "Shall I come sweet love to thee"*

BL, Add. 29481, fol. 20r:

Shall   I   com   sweet   love   to   thee   when   thy

1618/3, no. 17:

Shall   I   come sweet   Love   to   thee,   When   the

eve-   ninge   beames   are   sett   shall   I   not ex-

ev'-   ning   beames   are   set?   Shall   I   not   ex-

clu-   ded   be   will you   finde   no   fain- ed

clu-   ded   be?   Will you   finde   no   fain-   ed

let   let   not   for   pit- tie a- ny   more   tell the   longe

lett?   Let me   not   for   pit-   ty   more,   Tell the   long,   long

howers   tell the   long   howers   at the   door

houres,   tel   the   long   houres   at   your   dore.

"Avertimenti per li passaggi" and the summary in Harrán 1986: 276–80). Nevertheless, this approach to fitting words to notes does exist as part of late Renaissance practices, even though Dowland would have called the musicians responsible "blinde."

GRACES

In addition to providing a wealth of information on divisions, a number of the sources illustrate the use of graces in the early seventeenth century. Fortunately, many of the graces in these documents have been fully written out, and this allows us to achieve a reasonably secure interpretation of the stylized signs many copyists and print-ers employed to represent the ornaments. For example, the graces commonly sung in England during this period remained in vogue for much of the century, as later sources confirm, and they equate directly to ornaments found in late sixteenth- and early seventeenth-century Italian documents. The written-out graces include the shake, relish, cadent, elevation or fall, backfall, and springer, whereas the stylized signs include the shake, cadent, elevation, springer, and beate. The signs and their interpre-tation, as derived from various later seventeenth-century English writers, appear in Example 3.20, and this table agrees, for the most part, with written-out graces notated in both English and Italian sources (Example 3.21).

Several English song manuscripts write out the shake as a cadential ornament (Example 3.21 1b), and all three sources that contain "This merry pleasant spring" (the Turpyn songbook, Egerton 2971, and Christ Church 439) use it to depict the word "quiver" (Example 3.21 1a). Although I have not found identical passages in Italian sources, Casa employs similar cadential ornamentation (Example 3.21 1c, 1d). The relish occurs only in Christ Church 87 but not in the form described by later seventeenth-century writers; rather it conforms to Thomas Robinson's explana-tion (1603) of the grace as an upper-note figure (Example 3.21 2). Both English and Italian sources notate the cadent in an identical fashion (Example 3.21 3a, 3b, 3d, 3e), the earliest example of the fully written-out grace in the English song manuscripts dis-cussed here coming from the Turpyn songbook (Example 3.21 3c). Elevations or falls, however, occur in a wide variety of forms. The most common configuration in English sources is that shown in Example 3.21 4a, b, where singers apply the grace to long as well as short notes, but the elevation also appears in the form given in Example 3.21 4c. Moreover, vocalists sometimes extend elevations beyond the interval of a third to encompass a fourth (Example 3.21 4d), a fifth (Example 3.21 4e), or even an octave (Example 3.21 4f). Yet quite a different type of elevation, the dotted form, exists in the English and Italian sources (Example 3.21 4g to 4k). Although in Example 3.21 4g the copyist does not clarify whether the grace should be performed before the beat or on

EXAMPLE 3.20 *Graces from later seventeenth-century English sources*

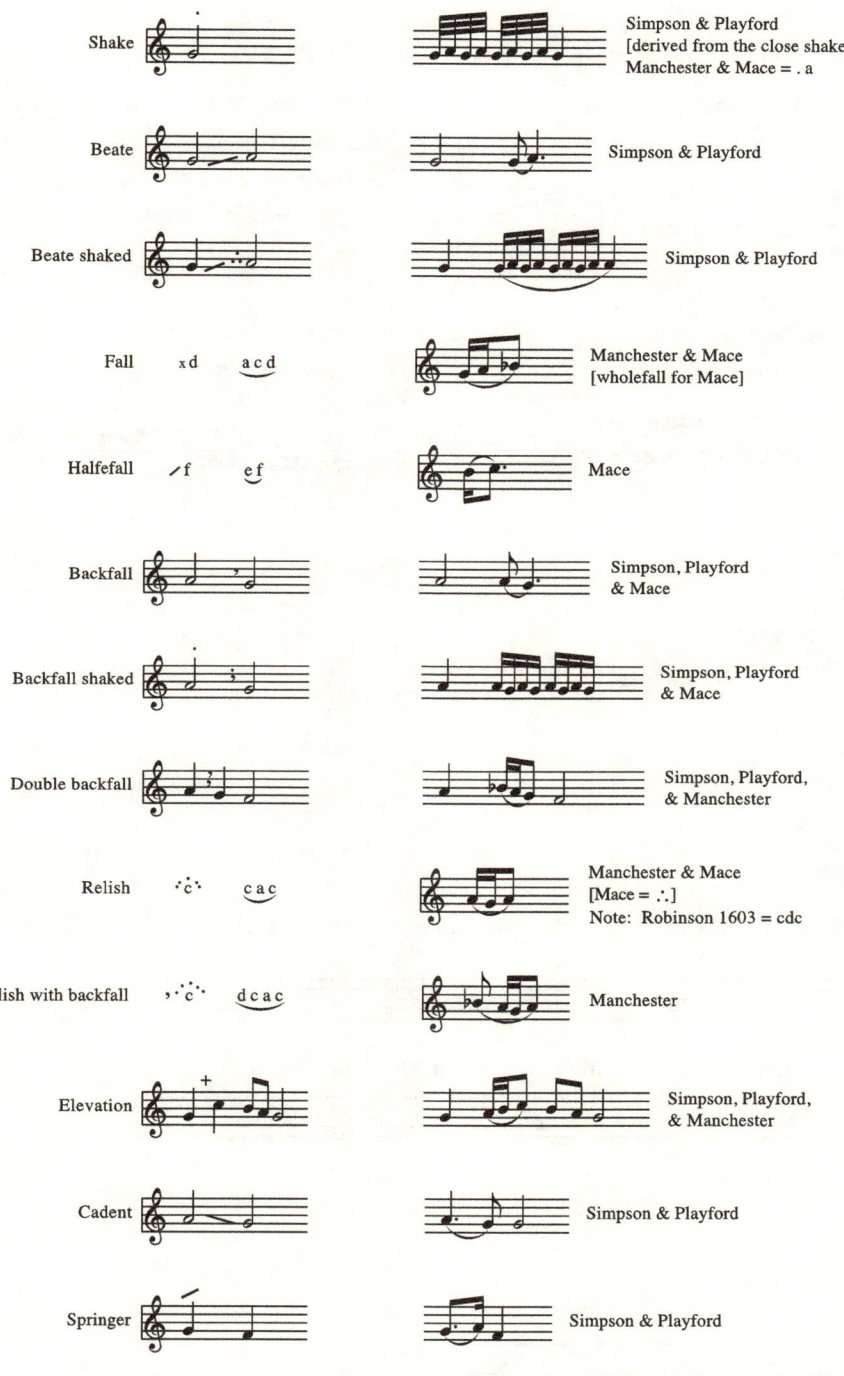

Sources: Manchester. Public Library, Watson Collection, Ms. 832 Vu 51 [*c.* 1660]
Simpson, Christopher. *The Division-Viol*. London, 1665
Playford, John. *An Introduction to the Skill of Musick*. London, 1674
Mace, Thomas. *Musick's Monument*. London, 1676

EXAMPLE 3.21 *Written-out graces*

1. Shake

English

a) Anon., "This merry pleasant spring"

Christ Church 439, p. 42

b) Ferrabosco, "Drowne not with teares"

Egerton 2971, fol. 14r

Italian

c) de Rore, "Ben qui si mostra"

Casa 1584; Erig 1979: 232

d) Crecquillon, "Oncques amour"

Casa 1584; Erig 1979: 127

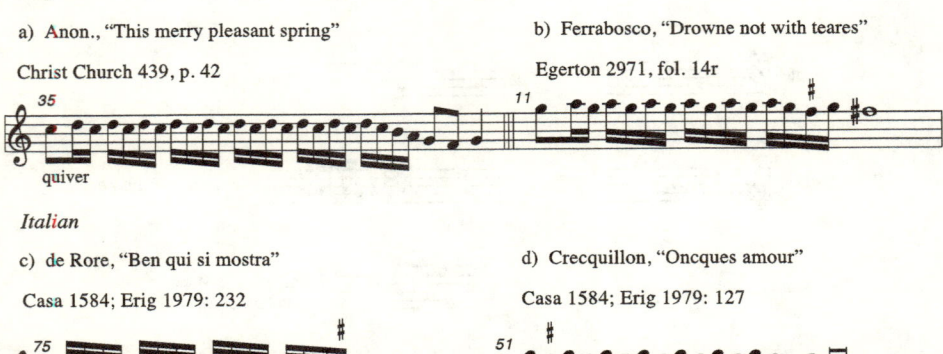

2. Relish

English

Anon., "Eyes gaze no more"

Christ Church 87, fol. 9v

3. Cadent

English

a) Campion, "Silly boy"   b) Morley, "With my love"   c) Parsons, "No griefe"

BL, Add. 24,665, fol. 50v   Christ Church 439, p. 37   Turpyn, no. 6

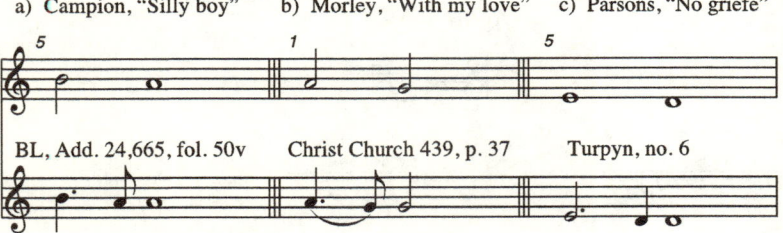

Italian

Palestrina, "Io son ferito"

d) *124*   e) *126*

Bovicelli, 1594; Erig 1979: 265

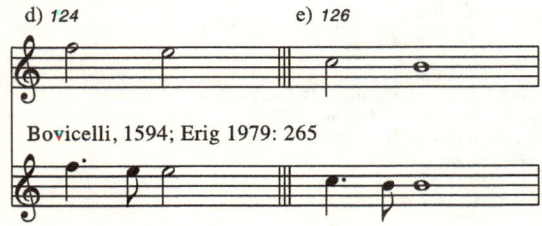

4. Elevation or Fall

English

a) Batchelar, "To plead my faith"   b) Anon., "Art thou that she"   c) Anon., "Eyes gaze no more"

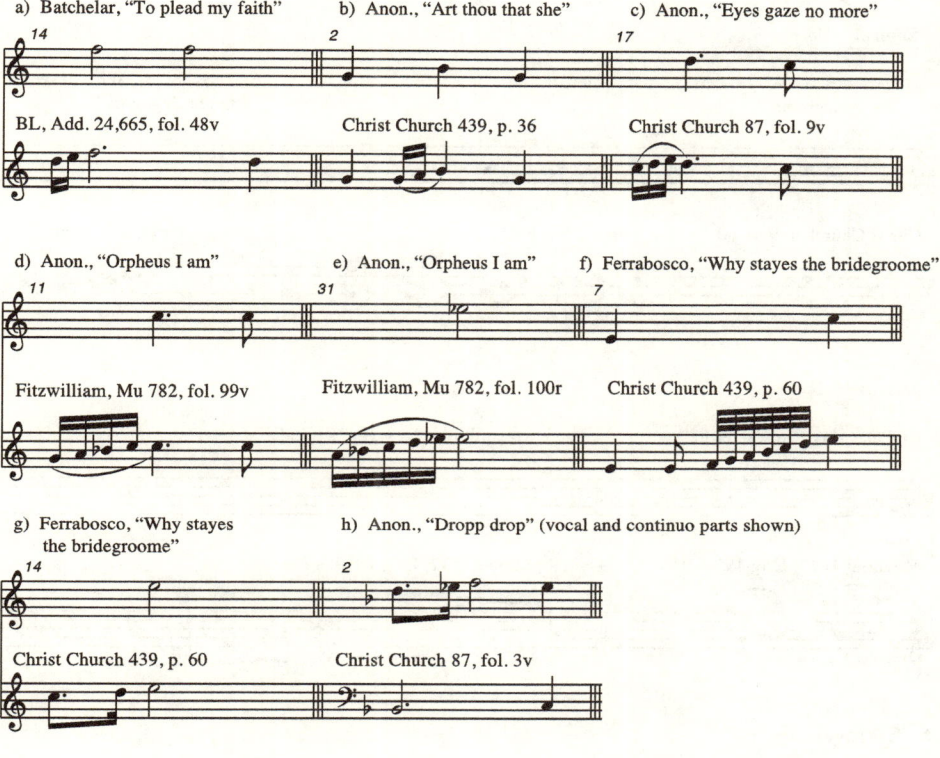

BL, Add. 24,665, fol. 48v   Christ Church 439, p. 36   Christ Church 87, fol. 9v

d) Anon., "Orpheus I am"   e) Anon., "Orpheus I am"   f) Ferrabosco, "Why stayes the bridegroome"

Fitzwilliam, Mu 782, fol. 99v   Fitzwilliam, Mu 782, fol. 100r   Christ Church 439, p. 60

g) Ferrabosco, "Why stayes   h) Anon., "Dropp drop" (vocal and continuo parts shown)
   the bridegroome"

Christ Church 439, p. 60   Christ Church 87, fol. 3v

Italian

i) Palestrina "Io son ferito"   Palestrina "Pulchra es"

j) *32*   k) *62*

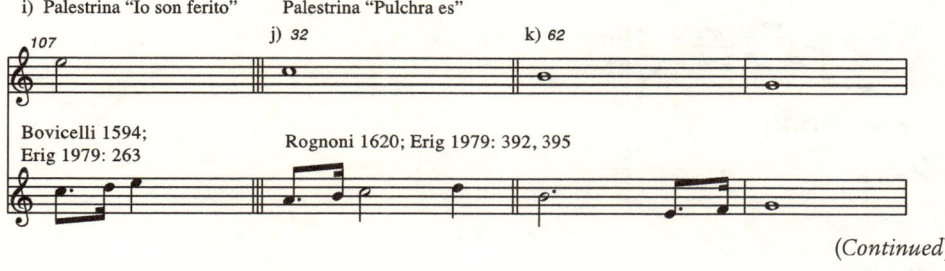

Bovicelli 1594;   Rognoni 1620; Erig 1979: 392, 395
Erig 1979: 263

(Continued)

EXAMPLE 3.21 (*Continued*)

5. Backfall

English

a) Ferrabosco, "Why stayes the bridegroome"   b) Anon., "You that have"   c) Ferrabosco, "Why stayes the bridegroome"

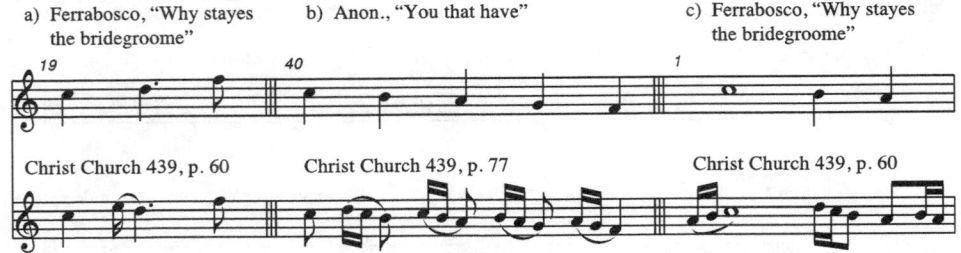

Christ Church 439, p. 60   Christ Church 439, p. 77   Christ Church 439, p. 60

Italian

d) Palestrina, "Io son ferito"   e) Crecquillon, "Ung gay bergier"

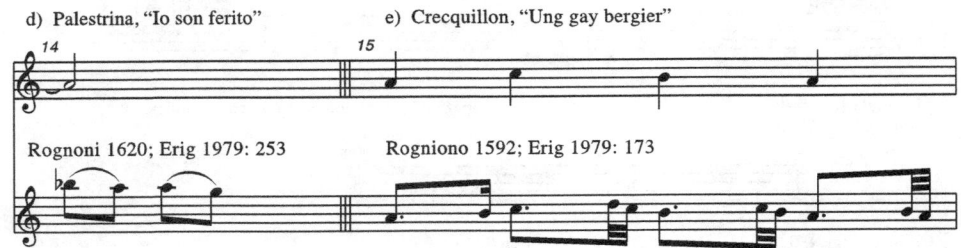

Rognoni 1620; Erig 1979: 253   Rogniono 1592; Erig 1979: 173

6. Springer

English

a) Anon., "Where wit"

Tenbury 1018, fol. 11v

Italian

b) Palestrina, "Io son ferito"

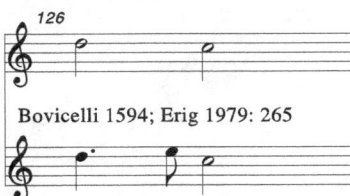

Bovicelli 1594; Erig 1979: 265

the beat, Example 3.21 4h shows the ornament starting on the beat (as the sources in Example 3.20 illustrate) and taking time away from the note being embellished. Italian sources confirm this reading (Example 3.21 4i, 4j), but before-the-beat interpretations also exist (Example 3.21 4k). Backfalls appear in two forms: the single (Example 3.21 5a, 5d) and the double (Example 3.21 5b, 5c, 5e). In the one English source that writes out a single backfall, Christ Church 439 (Example 3.21 5a), the grace note seems to be of a short duration in relation to the main note (as the later sources in Example 3.20 indicate), but in one of the Italian sources, Rognoni 1620 (Example 3.21 5d), both the grace note and the main note receive the same duration. Interestingly, Christ Church 439 provides examples of written-out double backfalls, as well. In Example 3.21 5b, the manuscript clearly indicates a before-the-beat performance (in opposition to the later English sources shown in Example 3.20), with at least one Italian source (Example 3.21 5e) supporting this interpretation, but Example 3.21 5c shows an on-the-beat performance. The final grace to be discussed, the springer, occurs in Tenbury 1018, where the singer uses it in series to decorate a descending melodic line (Example 3.21 6a), and this grace also appears in Italian sources, especially Bovicelli 1594 (Example 3.21 6b).

In addition to writing out a number of graces in full, English manuscripts use stylized signs to indicate five ornaments (Example 3.22). When viewed in relation to Examples 3.20 and 3.21, the realization of these signs presents only one problem. The primary difficulty concerns whether the shake should begin on the main note or its upper neighbor. This is especially problematic when the upper neighbor precedes the note to receive the shake (Example 3.22 Shake a, b, c), and one of the normal practices may have been to begin the shake with a backfall (Example 3.20, backfall and shake). For this reason, I have suggested two solutions for each example. But without knowing the precise configuration of the ornament the copyists intended to suggest by the sign, all solutions must remain speculative. Furthermore, the interpretation of two of the signs in Example 3.22 has been aided by Edward Bevin's table of ornaments entitled "Graces in play," in the keyboard manuscript British Library, Add. 31403 (fol. 5r; Example 3.23). David Wulstan (1985: 130–31) argues that Bevin's table belongs to the second quarter of the seventeenth century and that because the section of Add. 31403 that Bevin copied contains works by Bull, Gibbons, Byrd, and others, the signs may reflect earlier practices. Wulstan's hypothesis may very well be correct, for written-out graces in both the English and Italian vocal sources discussed above corroborate his suggestion. Apparently, then, singers and keyboard players employed some of the same graces. Moreover, the hook at the right end of the second stroke in measure one seems to instruct performers to conclude the grace with a backfall, whereas the hook at the left end of the double stroke in measure two probably indicates that the shake should begin with a backfall, that is, should start on the upper note.

EXAMPLE 3.22 *Grace signs*

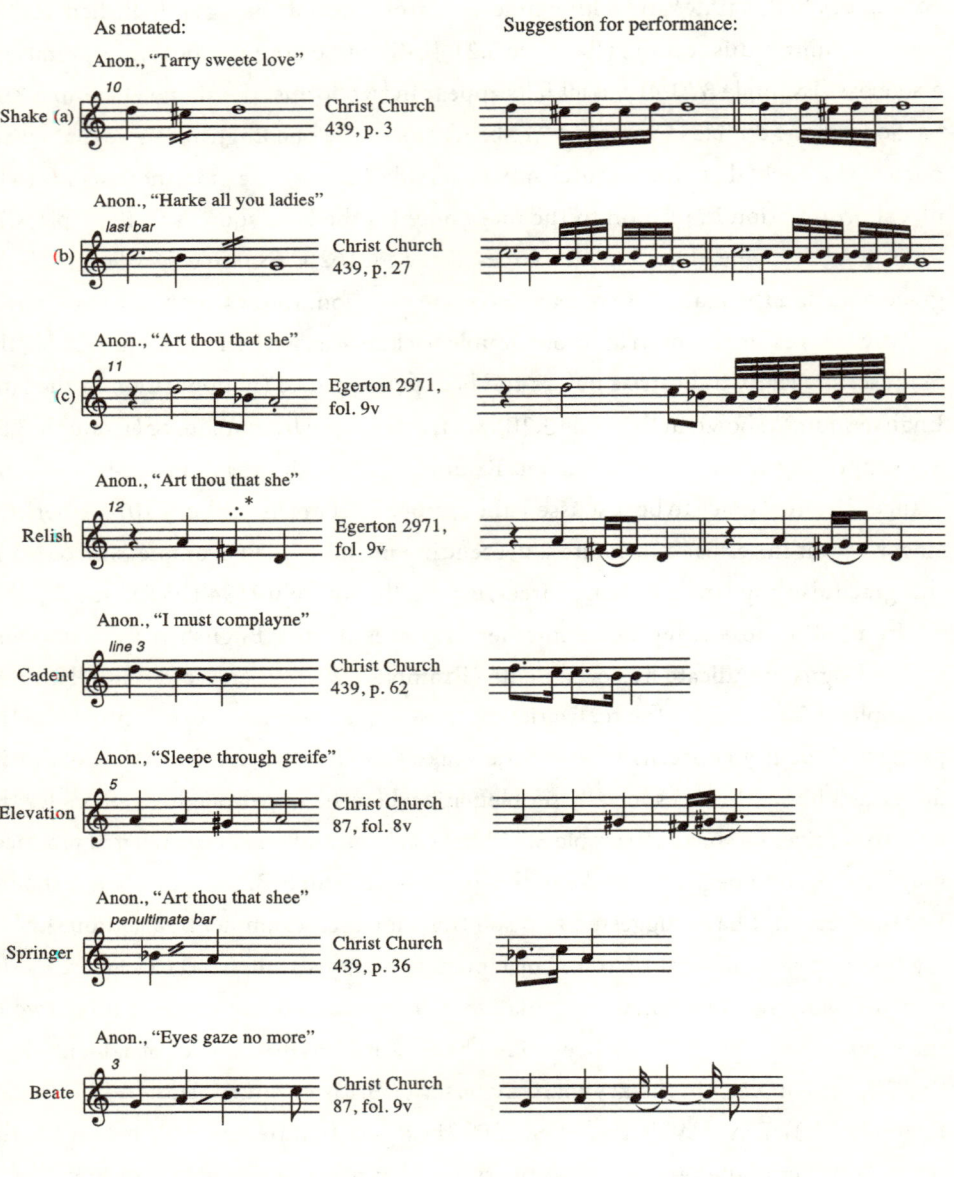

* Sign interpreted according to Mace.

In the English song manuscripts, copyists frequently intermingle graces and divisions, and Ferrabosco's "Why stayes the bridegroome" (Christ Church 439; Example 3.17) provides an excellent example of how singers in the second decade of the seventeenth century combined graces and divisions to create a highly ornate reading of a lute song. Almost half the notes receive one form of

EXAMPLE 3.23 *"Graces in play"*

embellishment or another, the style of ornamentation extending from single-note graces to elaborate divisions that expand cadential passages. Elevations abound (mm. 1, 3, 7, 9, 13, 14, 17, 18, 20, and 21) and both single (mm. 14 and 19) and double (mm. 1 and 18) backfalls appear. At one point (m. 15), where the copyist slurs the notes of the original melody together, the singer can produce the effect of a backfall occurring before the beat simply by observing the slurs. And in typical early seventeenth-century fashion, the vocalist expands each main cadence (mm. 5–6, 10–11, 15–16, and 23–24) through divisions, the most elaborate decoration being saved for the final cadence.

PART SONGS

In part songs, performers applied divisions in much the same way as in solo song, except that each singer needed to avoid conflicting with the other parts. Giovanni Camillo Maffei discusses the embellishment of part songs in the first book of his *Delle lettere* (1562), not only giving five rules for applying divisions to madrigals but also completely embellishing Francesco de Layolle's "Lasciar il velo" as an example of his approach (Example 3.24). Maffei's five rules, which echo some of the observations Hermann Finck (1556: V, fol. Ssiv) made six years earlier, are:

1. "do not make divisions in places other than cadences"/"non si facciano passaggi in altri luoghi, che nelle cadenze" (p. 58)
2. "in a madrigal, do not make more than four or five divisions"/"nel madrigale non si facciano più di quattro, o cinque passaggi" (58–59)

3. "the division should occur on the penultimate syllable of the word, so that when the word finishes the division also ends"/"si debba far il passaggio; nella penultima sillaba della parola, accioche, co'l finimento della parola, si finisca ancho il passaggio" (59)

4. "it is more pleasing to make a division on the word where the syllable 'o' is found"/"piu volontieri si faccia il passaggio, nella parola, e sillaba dove si porta la lettera, o" (59–60)

5. "when one finds four or five people singing in consort, one [singer] should yield to the other, because if two or three make divisions all at once, it would confound the harmony"/"quando si ritrovano quattro, o cinque di conserto, mentre cantano, l'uno debbia dar luogo all'altro; per che se, due o tre tutti in un tempo passaggiassero, confonderebbono l'armonia" (61)

EXAMPLE 3.24 *Francesco de Layolle, "Lasciar il velo"*

(*Continued*)

EXAMPLE 3.24 (*Continued*)

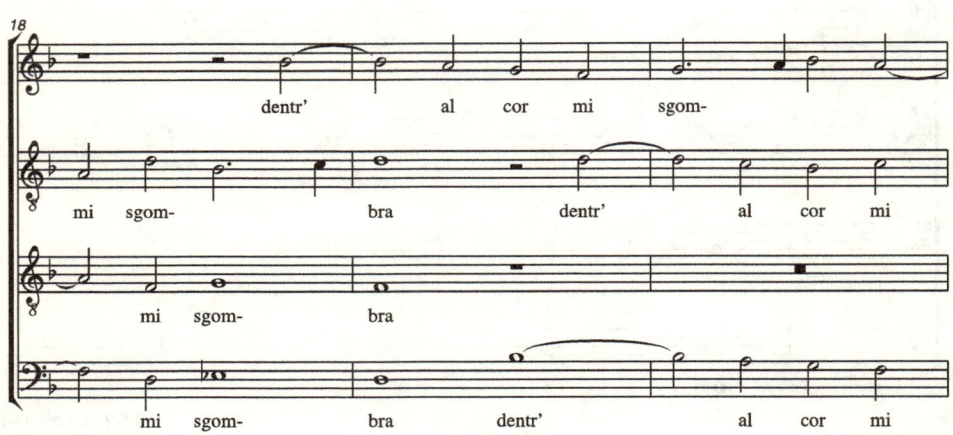

bra

sgom- bra al cor mi sgom-

dentr' al cor mi sgom-

sgom- bra dentr' al cor mi sgom-

Mentr' io por- ta- va i bei pen- sier ce- la-

bra Mentr' io por- ta- va i bei pen- sier ce- la-

bra Mentr' io por- ta- va i bei pen- sier ce- la-

bra Mentr' io por- ta- va i bei pen- sier ce- la-

(Continued)

EXAMPLE 3.24 (*Continued*)

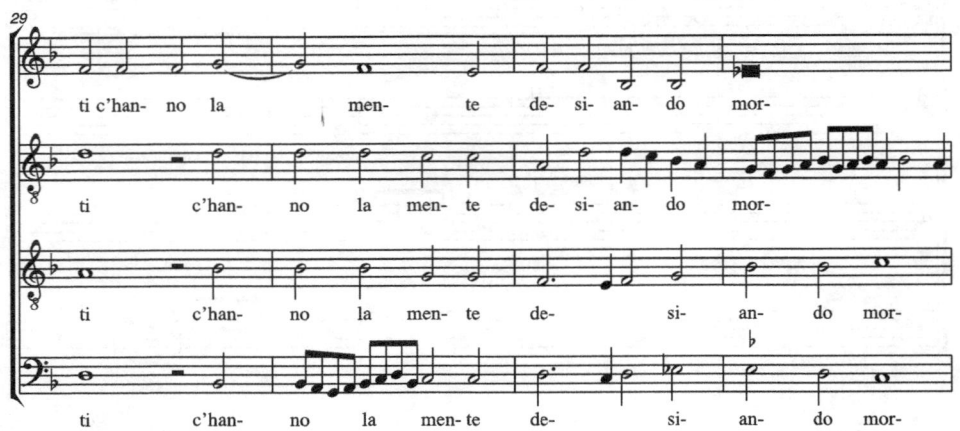

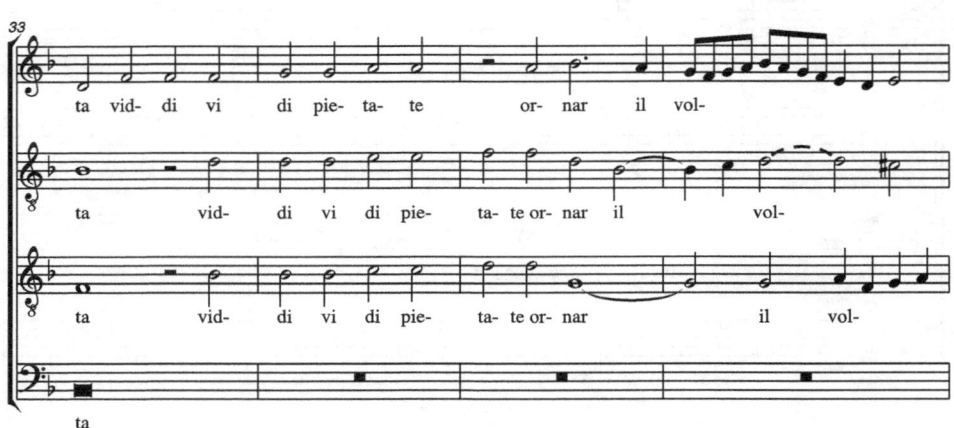

to Ma poi ch'a- mor di me vi fe- ce ac- cor-
to Ma poi ch'a- mor di me vi fe- ce ac- cor-
to Ma poi ch'a- mor di me vi fe- ce ac- cor-
Ma poi ch'a- mor di me vi fe- ce ac- cor-

ta fur' i bion- di ca- pell' all-
ta fur' i bion- di ca- pel- li fur' i bion-
ta fur' i bion- di ca- pell' all- hor ve- la- ti
ta fur' i bion- di ca- pell' all- hor ve- la- ti fur' i bion-

(*Continued*)

EXAMPLE 3.24 (*Continued*)

Quel- che piu de- si- a- va in voi m'e tol-
de- si- a- va in voi m'e tol-
che piu de- si- a- va in voi m'e tol-
de- si- a- va in voi m'e tol-

to Si me go- ver- na'l ve- lo
to Si me go- ver- na'l ve- lo che
to che per mia mor-
to che per mia

(*Continued*)

EXAMPLE 3.24 (*Continued*)

The embellishments Maffei added to Layolle's madrigal certainly follow this advice, for he reserves the divisions for cadential passages, applies them sparingly in no more than one voice at a time, and generally places them on penultimate syllables, predominantly on the vowel "o." Moreover, the figural patterns he employs largely adhere to the simpler ones given in Examples 3.9 and 3.10.

As the writers quoted at the outset of this section indicate, listeners in the sixteenth and early seventeenth centuries considered ornamentation to be a highly desirable attribute of performance, and modern singers might wish to gain facility in this area as well. The question we probably should ask ourselves is, however, "Just how 'blind' should our divisions and graces actually be?" In other words, which historical model(s) should we follow? The surviving documents present us with two main options: we can add embellishments that do not alter the basic structure of the vocal lines, or we can sing with highly elaborate figuration. Both of these practices find precedence in the sixteenth century, and even if we decide not to add any ornamentation at all, we will still remain within the customs recorded at the time.

THREE

Action

T HE ART OF SPEAKING AND SINGING WELL, AS OUTLINED IN THE PRECEDING sections, could not reach perfection, of course, if it lacked action. Thomas Heywood (1612: fol. C4r) maintained that without action the other parts of oratory (invention, disposition, elocution, memory, and even pronunciation) remain imperfect (Heywood separates action from the other parts of *pronunciatio*). The invention of orators never would be so fluent and exquisite, their disposition and order never so composed and formal, their eloquence and elaborate phrases never so material and pithy, their memory never so firm and retentive, and their pronunciation never so musical and plausive, if void of "a comely and elegant gesture, a gratious and a bewitching kinde of action, a naturall and familiar motion of the head, the hand, the body, and a moderate and fit countenance sutable to all the rest." Heywood, in addition to stressing how important action involving the head, hand, and body is to speaking, tells us about the way *elocutio* and *pronunciatio* interrelate: "It [and here Heywood refers to the value of rhetoric for a young scholar] instructs him to fit his phrases [*elocutio*] to his action, and his action to his phrase, and his pronuntiation to them both" (fol. C4r). Clearly then, action as well as the other aspects of delivery must match the text. Thomas Wright (1604: 124) takes our understanding of action one step further, suggesting that speakers express the internal conceits and affections of the mind not only with words but also with actions, the two vehicles through which the orator penetrates the ears and eyes of listeners, thus gaining access to their souls. For this reason, he states, rhetoricians find the simple pronunciation of orations unsatisfactory. Indeed, they regularly enhance discourse by prescribing many rules of action, and this enables them to imprint affections much more deeply in the souls of listeners. Both words and actions, he concludes, spring from the same root, that is, understanding and affections. Heywood and Wright remind us of the importance of gaining knowledge of the rhetorical structure of texts and the passions those texts embody, since a detailed understanding of the text shapes our style of delivery.

Without a doubt, singers in the sixteenth century aligned themselves with orators and graced their delivery with action, for in the description of a performance by Fabio Orsini quoted earlier, Angelo Poliziano (1498: Bk. 12, fol. pviii) commented that the singer's "gesture was neither indifferent nor sluggish but yet not affected or offensive"/"gestus non otiosus, non somniculosus, sed nec vultuosus tamen, ac molestus." Similarly, vocalists active in late sixteenth-century Mantua received praise for the way they moved listeners "principally with facial expressions, glances, and gestures that appropriately accompanied the music and sentiment, and above all without disgraceful movements of the mouth, hands or body which would not address the purpose of the song"/"principalmente con azione del viso, e dei sguardi e de' gesti che accompagnavano appropriatamente la musica e li concetti, e sopra tutto senza moto della persona e della bocca e delle mani sconcioso, che non fusse indirizzato al fine per il quale si cantava" (Giustiniani c. 1628: 108). Along these lines, an anonymous account of a performance of Gabriele Bombasi's tragedy *Alidoro*, given in Reggio before Barbara of Austria on November 2, 1568, reported that one of the female singers in the chorus "had, in addition to a voice most delicate, a fair amount of a natural talent, ruled by art and great judgment. And at the right moments while she was singing, she always matched her face, eyes, gestures, and movements with the various conceits with which she had so gently enchanted [us], and she turned everyone's minds to fear, to hope, to rejoicing, to sorrow, as she wished"/"haveva questa donna, oltre la voce delicatissima, alquanto di natural dispositione regolata dall'arte, con sommo giuditio. Et mentre l'andava spargendo a certi luoghi, accompagnava sempre il volto, gli occhi, i gesti et i movimenti alla varietà de' concetti così gentilmente ch'innamorava, et volgeva gli animi di ciascuno a temere, a sperare, a rallegrarsi et attristarsi, come più le piaceva" (cited in Crocioni 1938: 37). Moreover, Emilio de' Cavalieri (1600: preface) expected singers to accompany words with gestures, and some twenty years later, Marin Mersenne (1623: column 1615; cited in Barnett 1987: 17) advised vocalists in France to "adapt the movement of the body, especially face and hand, [to the poetry,] otherwise the music will be imperfect and incomplete"/"Motum corporis, vultum praesertim, & manum cantui conformare debent, alioquin musica imperfecta, atque manca erit."

As these authors suggest, singers should employ appropriate gestures and avoid what in early seventeenth-century England Philip Rosseter had described as childish action. In defending the simple, "naked" ayre against its detractors, Rosseter (1601: "To the reader") asserts that singers should refrain from the sort of action exploited in comedies, stressing that a "manly cariage," both in setting words to notes and in reinforcing words with action, should be maintained:

But there are some [musicians], who to appeare the more deepe, and singular in their judgement, will admit no Musicke but that which is long, intricate, bated with fuge, chaind with sincopation, and where the nature of everie word is precisely exprest in the Note, like the old exploded action in Comedies, when if they did pronounce *Memeni*, they would point to the hinder part of their heads, if *Video*, put their finger in their eye. But such childish observing of words is altogether ridiculous, and we [musicians in Rosseter's day, that is, composers and singers] ought to maintaine as well in Notes, as in action a manly cariage, gracing no word, but that which is eminent, and emphaticall.[7]

Rosseter's attitude toward gesture dates back at least to the time of Quintilian, who (XI, 290–91) condemns those who use the hands to illustrate anything they may chance to say. Rosseter, of course, expresses an informed opinion, and his interest in the theatrical world manifests itself during the years 1609–1617, when he was one of the theatrical managers for the Children of Blackfriars, later called the Children of the Queen's Revels (Poulton 1980: 211–12; corrected in Wilson 1991: 580).

Although Rosseter's brief reference to action in singing does not tell us exactly what gestures should replace childish action, other writers on the subject echo and amplify his notions about gesture. Abraham Fraunce, for example, frames his opening remarks on action in a remarkably similar fashion: "The gesture must followe the change and varietie of the voyce, answering thereunto in everie respect: yet not so parasiticallie as stage plaiers use, but gravelie and decentlie as becommeth men of greater calling. Let the bodie therefore with a manlike and grave motion of his sides rather followe the sentence than expresse everie particular word" (1588: II, 3, fol. J3v). And John Bulwer maintains that even though "gesture must attend upon every flexion of the voice," it should not be demonstrated scenically (1644: 241). Moreover, Rosseter's example of parasitic action on words like "memeni" and "video" would find a place in Fraunce's description quite easily, for Fraunce suggests that action simply follow the sentence. Both Rosseter and Fraunce seem to imply the same thing. By selecting only the most important word in a phrase or sentence, a word that may embody the affection expressed in the entire sentence or phrase, one would, in fact, derive action from those "eminent and emphaticall" words that determine the character of the sentence.

We glean from these authors that a "manly cariage" is as appropriate for singing as it is for oration, and that the singing of ayres seems to have been more akin to oration than to acting. Treatises on oration, then, form a natural source from which to draw information on action in singing, and some of the most useful sources from the period discussing the art of gesture come from England. Those by Fraunce (1588) and Bulwer (1644), with information from Le Faucheur (1657) supplementing and corroborating the two earlier writers, provide the framework for understanding the action employed during the late Renaissance. Fraunce gives particularly detailed information about the motion of the head, and Bulwer provides a wealth of information on the hands and fingers, mentioning no less than 87 separate gestures, together with 137 other types of directions, and illustrating all this with numerous drawings of the hands and fingers. These writers, as well as others, suggest that action must be adapted to the voice, for gesture enriches the delivery by appealing to the eye in the same way that the voice speaks to the ear (Quintilian: XI, 250–51; Wilson 1553: 437; Wright 1604: 176; Bulwer 1644: 5). Fraunce even goes so far as to recommend following the "change and varietie of the voyce" in every respect (1588: II, 3, fol. J3v; see also Bulwer 1644: 241). On this basis, we today, in preparing to deliver a song, probably should determine the disposition of the voice first so that we will know which sorts of gestures will enhance delivery most effectively. The previous sections have documented the options open to performers concerning the voice, and now we must turn our attention to the action of the whole body.

General advice is not hard to find. All action, it seems, begins with a natural imitation of the person being impersonated: "Qualifie every thing [that is, every gesture] according to the nature of the person personated" (Heywood 1612: fol. C4r). Wright (1604: 179), as noted earlier, recommends careful observation of real life, for those who imitate best, act best: "looke upon other men appassionate, how they demeane themselves in passions, and observe what and how they speake in mirth, sadnesse, ire, feare, hope, &c, what motions are stirring in the eyes, hands, bodie, &c." Action, then, should reflect everyday life. Orators never considered gestures frozen positions they assumed at certain points in a sentence, but rather fluid motions of the hands, fingers, head, and so on, born from the thoughts and emotions that produce the words they spoke. Action should be, to borrow the words of Wright (1604: 179), an external image of the passion in the mind. But not all nations displayed the same temperament for action. According to Bulwer (1644: 250), Italians used too much gesture of the hand, and French action was full of "quick and lightsome expressions." But in Germany and England, countries with similar national complexions, "moderation and gravity in gesture is esteemed the greater virtue." Spaniards, however, although equally disposed to moderate and grave action, use the hands "as often [as] principals as accessories to their proud expressions." References to moderation and gravity permeate English writings on action. Wright (179), as quoted above, certainly advises orators to study "other men appassionate" but recommends that they "leave the excesse and exorbitant levitie or other defects, and keepe the manner corrected with prudent mediocritie." Fraunce and Rosseter employ words such as "grave" and "manly cariage" to describe the ideal approach to action (see above), and Bulwer (249), in recognizing national differences in temperament, advocates moderation in gesture, the golden mean being the best prescription for action.

Orators and singers should study the art of gesture assiduously, Bulwer and Le Faucheur suggesting practicing before a mirror (Bulwer 1644: 247; Le Faucheur 1657: 175). In learning action, however, one should imitate only the best orators and perfect the techniques through exercise: "Bend and wrest your arm and hands to the right, to the left, and to every part, that having made them obedient unto you, upon a sudden and the least signification of the mind you may show the glittering orbs of heaven and the gaping jaws of earth . . . [so that] you may be ready for all variety of speech" (Bulwer 246–47). Performers should, of course, plan gestures in advance, speakers/singers determining beforehand the type of action they will accommodate to the variety of the voice and the words. In preparation for applying action to a text, singers should analyze the text, following the simple formula I have adapted from Bulwer (244). First, take note of the dominant passion. Next observe how the main parts of the text relate to this central emotion. Then study individual sentences to determine the specific affections embodied in them. Finally, decide which words in those sentences need to be emphasized through gesture. But we should remember that Bulwer also stressed the absurdity of changing gesture frequently in the same sentence. Once orators and singers of the time understood the requirements of the text, they could turn to treatises on action to find detailed prescriptions for specific motions that would give them, to use Wright's phraseology (1604: 176), that visible eloquence of the body so necessary for the affection to pour forth by all means possible.

The "comely grace" to which Wright (176) and other writers refer concerned the whole body, that is, the stance of the orator, as well as motions of the head, eyes, eyebrows, shoulders, arms, hands, fingers, and feet. In general, one should stand upright and straight, "as nature hath appoynted," without wavering about (Fraunce 1588: fol. J3v), for orators considered the frequent changing of place and posture ridiculous. Nonetheless, one should "neither *stand* like a *Stock*, nor be as immoveable as a *May-pole*" (Le Faucheur 1657: 179). In fact, Fraunce (fol. K4v) considered it tolerable "to stirre a step or two" as long as this movement was seldom, the place was large, and the auditors were numerous. The head should retain its natural position (modestly upright), departing from this to enhance the expression of a particular affection. For example, Fraunce (fol. K1r) comments that shaking the head denotes grief and indignation, as well as compassion, and that a nod represents a token of a grant. But in order to show certain affections, Fraunce (fols. J4r and K1r) recommends combining the motion of the head with movement in the eyes, the eyes being the "chiefest force" in the countenance. Orators depict modesty best, he states, by holding the head down while casting the eyes in the same direction. Fraunce says little else about the eyes and nothing about the other parts of the face except that "the particular ordering is left to everie mans discretion" (fol. K2r).

Fortunately, Le Faucheur describes many of the motions to which Fraunce merely alludes. To depict anger, a fire must be seen in the eyes that makes them sparkle. Violent grief, on the other hand, should draw tears from the eyes (1657: 184). Ancient orators, Le Faucheur contends (185, 188–89), acquired the ability to counterfeit the *"Power of Weeping* and *shedding Tears"* in such abundance that when they left the stage their faces were "all over blurr'd with *Crying."* The method of producing tears he suggests involved keeping the imagination on real subjects and one's own private afflictions rather than on the *"Fables* or *Fictions* of the *Play."* Moreover, Le Faucheur asserts that orators found tears as appropriate for the pulpit as for the stage. Beyond tears, one should lift up or cast down the eyes according to the subject matter. When speaking of heaven and celestial powers, look up, but when referring to earth and terrestrial things, look down. Similarly, in honor one should look up, whereas in disgrace one should look down (1657: 191). The eyebrows might be contracted into a frown in sorrow, and one could dilate and smooth them in joy. They should be hung down, however, in humility and modesty (192). For certain powerful affections, such as detestation and abhorrence, orators accompanied the motion of the head with action in the hands. Both Bulwer and Le Faucheur recommend similar gestures for these passionate rejections (see also Fraunce 1588: fol. J4v). Bulwer (1644: 186–87) suggests thrusting the left hand forward with the palm turned out, the left shoulder raised, and the head turned to the right as a way of repelling distasteful objects. But orators can make this action even more passionate, he contends, if they thrust both hands out to the left side. For Le Faucheur (1657: 181), however, one rejects with the right hand, turning the head away to the left.

The hand is, of course, the most powerful gesticulatory agent available to orators and singers. Both Bulwer (1644: 239) and Le Faucheur (1657: 194) refer to it as the "chief instrument" of action, and Fraunce (1588: fol. K3r) maintains that, without the hand, gesture amounts to nothing. The casting out of the arm and the hand allows speech "to powre forth" and gives the figures contained in the text all the force, vigor, and efficacy they require (Fraunce fol. K2r; Le Faucheur 199–200). Orators used the hands in certain prescribed ways, however, and the three sources forming the basis of my discussion generally agree with one another on the principles of action that apply to the hand. Bulwer's extraordinarily detailed descriptions of the hands dominates my treatment of the subject, for his book probably contains the most thorough account of hand gesture to survive from the first half of the seventeenth century. The main vehicle for gesture was the right hand, the left being used as an accessory rather than a principal in action. In fact, Bulwer (234) notes that the left hand received its name because orators usually "left" it out. Nonetheless, Bulwer (247–48) did admit that orators could use the left hand alone, but its normal role, if employed at all, was to accompany the right hand, for when speakers used the hands together, they could exhibit much more affection. They should, however, never lift the left hand as high as the right (Le Faucheur 196–97). In fact, the hands and arms operated within a carefully defined physical space. The hand should not be raised above the eyes or fall below the breast, and the arms should not be stretched out sideways more than half a foot from the trunk of the body. Consequently, orators always kept the hands in view of the eyes, and their action consists of motions to the right, to the left, up, down, and forward. Apparently, they did not use backward or circular motions. Furthermore, gestures normally should pass from the left side of the body to the right and end on the right (Bulwer 240–41; Le Faucheur 198, 200–1).

These gestures, according to the divergent opinions of the two English writers Fraunce and Bulwer, could either anticipate, accompany, or follow the words. For Bulwer (1644: 17), orators conceived speech and gesture simultaneously in the mind, yet in delivery the hand appears first, giving shape to the thought before the words can complete it. In this way, action anticipates the words that both accompany and follow specific gestures. The addition of the words serves as a comment on and a fuller explication of the gesture and is so necessary for a complete understanding of action. Fraunce (1588: fol. K3r), however, maintained that hand gesture should follow rather than go before the words, and Le Faucheur held this view as well (1657: 198–99), emphasizing that one would not begin with gesture and that action of the hand should be completed before one finishes speaking. On this last point, Bulwer (1644: 240) seems to agree with Le Faucheur's contention that the hand would, so to speak, rise and fall with the sentence: "When the oration begins to wax hot and prevelent, the hand may be put forth with a sentence but must withdraw again with the same." Within the discourse orators should shun similitude of gesture, for uniformity of action corresponded to a monotonal voice (Bulwer 243). But do not use so much action that the hands remain perpetually in motion (224; Le Faucheur 201–2). The hands may, in fact, be idle for a time if no new affection arises, but long intermissions displease listeners (Bulwer 248). Bulwer (241) suggests keeping silences in the hand to intervals of, perhaps, three words. This undoubtedly would prevent orators and singers from changing gesture within a sentence too frequently, and certainly at the beginning of a discourse do not start abruptly with the hands unless, of course, the text warrants such action (Bulwer 240; Le Faucheur 195). Instead, the hand should break into gesture only after the orator has brought it forward softly, Bulwer considering this stretching forth of the hand a posture of preparation (173, 240; illustrated in Plate 3.3 C, E).

After preparing the hand, orators and singers could use it to heighten the passionate language of the text in a wide variety of ways. Bulwer describes dozens of specific postures for the hands and fingers, providing drawings for many of them (see Plates

3.1–3.5). These actions accompanied the affections present in the text, and although most of the descriptions apply to individual passions, certain gestures were of a more general nature, used to increase the vehemence of numerous affections. Bulwer, in fact, considers eight separate gestures appropriate for this latter purpose and illustrates the five postures of the fingers with drawings. In order to grace any matter with a loftier style, the "gentle and well ordered hand" should be "thrown forth by a moderate projection, the fingers unfolding themselves in the motion and the shoulders a little slackened" (174). Moreover, if one wishes to reinforce an emphatic declaration (asseveration), gently spread the hand on the stomach (179) or smite the hands together with a "certain kind of gravity" (189). But when one needs to stimulate or excite the listeners more, bring the two middle fingers under the thumb to create an action "instant and importunate" (199; Plate 3.5 D). Similarly, an argument can be urged and instantly enforced if the orator presses the left thumb down by the index of the right hand (200; Plate 3.5 W). A particularly effective method of driving "the point into the heads of the auditors" is to turn the extended right index down, while composing the rest of the fingers into a fist (202; Plate 3.5 P).[8] This same posture of the hand becomes a forceful indicatory action capable of showing many things (useful for scolding and indicating grief) when the orator holds the hand and arm in a horizontal position (201; Plate 3.5 M). Bulwer illustrates two other techniques for using the right index finger to increase vehemence: with it, apprehend the middle joint of the left index (200; Plate 3.5 I) or apprehend the upper joint of the left index, but in this last case, the next two fingers of the left hand should assume a slightly bowed position, with the small finger scarcely bent at all (200; Plate 3.5 H). As part of their general approach to gesticulation, speakers even may wish to mark the punctuation of the text with their hands. Bulwer suggests two procedures. Orators could distinguish commas and the "breathing parts of a sentence" with a "gentle percussion, now greater, now less, now flat, now sharp, according to the diversity of the affections" (181). But for the "close or period of a sentence" they might gently set the hands together "by a sweet approach, causing a low sound by their light encounter or complosion" (188).

However, orators designed most action of the hand to reinforce specific affections, and Bulwer's meticulous attention to detail allows us to recover with considerable accuracy the early seventeenth-century art of coupling manual and verbal rhetoric, particularly for England. In treating Bulwer's prescriptions for artificially managing the hand, I will group the techniques according to affection, discussing related passions as a group. This arrangement of the material allows us to comprehend the subtle ways in which the eloquently ordered hand helped produce a passionate style of delivery.

PLATE 3.1 *(A) Entreat; (B) Pray; (C) Weep; (D) Admire; (E) Applaud; (F) Indignation; (G) Explode; (H) Despair; (I) Indulge in ease; (K) Mental anguish; (L) Innocence; (M) Applaud the taking of money; (N) Resign liberty; (O) Protect; (P) Triumph; (Q) Demand silence; (R) Swear; (S) Declare emphatically; (T) Permit; (V) Reject; (W) Invite; (X) Dismiss; (Y) Threaten; (Z) Beg*

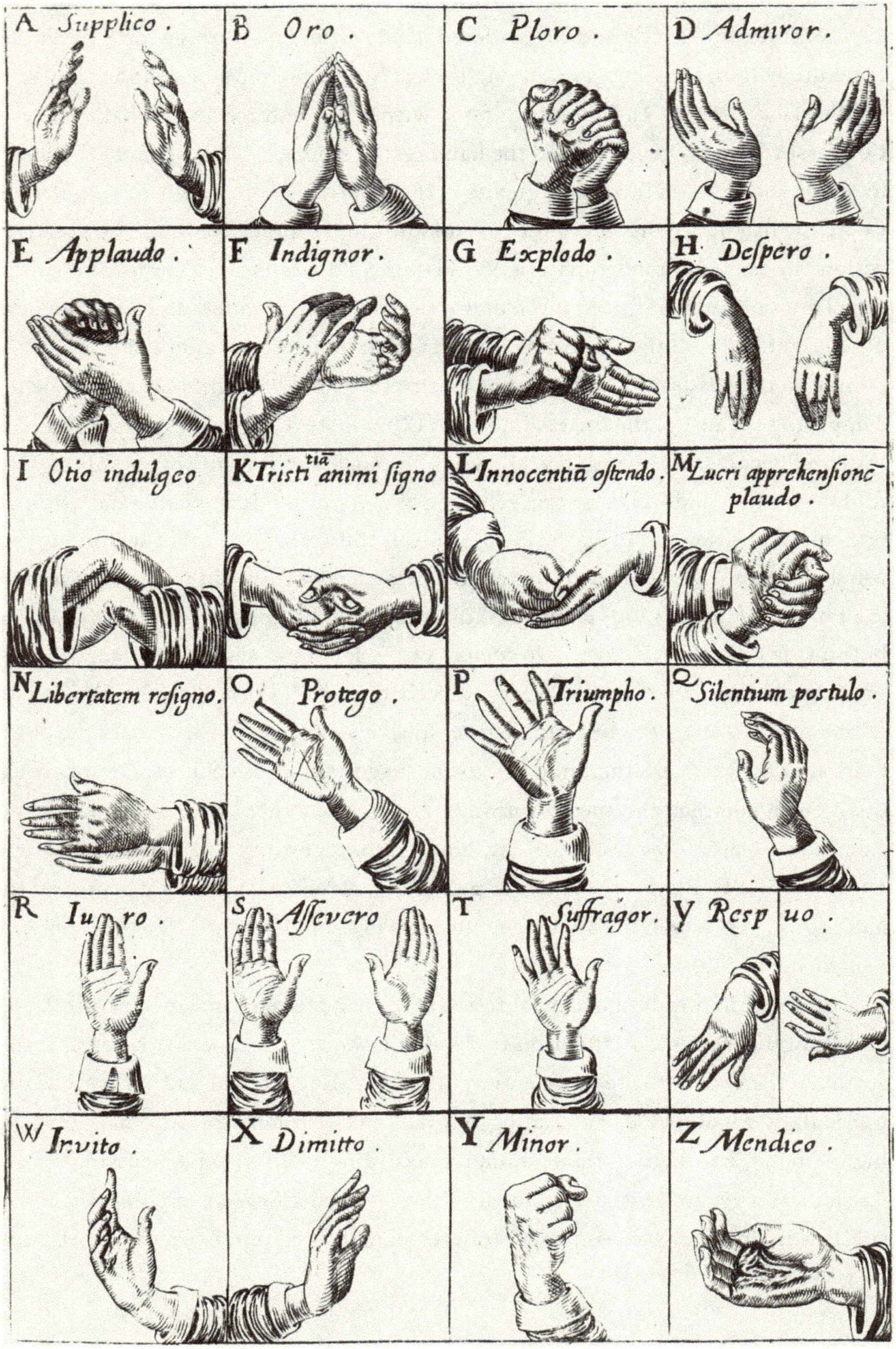

PLATE 3.2 *(A) Reward; (B) Bring aid; (C) Anger; D) Demonstrate that one does not have; (E) Chastise; (F) Fight; (G) Confide; (H) Impede; (I) Recommend; (K) Lead about; (L) Betray impatience; (M) Compel by repeated requests; (N) Shame; (O) Adoration; (P) Affirm one's conscience; (Q) Display contrition; (R) Fear with indignation; (S) Pledge one's faith; (T) Reconcile; V) Suspicion and hate; (W) Honor; (X) Greet with reservation; (Y) Show thievery; (Z) Bless*

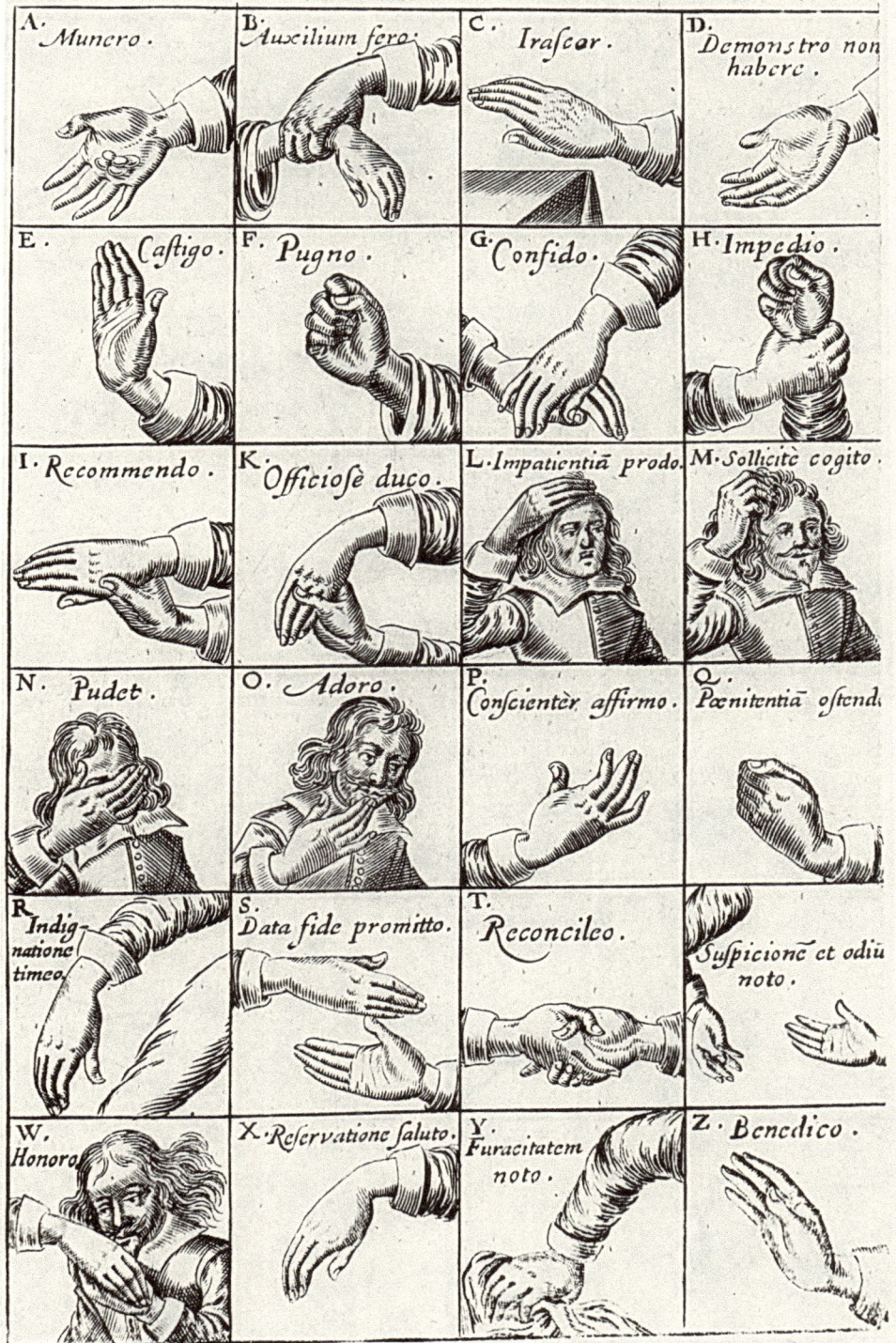

PLATE 3.3 *(A) Pacification; (B) Appease auditors; (C) Preparative gesture, convenient for exordium; (D) Show; (E) Preparative gesture; (F) Admiration; (G) Cheer, exhort; (H) Produce reasons; (I) Slight, undervalue; (K) Deprecate; (L) For speaking about oneself; (M) Abhor, repel; (N) Perspicuity; (O) Exclamation; (P) Antithesis; (Q) Digesting the arguments; (R) Benevolence; (S) Commiseration; (T) Show immensity; (V) More passionate detestation; (W) Extreme loathing; (X) Doubt; (Y) Grief, sorrow; (Z) Dismissal benediction*

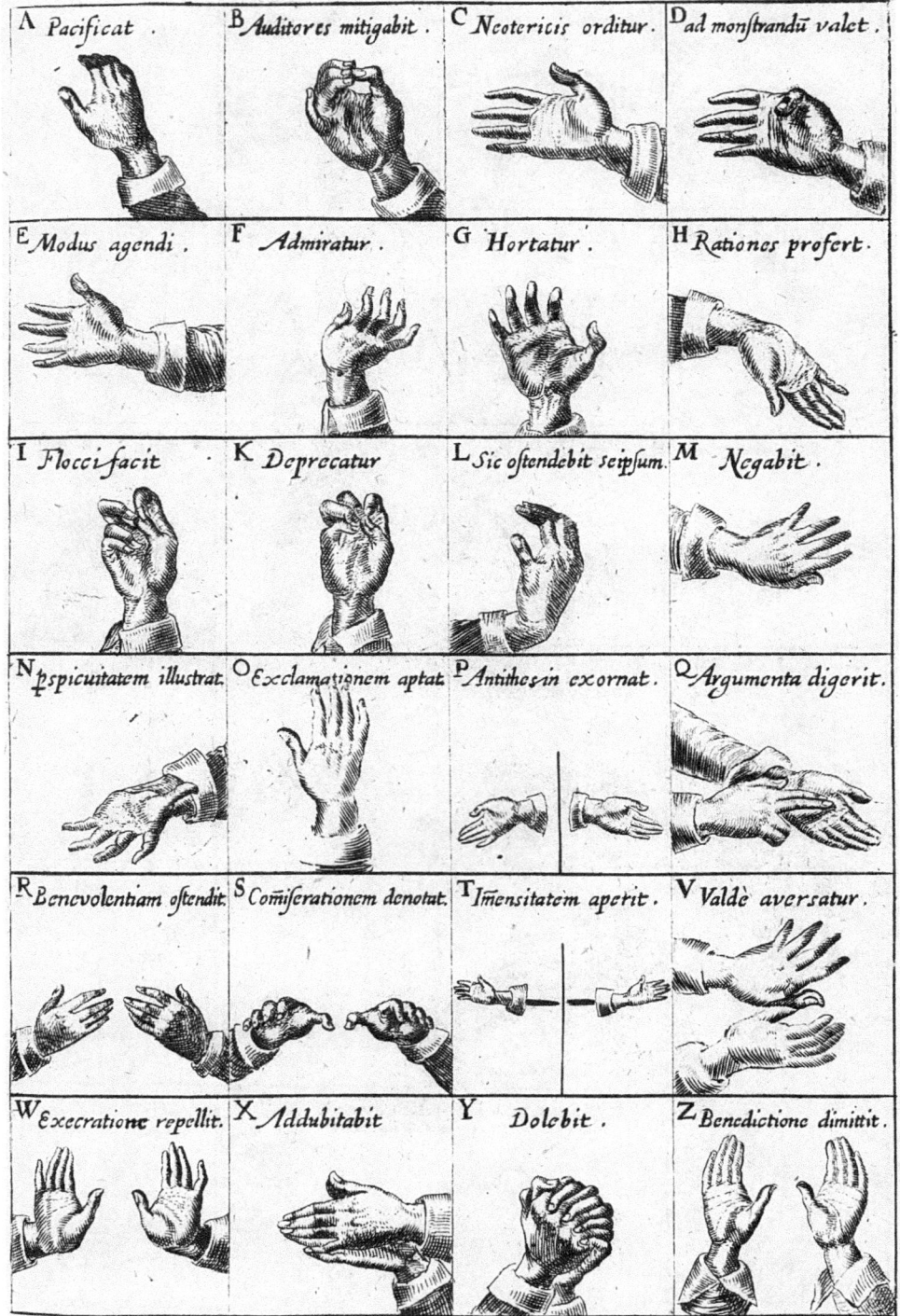

PLATE 3.4 *(A) Work in discovery; (B) Weep; (C) Approve; (D) Extol; (E) Show both sides; (F) Point; (G) Inflict terror; (H) Show silence; (I) Reprove; (K) Summon; (L) Disapprove; (M) Show hesitancy; (N) Betray weakness; (O) Provoke an argument; (P) Condemn; (Q) Impose irony; (R) Provoke contemptuously; (S) Betray avarice; (T) Resent a slight offense; (V) Betray mild anger; (W) Sign of folly; (X) Accuse of improbability; (Y) Give sparingly; (Z) Count*

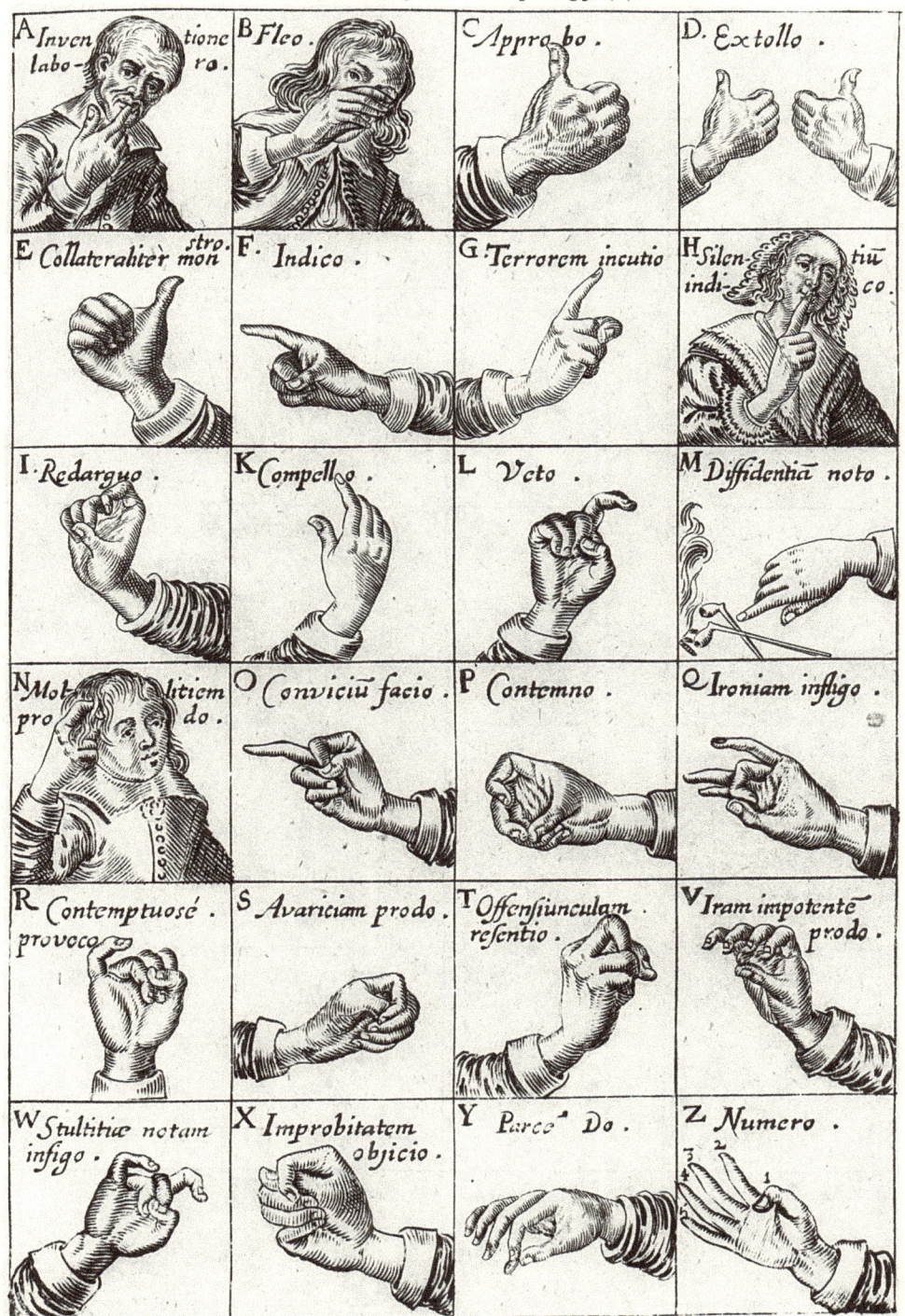

PLATE 3.5 *(A) Demand silence; (B) Hand fit for exordium; (C) Commodious for proem; (D) Urge; (E) Approve; (F) For enthymemes; (G) Show a small number; (H) Disputation; (I) For greater vehemence of a word; (K) Demonstration; (L) Magnanimity; (M) Forceful indication; (N) Threaten, denounce; (O) Confirm, refute; (P) Urge; (Q) Exaltation from splendid elocution; (R) Ironical intention; (S) For handling a matter lightly; (T) Explain subtle things; (V) Scoff, reproach; (W) Urge and instantly enforce an argument; (X) Number arguments; (Y) Denotes amplitude; (Z) To distinguish contraries*

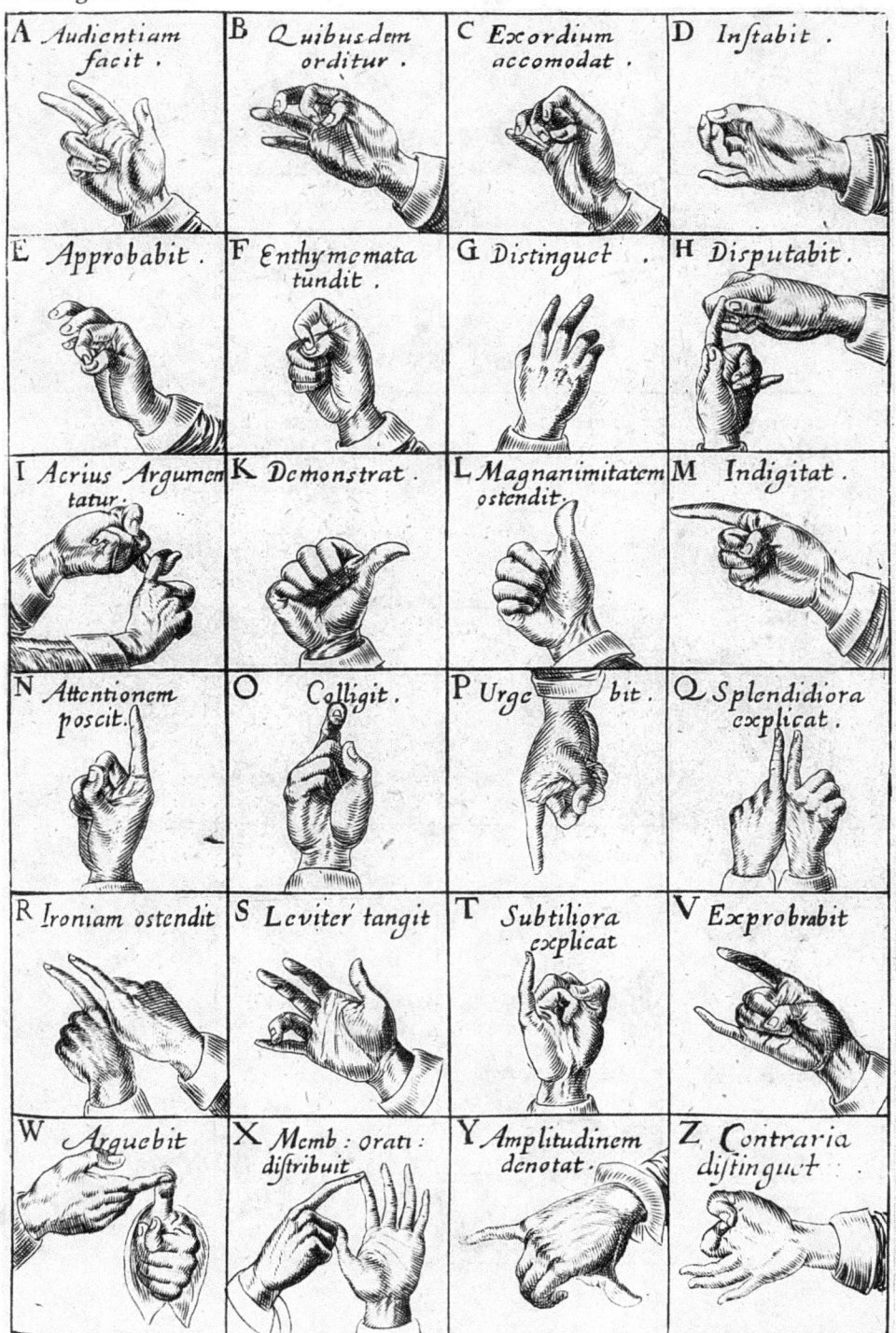

One of the largest groups of related affections encompasses grief, sorrow, sadness, despair, mental anguish, pity, and weeping. These affections, though similar, arise from such a variety of situations that orators needed a great number of hand gestures to accommodate them. A passionate application of the hand to the head demonstrates anguish, sorrow, grief, impatience, and lamentation, and brings action into line with the adage "where there is sorrow, there is the finger" (Plate 3.2 L). The beating of the head to which Bulwer refers serves to portray someone overcome with sorrow, as when a father learns that his son has died. To strike the forehead with the hand, however, produces an image of sadness particularly suited to great grief, the effect of which can be aided by weeping (183–84; this gesture may also be used to signify shame and admiration). Similarly, orators would often smite the thigh with the hand when enraged with grief. This gesture can, however, be used in fear, admiration, and amazement, as well (76–77; Plate 3.2 R). The other English writer to discuss this motion, Abraham Fraunce (1588: fol. K4v), noted the common employment of this gesture but felt that orators should use it to denote indignation. Furthermore, Fraunce also suggests that speakers could show "vehemencie of speach" by striking the ground with the foot (1588: fol. K4v). When grief became deeply settled in the "yearning bowels" and warranted a sharp and inflamed style, touch the breast with the fingertips (Bulwer 1644: 179). But when one wants to raise great motions in the minds of the auditors (grief, sorrow, repentance, and indignation) and draw tears from their eyes, strike the breast with an audible stroke (74, 182–83; Plate 3.2 Q, which gives the shape of the hand for smiting the breast). Orators could, of course, greatly enforce all these motions by tears, one of the visible manifestations of sorrow, itself a product of contradictory spirits in the brain. Tears flow forth when this contradiction strains together the moisture of the brain and brings that moisture to the eyes. From this act of weeping follows the folding and hard wringing of the hands, a gesture most appropriate for weeping and tears (32–33; Plate 3.1 C). Another gesture commonly used in crying is "to put [one's] finger in the eye" in order to rub or wipe away the tears (122–23; Plate 3.4 B).

Orators demonstrate despair, mental anguish, and pity with much gentler motions, however. When they appear with fainting and dejected hands, they produce a posture of, among other things, utter despair (Plate 3.1 H; the gesture also depicts fear, abasement of mind, and abject and vanquished courage), and if they hold the fingers inserted between each other, they show the mental anguish of those who have fallen into a "melancholy muse" (Plate 3.1 K). They demonstrate pity by extending and offering the right hand to someone (58) or by letting down the hand with the "intent to rear some languishing creature from off the ground" (59). But both palms held averse before the breast denotes commiseration (189; Plate 3.3 S).

A second broad category of related affections embraces those that listeners find more menacing: anger, abhorrence, rejection, dismissal, condemnation, disapproval, threat, and terror. An expression of the hand frequently used to direct anger at a specific person involves showing and shaking the bended fist at that person (52–53; Plate 3.1 Y). To explode in anger, however, one should clap the right fist on the left palm often (36; Plate 3.1 G). Similar violent motions, such as striking the table with the hand (59; Plate 3.2 C) or the pulpit with the hand bent into a fist (182), accompany impatient anger and vehement contentions, and the thigh smitten with the hand is a sign of one fuming with indignation (185). Indignation could, nevertheless, also be demonstrated by suddenly smiting the left hand with the right (35; Plate 3.1 F). One expresses mild anger, however, with the fingers formed into a talonlike claw in order to scratch those who have provoked a "cursed heart" (138; Plate 3.4 V). Bulwer continues this last description by cautioning that this motion presents "no manly expression of the hand" and pertains more properly to children and vixens prone to wreak their despite upon others.

To shake the hand back and forth, with bent brows, is an action of abhorrence (181), and a resilient hand that leads back to the left side of the body from where it descended makes an action suited to abomination (181). Detestation may be shown by holding up both hands with the palms averse (187; Plate 3.3 W), but orators may demonstrate a more passionate form of detestation by turning out both palms and projecting them to the left side (187; Plate 3.3 V). If, however, one simultaneously drove the palms out to either side, then the vehement effect of averseness would be doubled (187). In order to reject, negate, or repel some detestable thing, orators and singers may choose from at least three motions. First, the right hand may be driven to the left at the same time that the orator brings the left shoulder forward and inclines the head to the right (181). Second, while the head turns to the right, the left hand, with the palm turned backward, can be thrust forth from a raised shoulder in an act of repulsion (186–87; Plate 3.3 M). Finally, one can wag the back part of the down-turned hand in a sudden, jerky movement or simply turn out the palm of the hand to form a natural expression of denial (50–51; Plate 3.1 V). Similarly, to wag and wave the hand, this time raised, with the palm turned out becomes a gesture of dismissal (51–52, and it also may be used to bid farewell; Plate 3.1 X), but to clap the hand suddenly on the breast denotes a chiding rebuke (182). Another subtler way of showing disapproval does exist, however: simply raise the hand and bow the index finger away from oneself (130; Plate 3.4 L). But if one wished to condemn, slight, or insult, cast out the hand while snapping the middle finger sharply against the palm, causing an audible sound (134; Plate 3.4 P).

Actions born from these sorts of denunciations border on those that threaten, and at least some hand gestures served both purposes. To direct the hand toward the auditors with an impetuous agitation of the arm not only denounces but also threatens

(175), and to show and shake the clenched fist at the listeners does more than condemn and threaten, for it strikes terror in them (52–53; Plate 3.1 Y). Similarly, the index finger raised from a fist and brandished in a menacing way denounces, threatens, and incites terror (127, 202; Plate 3.5 N).

An equally important but gentler group of related affections encompasses love, adoration, admiration, faith, honor, loyalty, modesty, exaltation, and joyful exclamation. A gentle stroke of the hand, that is, drawing the hand "with a sweetening motion over the head or face of the party to whom we intend this insinuation," signifies affectionate love (66–67), and to press hard and wring another's hand becomes a natural expression of the amorous intentions of a lover who strives to imprint upon his mistress's hand a tacit hint of his affection (93; this gesture may also signify duty and reverence). But if one wished to express "an incredible ardor of love lodged in his bosom and cleaving to his very marrow," the orator would touch the breast with the fingertips (179). A degree of courtly solemnity could be maintained in showing adoration, however, simply by kissing the hand or the forefinger. Orators frequently use this sign of respect, Bulwer observes, in the formalities of civil conversation (73, 127–28; Plate 3.2 O). Moreover, to dearly cherish those we love, put forth both hands in an embrace (96). Speakers express faith, honor, and loyalty by apprehending and kissing the back of another's hand (97; Plate 3.2 W), whereas they demonstrate modesty by restraining and keeping in the hand (175; in ancient times, Bulwer maintains, orators kept the right hand within their cloaks as an expression of modesty). A more extravagant form of showing admiration, particularly the type that borders on amazement and astonishment, would be, however, to throw up the hands to heaven (33; Plate 3.1 D) or to strike the forehead with the hand (183–85; also suitable for shame and great grief). Another action convenient for admiration involves turning up the palm with the fingers joined together in preparation for reversing the position of the hand while spreading the fingers (177; Plate 3.3 F). If admiration is taken one step further and becomes exaltation, put out the raised hand and shake it "into a shout" (45; Plate 3.1 P). However, a slightly less flamboyant way of amplifying one's joy or making a congratulatory exclamation simply would involve raising the hand aloft (177; Plate 3.3 O). Yet the raised hand, especially when presented in a hollow manner and coupled with some sort of a grave motion of the wrist, could represent quite a different affection; that is, the act of raising the hand might cheer, exhort, embolden, or encourage (177; Plate 3.3 G).

In addition to discussing how the hands could heighten the passions in the text, Bulwer identifies a number of gestures that allow orators to use action for other purposes.[9] For example, the hands may request or invite. Stretching out the hands requests, entreats, or solicits (21; Plate 3.1 A), whereas putting forth the hand without any waving motion or beckoning with the hand invites or calls after (179). Furthermore, supplication, that is, entreatment, can be made more artificial if the speaker dejects both hands (187). When orators or singers need to speak of themselves, they should refer the hand to their own body (181; Plate 3.3 L), and to show contraries the turned-up hand could be transferred from the left side of the body to the right. Bulwer suggests two finger postures for this motion: while keeping the other fingers remiss, either bend in the thumb or join the top of the thumb to the middle of the nail of the index (177–78, 200; see Plate 3.5 Z for a drawing of the latter posture of the fingers). Another equally effective way speakers can show antithesis or opposition, however, involves having both hands alternately "behave themselves with equal art" in order to set off any matter (189).

Through the wide range of gesticulatory techniques that Bulwer and others describe, orators and singers conveyed their thoughts and passions to listeners with greater force and delight. The voice on its own achieved a great deal, of course, but when those who sought to move listeners augmented their voices with action, delivery reached its most persuasive state. The purpose of delivery, as we already know, was to speak or sing eloquently and act aptly so that the minds of auditors could be captured and inflamed. The eyes and ears became the windows to the soul, and orators and singers drew upon a vast arsenal of skills to help them penetrate deeply into the soul, moving it to experience whatever passions the text contained. I encourage singers today to acquire the same skills that singers in the sixteenth century possessed and to re-create those practices that allow us to place our intuitive emotional responses to both solo and part songs in a framework derived from the documents that transmit sixteenth- and early seventeenth-century culture to us. The principles of eloquent delivery, as discussed in this part of the book, now may be applied to specific works, and this will permit us to emulate our Renaissance counterparts: "please the Eye, charm the Ear, and move the Passions" (Le Faucheur 1657: 37).

NOTES

7. This preface may have been written by Thomas Campion, as the volume also contains his songs. Unfortunately, no reliable way exists for determining which man actually wrote the preface, and I simply presume that it was the work of Rosseter.

8. Abraham Fraunce (1588: fol. K4r) concurs, except that he advocates extending the middle finger. Fraunce (fols. K3v–K4r) lists several other positions of the fingers, and all these differ from Bulwer's use of the same or similar positions. For example, Bulwer's drawing in Plate 3.4 Q represents irony or mockery, whereas Fraunce describes it as an urgent and insistent gesture. Furthermore, the position shown in Bulwer's Plate 3.4 O is an expression of scorn and contempt, but for Fraunce it is simply an indicatory gesture, pointing at or showing something.

9. Bulwer (1644: 214–38) also includes a lengthy section called "The Apochrypha of Action," which lists those things that truly fall outside rhetorical decorum.

PASSIONATE AYRES PRONOUNCED

The *Prosopopoeia* in England

Henry peacham the younger (1622: 103) probably suggested the most compelling reason for applying principles derived from *elocutio* and *pronunciatio* to the lute-song repertoire of the late Renaissance when he asked, "What . . . [are] passionate Aires but *Prosopopoea's?*" In a *prosopopoeia*, the singer feigns the affections and nature of the imaginary person in the text, using tools of delivery derived from *pronunciatio* to transport listeners to that state of mind, and if we take Peacham's advice and approach each song as a *prosopopoeia*, we might begin to understand sixteenth-century performance conventions more from within Renaissance culture. Indeed, since passionate ayres exhibit the highest style, they provide us with an ideal vehicle for learning how to perform the music from an historically informed perspective. Figures copiously decorate these songs in the same way that they adorned the orator's discourse, and both singers and orators made passionate ornaments manifest through voice and action. Figures, after all, helped both speakers and singers move and delight listeners, and if we acquire the skills necessary for delivering passionate ayres well, then songs in simpler, plainer styles should present few difficulties. In fact, Thomas Campion elegantly captured the effect singers should have on listeners ("When to her lute Corrina sings," Rosseter 1601: no. 6):

> When to her lute Corrina sings,
> Her voice revives the leaden stringes,
> And doth in highest noates appeare
> As any challeng'd eccho cleere,
> But when she doth of mourning speake,
> Ev'n with her sighes the strings do breake.

And as her lute doth live or die,

Led by her passion, so must I,

For when of pleasure she doth sing,

My thoughts enjoy a sodaine spring,

But if she doth of sorrow speake,

Ev'n from my hart the strings doe breake.

Perhaps two of the most sublime and pithy expressions of the passionate ayre remain John Dowland's "Sorrow stay" (1600: no. 3) and "In darknesse let mee dwell" (R. Dowland 1610: no. 10). Dowland imbued these ayres with all the rhetorical artifice one would expect to find in a *prosopopoeia*, and a successful performance of them depends on the singer's ability to feign the affections in the texts and use the musical and rhetorical devices the songs contain to create the persuasive style of delivery they demand. In preparing to perform these songs, then, I suggest that singers follow the approach recommended in treatises of the era. First, consider the passions of the poem. Note the dominant affection and determine how the main parts of the text relate to this central passion. Then study individual sentences to discover the specific affections embodied in them. At the same time, observe the figurative language with which sentences have been decorated and decide which words require emphasis. Do not overlook the punctuation, for it is the vehicle through which one articulates the structure of the discourse, and the observance of it enables listeners to comprehend the thoughts and emotions of the texts easily. At this point, the study of the structure of the text should be complete. Next, one would decide how to "pronounce" the poem, taking care to match voice and gesture to the passions it contains. This leads singers, of course, to the very useful exercise of presenting the text as a dramatic reading, for as Campion (1613/1: "To the Reader") says of the ayres in his first two books, "not everything of ours in these books is good, but neither is it bad; by this rule, if it [the song] pleases, you may sing it, also you may read it aloud"/"omnia nec nostris bona sunt, sed nec mala libris; si placet hac cantes, hac quoque lege legas." When singers can deliver the poem convincingly in the spoken realm, the basis for delivering it as a song has already been established. They now can determine how much of the spoken delivery actually will transfer to the song itself. To do this, the singer must consider the nature of the musical setting carefully. What rhetorical devices in the poem have been reinforced by melodic or harmonic figures? In what other ways does the music reflect the sentiments of the text? How does the punctuation in the poem control musical phrasing and articulation? Remember that musical notation throughout the sixteenth century was not overly fussy. Composers rarely notated subtleties of articulation and phrasing, and neither composers nor performers specified tempo or dynamics. After studying the manner in which the songwriter set the text to music, the singer can make the final decisions for delivering the poem as a song. During the last stage in the process of preparing a song for performance, the vocalist commits the piece and its style of delivery to memory.

To demonstrate how all this may be applied to the lute-song repertoire, I will discuss Dowland's "Sorrow stay" and "In darknesse let mee dwell" and show various ways in which singers might communicate the passionate sentiments of the poems to listeners, while rooting their interpretations in historical documents. The discussion follows the approach outlined above, and because I firmly believe that a careful study of the poem should precede singing, I treat the poetry first. But in doing so, I concentrate only on those figures and passionate ornaments that speakers and singers actually need to make manifest through voice and gesture. However, even though I strongly advocate that singers should master the poem first, learning to read it aloud, I do not wish to labor the point; therefore, I treat speaking and singing separately in only one of the songs, "Sorrow stay."

Both of the poems Dowland set belong to the form of persuasion known as pathos, discourse designed to arouse certain states of mind in the listener by appealing to the emotions that color the judgment. Rhetoricians grouped those figures that functioned to stir the affections under the generic heading *pathopoeia*. Henry Peacham the Elder (1593: 143–45) discusses the term:

Pathopeia, is a forme of speech by which the Orator moveth the minds of his hearers to some vehemency of affection, as of indignation[,] feare, envy, hatred, hope, gladnesse, mirth[,] laughter, sadnesse or sorrow: of this there be two kindes. The first is when the Orator being moved himselfe with anie of these affections (sorrow excepted) doth bend & apply his speech to stir his hearers to the same: and this kinde is called Imagination. . . . The other kind of Pathopeia, is when the Orator by declaring some lamentable cause, moveth his hearers to pitie and compassion, to shew mercy, and to pardon offences. . . . A serious and deepe affection in the Orator is a mightie furtherance and helpe to this figure, as when he is zealous, and deeply touched himselfe with any of those vehement affections, but specially if he be inwardly moved with a pitifull affection, he moveth his hearers to the same compassion and pitie, by his passionate pronuntiation. . . . This figure pertaineth properly to move affections, which is a principall and singular vertue of eloquution.

I give the poems of each song below, together with the words as set by Dowland.

"Sorrow stay," undecorated poem (reconstructed following the example from Coprario 1606 cited below)

> Sorrow stay, lend true repentant teares,
>> To a woefull wretched wight,
> Hence, dispaire with thy tormenting feares:
>> O doe not my poore heart affright,
> Pitty, help now or never,
>> Mark me not to endlesse paine,
> Alas I am condempned ever,
>> No hope, no help, ther doth remaine,
> But downe, down, down, down I fall,
>> And arise, I never shall.

Words as set by Dowland (I have supplied the punctuation in brackets to help articulate the sense of the sentences and to bring the textual pointing in line with Dowland's musical punctuation):

> Sorrow sorrow stay, lend true repentant teares,
>> To a woefull, woefull wretched wight, [.]
> Hence, hence dispaire with thy tormenting feares:
>> Doe not, O doe not my heart poore heart affright, [.]
> Pitty, pitty, pitty, pitty, pitty, pitty, help now or never,
>> Mark me not to endlesse paine, mark me not to endlesse paine,
> Alas I am condempne'd, alas I am condempne'd, I am condempned ever, [:]
>> No hope, no help, ther doth remaine, [.]
> But downe, down, down, down I fall,
> But downe, down, down, down I fall,
>> Downe and arise, downe and arise, I never shall, [.]
> But downe, downe, downe[,] downe, I fall,
> But downe, downe, downe[,] downe, I fall,
>> Downe and arise, downe and arise, I never shall.

"In darknesse let mee dwell," undecorated poem (as printed four years earlier in Coprario 1606, no. 4)

In darknesse let me dwell, the ground shall sorrow be,
The roofe despaire to barre all chearefull light from me,
The walles of marble black that moistned stil shall weepe,
My musicke hellish jarring sounds to banish frendly sleepe.
  Thus wedded to my woes, and bedded in my tombe,
    O let me dying live till death doth come.

  Words as set by Dowland:

In darknesse let mee dwell, The ground, the ground shall sorrow, sorrow be,
The roofe Dispaire to barre all, all cheerfull light from mee,
The wals of marble blacke that moistned, that moistned still shall weepe, still shall
weepe,
My musicke, My musicke hellish, hellish jarring sounds, jarring, jarring sounds to
banish, banish friendly sleepe.
Thus wedded to my woes, And bedded to my Tombe,
O let me living die, O let me living, let me living, living die, Till death, till death doe
come,
till death, till death doe come, till death, till death doe come,
In darknesse let mee dwell.

In order to further the persuasive quality of the vehement affections expressed in the texts
of the two songs, Dowland amplifies the basic structure of the poetry by creating figures not
present in the poems. My discussion of the amplificatory devices in the two texts assumes
that Dowland adapted preexisting poems, but since the authorship of these poems remains
unknown, the possibility arises that Dowland may have penned these verses himself with
the figures of repetition forming part of his original conception. This is unlikely, however,
in the case of "In darknesse let mee dwell." As noted above, Coprario set the same poem,
with a few variants, to music four years earlier, and Dowland might have used Coprario's
publication as his source for the text. Interestingly, the publisher prints the complete poem
below the music, stripped of the few textual devices Coprario added in his setting, and the
inclusion of the unembellished text clearly demonstrates how both Coprario and Dowland
employed rhetorical figures to expand the basic structure of the poem.

  Although no undecorated model of "Sorrow stay" appears to exist, I presume that
Dowland's text represents a version amplified by rhetorical devices. Indeed, the expansion of a basic text seems to have been a procedure commonly employed by Dowland,

for over half of his solo songs augment the vehemence of persuasion through figures of repetition. Dowland's frequent use of *epizeuxis* (the immediate restatement of a word or phrase for greater vehemence), for example, embodies a compositional decision to stress and thus elicit in listeners the state of mind associated with that word or phrase. Various passages in both texts exemplify the procedure. At the opening of "Sorrow stay," the repetition of the word "sorrow" draws attention to and establishes the character of the ruling passion. Later, the reiteration of "pitty" reinforces this state of mind and categorizes the poem as Peacham the Elder's second type of *pathopoeia*, a lamentable cause that moves listeners to pity and compassion. Similarly, the restatements of "mark me not to endlesse paine," "alas I am condempned," "but downe, down, down, down I fall," and "downe and arise" emphasize the significance of these phrases.

Dowland's amplification of "In darknesse let mee dwell," in addition to the pervasive use of *epizeuxis*, involves another figure of repetition. As mentioned earlier, through *anadiplosis*, that is, the repetition of the last word of one phrase at the beginning of the next, the line "The roofe Dispaire to barre all cheerfull light from mee" becomes "The roofe Dispaire to barre all, all cheerfull light from mee." But as one would expect of a composer who has mastered both musical and verbal rhetoric, Dowland increases the artificiality of the poem by other means, as well. Rhetoricians called the device he uses to end the song *epanalepsis* (a unit that begins and ends with the same expression), and the words "In darknesse let mee dwell," which open and close the song, form a striking proposition to be considered at the beginning and to be remembered at the end. In addition, he employs *anastrophe* (a preposterous ordering of words that runs contrary to normal speaking; Sherry 1550: 31) to change the word order of Coprario's poem from "O let me dying live" to "O let me living die," thereby accentuating the underlying torment of the text (the possibility that Dowland himself may have reversed the order is suggested in Poulton 1982: 319, though Poulton did not comment on the rhetorical significance of this change).

Undoubtedly, knowledge of these devices helps singers deliver these poems effectively, both as dramatic readings and as songs, and I now wish to consider each song separately, illustrating in the process how the principles outlined in *elocutio* and *pronunciatio* form the basis of both eloquent speaking and singing. I do not intend my suggestions to be prescriptive, for vocalists may apply the principles of eloquent speaking and singing in various ways.

JOHN DOWLAND, "SORROW STAY"

As I indicated before, the central passion in this poem revolves around sorrow, and words like "teares," "dispaire," "tormenting feares," "pitty," and "endlesse paine" condemn this "woefull wretched wight" to a life without hope or help in which he falls steadily downward, never to rise again. The amplificatory devices mentioned above aid the singer in delivering the text of the song as spoken verse, and our knowledge of both voice and gesture can help us create a passionate delivery suitable to the affections of the poem. However, in this portion of my discussion I will concentrate on the voice, leaving gesture until I consider the song itself.

The tonal quality of the voice appropriate for someone in this state of mind (based on Table 3.1) might be described as doleful and grave, that is, a voice "fetcht from the bottome of the throate, groaning," interrupted with woeful exclamations and some-times breaking off abruptly with a sob or a sigh. Dowland begins by immediately ampli-fying the concept of sorrow through *epizeuxis*, a figure in which the speaker delivers the repeated word with a "different sound," pronouncing it "far louder and stronger." I suggest, however, that if a speaker consistently took the same approach to pronounc-ing *epizeuxis* every time it appeared in Dowland's text, delivery would become far too predictable. At times, one certainly might wish to utter the repeated word louder and stronger, but on other occasions an alteration of the tone color of the voice might be just as effective. At any rate, however the speaker decides to pronounce the *epizeuxis*, the repeated word really must receive some sort of emphasis, for without emphasis the figure becomes meaningless. The repetitions of "woefull" and "hence," therefore, should be stressed but perhaps in a way different from the utterance of "sorrow." In the fourth line of the text, however, the repetition "doe not, O doe not" presents a spe-cial case, for it combines *epizeuxis* with *ecphonesis* (exclamation). The exclamatory "O" preceding the repetition of "doe not" calls for the speaker to deliver this word with a louder and more passionate accent. But these woeful exclamations, a characteristic feature of texts dealing with sorrow, become even more passionate when one separates them from other parts of the sentence through a sob or a sigh (either before or after the interjection). In uttering the whole phrase, speakers might wish to align themselves with John Hart's method of delivering exclamatory outbursts: begin the phrase loudly, as the interjection demands, and end it with a lower volume. Similarly, the six itera-tions of "pitty" draw attention to this word most vehemently and remind us that rheto-ricians designed emphatic devices to heighten the expression of the sentiment on each repetition of a word. In pronouncing this application of *epizeuxis*, one needs to decide whether to reserve the strongest utterance of "pitty" for the final statement of the word or whether some other combination of gradations in volume, alterations in the tonal quality of the voice, changes in speed of delivery, and so on would be just as effective in moving listeners to feel pity for the "wretched wight" the speaker represents.

Repetitions of whole phrases serve the same purpose. For example, the line "Alas I am condempne'd, alas I am condempne'd, I am condempned ever" uses graduated *epizeuxis* to lead listeners to the climactic assertion "I am condempned ever." Speakers achieve momentum in this passage through their pronunciation of the figure, the colon allowing them to pause at the climax just before being driven to utter the conclusion of the thought, "no hope, no help, ther doth remaine." Dowland augments the vehement effect of the following descent into despair with *epizeuxis*, punctuating every repetition of the word "down," like the word "pitty," by commas (*articulus*). Varying the length of pause between repetitions gives performers ample opportunity to alter the sense of the word, if so desired, on every reiteration (mainly through changes in the tonal quality of the voice, volume, and speed of delivery). By the end of the period, the protagonist is resigned to remain in the depths of despair, and the speaker might utter the words "I never shall" so as to capture the bleak reality of the situation. Undoubtedly, singers will wish to hone their skills in delivering song texts as spoken dramatic readings through further experimentation, but remember, writers in the sixteenth and seventeenth centuries considered practice the key to success—repeat a sentence over and over until it can be pronounced "according to *Art*" (Le Faucheur 1657: 214).

Dowland reveals his sublime mastery of affective persuasion in this *prosopopoeia* by coupling words and notes so artfully that one seems to complement the other almost perfectly, making the singer's task so much easier (Example 4.1). Dowland places the song in the transposed *protus* mode (that is, he composed the vocal line in the Hypodorian mode transposed to G), and he divides the song into three large sections, each ending with a strong cadence on the final of the mode, the conclusiveness of these cadences being reinforced by a raised third in the lute part (mm. 1–10, 11–22, and 22–26, repeated in a slightly extended form). These pauses, the musical equivalents of the full stop (*periodus*) in language, mark the main resting points in the musical discourse. Dowland further subdivides these three periods into a number of commas and colons, the smaller members focusing the listener's attention on specific ideas and affections. Each member, of course, requires an individual approach to its delivery, and this leads me to consider the members separately.

Dowland begins the song in reciting style, supporting the voice with simple chords. He enhances the vehement effect of the text's *epizeuxis* with musical *climax*, and the interaction of these two figures colors my approach to delivering the proposition to be considered: "sorrow sorrow stay." A slow arpeggiation of the opening G-minor chord invites the singer to implore sorrow to stay and hints at the grave subject matter to follow, passions for which the singer probably should adopt a doleful tonal quality of voice. Dowland's melody, a descending two-note figure (rhythmically long-short), allows the singer to adapt one of the devices Giulio Caccini mentions as important for moving the affections of listeners, that is, crescendo on the first note of the figure and decrescendo on the second.[1] On the repetition of the word "sorrow" and its corresponding musical figure, the crescendo might become even more exaggerated in order to conform to the

EXAMPLE 4.1 *"Sorrow stay"*

Sor- row sor- row stay, lend true re- pen- tant

teares, to a woe- full, woe- full wretch- ed wight, [.]

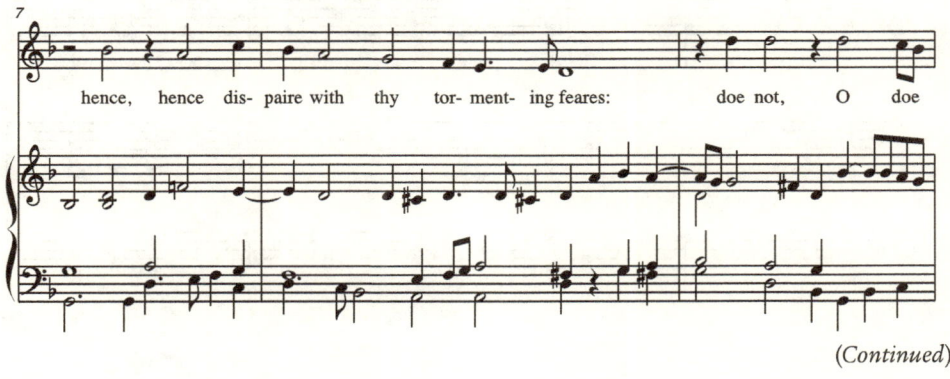

hence, hence dis- paire with thy tor- ment- ing feares: doe not, O doe

(Continued)

EXAMPLE 4.1 (*Continued*)

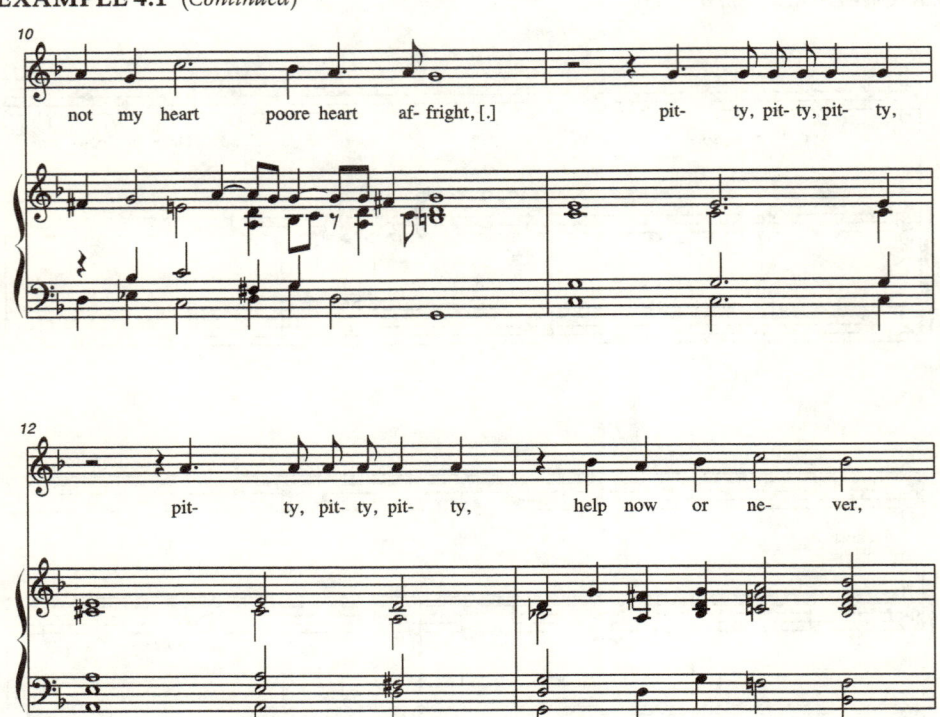

not my heart   poore heart   af- fright, [.]   pit- ty, pit- ty, pit- ty,

pit-   ty, pit- ty, pit- ty,   help now   or   ne-   ver,

mark me   not   to   end- lesse   paine,   mark me   not   to   end- lesse   paine,

(Continued)

EXAMPLE 4.1 (*Continued*)

normal delivery of *epizeuxis* (in which a speaker would deliver the repeated word with a louder voice). Moreover, singers can create a particularly poignant effect if they reach the peak of the first crescendo at the same time that the lutenist, in arpeggiating the chord below, plays the highest note of that chord (A), thereby accentuating the dissonance Bb/A. In the repetition of the figure, the performers can achieve the same effect between the singer's A and the lutenist's Bb.

The hand, of course, should reinforce the passionate appeal of the voice, and when executed in a natural and unaffected manner (as opposed to the statuelike poses some singers adopt today), gesture should not seem strange or archaic to modern audiences. In fact, if we take the advice of Thomas Wright seriously and observe people "appassionate" in our own age, then we soon discover that period gesture really is not very far removed from current practices. Action based on historical principles will and does, I believe, reinforce the passions of the text just as realistically as Wright, Rosseter, and others described. Several gestures seem appropriate for the opening of the song, and Thomas Hobbes (1637: 118) comments on the use of action to enhance figures of repetition: "But in *Pleadings* [that is, orations to the people as distinct from judicial pleading], by the helpe of Action and by some change [of voice] in the *Pleader*, Repetition becomes Amplification." From its resting point in front of the chest, vocalists might bring the hand forward softly as an act of preparation (Bulwer 1644; Plate 3.3 C, E). They would then transform this preparatory gesture into the posture for sorrow and grief at the moment they utter the first "sorrow" (Plate 3.3 Y). But the final word of the proposition, depending on the singer's interpretation of the text, might be graced in more than one way. The hand could invite sorrow to stay (Plate 3.1 W), it could beg sorrow to stay (Plate 3.1 Z), or it could command sorrow to stay (Plate 3.5 M). The vocalist may wish, however, to dispense with the preparatory gesture, preferring to create a more vehement effect at the outset by beginning abruptly with the posture for sorrow and grief. The only melodic ornamentation I would suggest for this passage, if one wished to add any embellishment at all, would be an elevation to the first note of the melody encompassing the interval of a third. Singers should probably duplicate this elevation for the repeat of "sorrow" in order to preserve the integrity of the musical figure Dowland composed.

After the performers have delivered this rather arresting *propositio* in a free manner, the lutenist can establish a slow tempo, one that parallels the grave and doleful tonal quality of voice the text demands (perhaps a crotchet or quarter note = 80–88), through the dotted figure that begins just as the singer finishes delivering the initial statement of the poem. The next textual phrase ("lend true repentant teares, to a woefull, woefull wretched wight") could be graced with purely melodic embellishments and with action that amplifies the underlying sentiments of the words. Specifically, singers might borrow from Christ Church 439, a manuscript that preserves the song only up to the first iteration of "woefull," the under-third elevations on "lend" and "-pen-" of "repen-tant," while reinforcing the meaning of the words with three separate hand gestures. Vocalists can show the torment they feel as they deliver the words "lend true repen-tant teares" through the posture for mental anguish (Plate 3.1 K), and the repetition of "woefull," in addition to receiving emphasis by inserting a pause at the comma, may be stressed through one of the finger positions for urging an argument (for example, Plate 3.5 D). They can then transform this latter gesture into the posture for speaking about oneself (Plate 3.3 L) on the words "wretched wight," the hand returning to the resting position before they finish singing "wight." The lutenist draws the period to a close, and the cadence at the beginning of measure 7 probably should be observed through a clear, but short, pause after the cadence note.

Dowland follows the punctuation of the text quite closely in the second period (mm. 7–10), as he composes rests into the melody for the commas at "hence" and "doe not" and represents the colon at "feares" through a cadence on the fifth above the final of the mode, thus giving the musical expectation that much more remains to be spoken. In fact, the lutenist pushes the song forward at this point with a new figure that leads the singer to an exclamatory outburst. The music written for the exclamation, the melodic equivalent of John Hart's loud beginning and soft ending, brings the first large section of the piece to a full and perfect close on the final of the mode (with a raised third in the lute part; end of m. 10). The repetition of "hence" at the beginning of this period might be enforced by uttering it with more intensity in order to prepare for an emphatic asser-tion of "dispaire," and singers could show "dispaire" itself with fainting and dejected hands (Plate 3.1 H). I suggest that vocalists deliver the interjection "O" in the Italian tradition with an *esclamazione*, specifically by a quick decrescendo followed by a rapid crescendo. This will create the emotional outburst Dowland seems to have intended, and the singer can increase the passionate force of the interjection by raising the hand aloft (Plate 3.3 O). In this case, one might leave the hand extended until near the end of the phrase, returning it to the resting position at the cadence. At this point, the vocalist should make a lengthy pause to give listeners enough time to reflect on the entire text that has been delivered. And at both cadences in this section ("feares" and "affright"), singers could apply subtle embellishments, perhaps in the form of discrete figures that would not obscure Dowland's melody, especially since he seems to have preferred the "old manner" of ornamentation.

Dowland returns to the reciting style to set the reiterations of the word "pitty." He divides the repetitions into two groups of three words and introduces musical *climax* to heighten the persuasive qualities of the textual *epizeuxis* (a stepwise ascent for the second group of three iterations of "pitty"). The carefully graduated increment of the rising *climax* not only increases the vehemence of the passion embodied in the word "pitty" but also suggests a manner of delivery appropriate for this passage. The singer persuades the listener by degrees, as it were, and might underscore the first group with one of the postures for reinforcing the vehemence of the word (for example, Plate 3.5 D) and utter the second group with greater intensity, emphasizing each reiteration of the sentiment by driving the extended right index down (Plate 3.5 P). The reason Dowland dwells on "pitty" becomes clear as the phrase continues. The protagonist asks "pitty" for help—now or never—and singers probably should draw attention to the antithetical nature of the text. They might very well stress the words "now" and "never" and transfer the gesture for distinguishing contraries from the left side of the body to the right (a suitable finger posture is given in Plate 3.5 Z).

The "woefull wretched wight" then implores "pitty" to "mark me not to endlesse paine" (mm. 14–15), and textual *epizeuxis* coupled with musical *palillogia* (the repetition of a melodic fragment at the same pitch) augments the expression of this sentiment. Here the freedom of the reciting style gives way to a slow tempo that parallels the sense of the words. For the repetition of "mark me not to endlesse paine," the separation of the second statement of the phrase from the first, so clearly indicated by Dowland in the vocal part, probably should be delayed slightly so that the articulation occurs after the lutenist plays the ultimate note of the phrase, that is, after the B♭ (the third crotchet or quarter note of m. 15). This reiteration, delivered with increased vehemence in the voice and reinforced by a forceful indicatory action in which the extended index finger admonishes pity not to inflict endless pain (Plate 3.5 M), prepares the listener for the exclamatory "alas I am condempne'd" (mm. 16–17). "Alas" is, of course, one of the interjections that convey emotional outburst, and singers should emphasize it with both the voice and the hand. They might raise the hand aloft for the interjection (Plate 3.3 O) and direct it toward themselves for the remainder of the phrase (Plate 3.3 L). Once again, Dowland combines textual *epizeuxis* with musical *palillogia*, and these devices, together with the style of delivery they suggest, lead listeners to the climactic moment of the passage, "I am condempned ever" (mm. 19–20). Singers can make the protagonist's increasing agitation, so carefully constructed by Dowland in an incremental way, even more vehement if the speed of delivery, that is, the tempo, accelerates for "I am condempned ever." A passionate application of the hand to the head (Plate 3.2 L) will help these words inflame the minds of listeners. Dowland ends the musical phrase with a cadence on the fifth above the final of the mode, the musical equivalent of a colon, and a pause at this point (by singer and lutenist) allows the accumulated energy to dissipate, leaving listeners to anticipate what follows.

Dowland returns to the reciting style (mm. 20–22), introduced through the lutenist's G-minor chord in the middle of measure 20, for the faltering realization that "no hope" and "no help" remain. Ascending musical *climax* (the stepwise repetition of a melodic fragment) accompanies these words and ensures that both singer and listener understand their implication—not only is there no hope but also there is no help for this "woefull wretched wight"—and perhaps vocalists could utter "no help" with even more anguish. In fact, they can underscore the greater vehemence of "no help" with a gesture that instantly enforces a word or idea such as the one shown in Plate 3.5 I. Moreover, ample space should be left between the utterances so that singers can deeply impress the increasing desperation of the protagonist, intensified through sighs or sobs, upon the souls of listeners. They might deliver the closing words of this period with the utmost dismay and follow them by the long pause the musical cadence suggests, for listeners now have a weighty matter on which to reflect.

But, of course, Dowland has not yet completed the story. The singer still must disclose the consequences of being condemned without hope or help, and the music Dowland composed for this purpose depicts the plight of his "wretched wight" quite literally. The descending minim (half note) line perfectly captures the sense of "but downe, down, down, down I fall," and singers can deliver the minims most affectively when they perform a crescendo and decrescendo on each one, the articulations required by the commas (*articulus*) helping them draw attention to each step of the steady descent. Listeners could feel the passion of each repetition of "downe" even more strongly, however, if the performer enforces the voice with an urging and pressing gesture (Plate 3.5 D). Dowland further reinforces the pathos of the situation through musical *palillogia* (the repetition of a melodic fragment at the same pitch), but the suffering soon turns to hope as the protagonist begins to rise out of the depths of despair ("downe and arise"). This proves to be false hope, however, for the words "I never shall" crushes it immediately. Dowland designs the rising vocal line, repeated by means of musical *synonymia*, to reflect this feeling of hope, and singers can enhance its delivery in two ways. First, they can heighten the irony of this phrase through the gesture for triumph (Plate 3.1 P), and second, they can reinforce the notion of hope by gradually increasing the speed of delivery (tempo) during the second statement of "downe and the rise." The lutenist can then carry forward the excitement and anticipation generated through this latter effect by continuing to accelerate the tempo (while the singer holds the long D) until the musical phrase comes to a close on the second full crotchet (quarter note) of measure 25. At this point, singers may wish to refer the hand to themselves, using the time taken up by this action to allow the accumulated energy of the preceding phrase to subside before delivering "I never shall," the words that portray the bleak reality of the situation.

Dowland reinforces the passions embodied in this remarkable conclusion to the poem through a repetition of the entire period, and this creates a tripartite structure of more or less equal proportions within the song. The performers may wish to deliver the repeated material in a similar fashion, except that because Dowland doubled the length of the singer's D on the reiteration of "arise," the lutenist's acceleration of tempo takes place over a longer musical phrase. This makes the introduction of a ritardando by the lutenist appropriate just before the singer utters the final "I never shall." The only melodic embellishments I would suggest for the last two large sections of the piece are discrete cadential figures on "doth remaine" and "never shall."

JOHN DOWLAND, "IN DARKNESSE LET MEE DWELL"

The author of "In darknesse let mee dwell," just like the author of "Sorrow stay," infused the poem with images of sorrow and grief. The striking *propositio* invokes a sense of foreboding right at the outset, and the words that follow depict someone so consumed with woe that the person's very existence seems a living death. Not only does the ground embrace sorrow but the roof of despair bars all light, the walls weep, and, perhaps worst of all, music has become a hellish cacophony. The protagonist's fate is sealed, however, and this person is resigned to living in darkness until death. Dowland intensifies these grave sentiments with numerous figures of repetition, and as in "Sorrow stay" these figures serve to transport the poem from the world of the written word to the realm of musical oration.

Dowland again chooses the transposed *protus* mode for setting a text dealing with grief, but for this passionate ayre he transposes the Hypodorian mode to A rather than G (Example 4.2). He divides the song into two large sections and clearly marks the two parts by means of a double bar line. These sections encompass a number of commas, the very first one being for the lute alone. The lutenist's preamble, the musical equivalent of the rhetorician's *exordium* (the beginning of an oration, which serves to prepare the audience to listen with interest), establishes the character of the song right from the first notes, for the opening musical gesture, an A-minor chord, serves to equate a doleful harmony with a woeful subject. Proceeding from this musical gesture, the lutenist establishes a tempo that reflects the grave subject matter of the poem (perhaps a crotchet or quarter note = c. 92). At the close of this preamble, the singer's initial note emerges, almost imperceptibly at first, from the A-minor chord on which the lutenist cadences. Dowland uses the singer's opening statement to close the song as well, and this creates the musical counterpart of rhetorical *epanalepsis* (the relationship between rhetorical and musical figures in this passage is discussed in *Elocutio* in conjunction with Example 2.19).

To intensify this opening image of grief, singers might shake their head while contracting their eyebrows into a frown. At the word "mee," they could direct their right hand toward themselves and then take care to observe the abrupt termination, the musical counterpart of *aposiopesis*, which closes the phrase. Dowland deliberately writes a remarkably short resolution to the *syncope* (suspension), and

EXAMPLE 4.2 *"In darknesse let mee dwell"*

The roofe Dis- paire to barre all, all cheer- full light from mee,

The wals of mar- ble blacke that moist- ned, that

moist- ned still shall weepe, still shall weepe,

(Continued)

EXAMPLE 4.2 (*Continued*)

to my woes, And bed- ded to my Tombe,

O   Let me liv- ing die,

O   let me liv- ing, let me liv-   ing, liv- ing die,

(Continued)

EXAMPLE 4.2 (*Continued*)

the duration of this note should be no longer than the crotchet (quarter note) specified, for he may very well have intended this hasty abandonment to convey to listeners that even at the outset the protagonist's sorrow has almost become too great
for the delivery to continue. In fact, singers can demonstrate the overwhelming
torment they feel most vehemently if they utter the last note as a sob. Dowland
separates the vocalist's opening phrase from the next one with a minim (half note)
rest in both the voice and lute parts, and this leaves listeners ample time to consider
the *propositio*.

The following textual phrases explain why the protagonist wishes to dwell in darkness, and the singer's increasing despair gradually emerges as the poem unfolds. For "the ground, the ground shall sorrow, sorrow be," in addition to pronouncing the punctuation, the singer should emphasize each of the two uses of *epizeuxis* and demonstrate the underlying sentiment perhaps through the gesture for sorrow (Plate 3.3 Y). This phrase, like the previous one, seems to stand alone, and singers might bring it to a close with a slower speed of delivery, that is, a slowing of the tempo through a ritardando, for the words "sorrow be." The next section ("the roofe Dispaire to barre all, all cheerfull light from mee") begins afresh, as it were, with a new melodic figure in the accompaniment. Here, vocalists can illustrate the growing despair of their situation by lowering their right hand to the position for mental anguish (Plate 3.1 K). Dowland separates the *anadiplosis* in the middle of this phrase, that is, the reiteration of "all," through a rest in the vocal line, and this enables the singer to emphasize the repetition with a sigh, as well as with increased intensity or volume. By the time the vocalist utters "the wals of marble blacke that moistned, that moistned still shall weepe, still shall weepe," the third statement to amplify the passion of despair, grief almost certainly has become well settled in the "yearning bowels," and singers can demonstrate this most vehemently by touching the fingertips to the breast. The crotchet (quarter note) rest in the vocal line, which breaks up the words "that moistned still shall weepe," undoubtedly represents a sob, and the comma at the end of this phrase allows the vocalist time to sigh (using that sharp intake of breath characteristic of Elizabethan and Jacobean sighing) at the high point of the phrase (both musically and emotionally), before reinforcing the passionate appeal of the words by repeating "still shall weepe."

Dowland captures the final and most damning depiction of the protagonist's grief with the words "My musicke, My musicke hellish, hellish jarring sounds, jarring, jarring sounds to banish, banish friendly sleepe." Singers might utter the *epizeuxis* employed at the beginning of this phrase with a most anguished tonal quality in the voice, as this would serve to heighten the realization that even music has become tormented. Performers, of course, speak of themselves at this point, and I suggest that they direct the hand inward. But for the words "hellish, hellish jarring sounds, jarring, jarring sounds" they might adopt one of the postures for urging and enforcing the sense of the words (for example, Plate 3.5 D). At the words "to banish, banish friendly sleepe," however, the singer could use the left hand to repel the idea of sleep being banished (Plate 3.3 M). Moreover, the speed of delivery might quicken somewhat for the hellish jarring sounds, and the lutenist should take care to emphasize the descending chromatic line that symbolizes the singer's plight. In general, the tonal quality of voice in this passage probably should reflect the nature of the words and tend to harshness. But the tone might very well soften somewhat for the words "friendly sleepe," and the singer could add discrete ornamentation on the dotted minim (half note) just before the cadence note B. These final thoughts draw the first part of the song to a close with a cadence on the fifth above the final, and this leads listeners to expect much more to be spoken on the subject.

The second part opens with an A-major chord, and this sudden shift of *concentus* (vertical sonority) away from the minorish character of the mode may lead listeners to anticipate brighter sentiments. But this turns out to be a false expectation, for Dowland keeps them firmly anchored, both in text and in music, to the passion of grief. However, the second part does seem to require a slightly faster speed of delivery, and a fairly lengthy pause between the two parts of the song enables listeners to reflect on the previous statements before the performers introduce new ideas. Right from the outset of this section, completely overcome with grief, singers resign their liberty, becoming wedded to their woes and bedded to their tombs. The hands held forth together (Plate 3.1 N) naturally express this state of mind and powerfully enforce the passionate appeal of the words. In fact, vocalists might select the word "woes" for particular emphasis through a quick crescendo and decrescendo. This submission to sorrow leads the singer to explode in grief with the exclamation "O Let me living die," and Dowland's setting of these words may have been influenced by one of Giulio Caccini's songs (Example 4.3a and b). Hence, an *esclamazione*, coupled with the explosive gesture of clapping the

EXAMPLE 4.3 *(a) R. Dowland 1610, "In darknesse let mee dwell"; (b) Caccini 1602, "Cor mio, deh non languire"*

left palm with the right fist (Plate 3.1 G), seems most appropriate for intensifying this sudden outburst. Dowland repeats the words through musical *climax* and extends the entire phrase by means of *epizeuxis*. For the second exclamation, the vocalist could add an under-third elevation, while raising the hand aloft, and use the punctuation that separates the repeated words and phrases to draw attention to the increasing emphasis placed on the word "living."

Dowland does not complete the textual idea that began in the exclamation, how-ever, until his protagonist utters "till death, till death doe come." The singer needs to emphasize the *epizeuxis* in this phrase, and Dowland further draws attention to the sen-timent expressed in the passage by repeating it twice, the first time using musical *palil-logia* to underscore the text and the second time employing a melody that lends itself to further intensification during its delivery. Each iteration, separated by commas, should be more anguished than the previous one, and the performer could reinforce the third statement through a crescendo on the dotted semibreve (whole note), articulated at its highest point, just before the *epizeuxis*. Moreover, singers can most strikingly enhance the incremental progression of intensification that Dowland's melodic design suggests if they organize their hand gestures in a similarly progressive manner. For the first itera-tion, they might assume a posture of extreme loathing (Plate 3.3 W), placing the hands a short distance from the chest. On the second statement, the hands could be pushed out a little further, but on the third iteration, they can show the utmost detestation by driving the hands out to the left side while turning the head to the right (Plate 3.3 V).

However, to surprise and delight listeners with the *epanalepsis* that closes the song, the two performers might wish to give the impression that the song concludes at the lutenist's cadence at the beginning of the second last measure. Singers can achieve this effect most persuasively if they deliver the final utterance of "till death doe come" as if it actually were the last statement of the song, the lutenist seeming to bring the piece to a close on the final of the mode placed in the penultimate measure. But Dowland toys with the listeners' expectations here, for although the performers certainly can approach this cadence as though it were the final one, Dowland carefully avoids the cadence by leaping from G♯ to C. At this point, listeners will be unsure of what to expect next, and a pause after the lutenist's cadence serves to heighten their anticipation, the follow-ing *epanalepsis* truly delighting their ears while stirring their minds. Undoubtedly, the repetition of "In darknesse let mee dwell" reminds listeners of the *propositio* and leaves them with a weighty matter to ponder. In fact, only at the end of the song does Dowland impress the full force of his abrupt termination on listeners and clarify the reason for his incorporation of the musical counterpart of *aposiopesis*. This figure enables the singer to penetrate deeply into the souls of listeners with a powerful demonstration of the depth to which grief has settled, sorrow so great that the performer really cannot continue even though the musical cadence that underpins this device (on the fifth above the final of the mode) leads listeners to expect more to be spoken on the subject. Singers can enhance the effect of the abrupt termination most vehemently if they simultaneously drive the hands out to either side in a violent motion designed to double the passion of abhorrence, while they utter the last note of the song as a sob.

NOTES

1. For a fuller discussion of Caccini's passionate manner of singing crescendo and decrescendo ("il crescere e scemare della voce") and *esclamazione,* see the section below, "Giulio Caccini, Deh dove son fuggiti." Both "Sorrow stay" and "In darknesse let mee dwell" contain a number of passages that show Italian influence. This is particularly true of the passages in reciting style and one phrase in "In darknesse let mee dwell" that may have been derived directly from Caccini (see Example 4.3 below). Dowland had traveled to Italy, and one should not be surprised to find Italian traits in his music. I will suggest, therefore, Italianate devices where appropriate.

Affetto cantando and Consort Singing in Italy

GIULIO CACCINI, "DEH DOVE SON FUGGITI"

In the preface to *Le nuove musiche* (1602: "A i lettori," unpaginated), Giulio Caccini laid out the principles he used for singing in a style he described as wholly passionate ("cantare . . . tutta affettuosa"). Caccini had been composing music suited to passionate singing ("affetto cantando") since the mid-1580s,[2] and by 1602 he had grown tired of the "torn and corrupted" ("lacere, e guaste") versions of his songs in circulation and decided not only to publish the songs himself but also to give at least a partial explanation of how he performed them.

In these songs, Caccini sought to compose music that imitated the ideas behind the words ("ho sempre procurata l'imitazione de i concetti delle parole"), and the manner of delivery he used to move the passions of listeners paralleled his musical/textual structures. In fact, he felt that in order to compose and sing well in this new style, the composer/performer needed first to understand the poet's conception, then to imitate the words with affective music, and finally to sing those words passionately. Through his songs, Caccini believed he had introduced a type of music that allowed vocalists almost to speak in tones, especially if they employed a certain noble negligence in their delivery ("una sorte di musica, per cui altri potesse quasi che in armonia favellare, usando in essa . . . una certa nobile sprezzatura di canto"). As he explained in his 1614 publication *Nuove musiche e nuova maniera de scriverle* ("Alcuni avvertimenti," unpaginated preface),

negligence ["sprezzatura"] is that elegance which is given to song through the transgression of several quavers [eighth notes] or semiquavers [sixteenth notes]

on various strings [pitches], like those [transgressions] made in tempo. It removes
from song a certain confining rigidity and dryness; thus it renders [song] pleasing,
free, and airy, just as in common speech, eloquence and fecundity [abundant vari-
ety] make the matters on which one speaks easy and pleasant.

La sprezzatura è quella leggiadria la quale si da canto co'l trascorso di più crome,
e simicrome sopra diverse corde co'l quale fatto à tempo, togliendosi al canto una
certa terminata angustia, e secchezza, si rende piacevole, licenzioso, e arioso, si
come nel parlar comune la eloquenza, e la fecondia rende agevoli, e dolci le cose di
cui si favella.

The elegance this freedom of rhythm and tempo produced was, of course, not new in
Caccini's time; singers had used these techniques of liberating music from the written
page for decades. In the middle of the sixteenth century, for instance, Loys Bourgeois
(1550: ch. 10, "De chanter les demiminimes") commented on the grace performers could achieve by lingering slightly longer on the first note of an equally notated
pair of "demiminimes" (quarter notes) or "fuses" (eighth notes; see also Thomas de
Sancta Maria 1565: I, 19, fol. 45v). Indeed, a number of the passages quoted in the
Introduction ("An Age of Rhetorical Persuasion") document this free manner of performance throughout the sixteenth century, and in creating something "new," Caccini
had tapped into a tradition that extended back to at least the late 1400s. In 1602, he
simply included the notion of *sprezzatura* within his broader concept of *affetto*, and in
1614, he defined what he meant by the term *affetto*:

passion in one who sings is nothing other than this: by the power of certain notes
and varied accents, together with the moderation of soft and loud, an expression of
the words (and their meaning) that one takes the liberty to sing, acts to move the
affections of the listener.

lo affetto in chi canta altro non è che per la forza di diverse note, e di vari accenti co'l
temperamento del piano, e del forte una espressione delle parole, e del concetto, che
si prendono à cantare atta à muovere affetto in chi ascolta. ("Alcuni avvertimenti.")

Caccini went on to say that singers should take note of the various passions in the text
and let the changes of meaning from one moment to another guide them, so they could
avoid clothing the bridegroom and the widower alike ("one is not satisfied to represent
the bridegroom and the widower, so to speak, with the same clothes"/"la medissima
veste (per dir cosi) uno togliesse à rappresentare lo sposo, e'l vedovo"). His position
remained unchanged from the one he had advocated in *Le nuove musiche*: a thorough

understanding of the ideas and emotions present in the words would help singers know when to use more or less *affetto*. The fundamental elements of this *affetto cantando* included crescendos and decrescendos, *esclamazioni, trilli*, and *gruppi* ("il crescere e scemere della voce, l'esclamazioni, trilli, e gruppi"; 1602: "A i lettori"). He described *passaggi*, however, particularly the indiscriminate use of them, as a tickling of the ear, a nonessential part of good singing: "*passaggi* have not been devised because they are necessary for a good manner of singing, but I believe more for a certain tickling of the ears of those who understand little about singing with passion"/"passaggi non sono stati ritrovati per che siano necessarii alla buona maniera di cantare, ma credo io più tosto per una certa titillatione à gli orecchi di quelli, che meno intendono che cosa sia cantare con affetto."

He opened his discussion of professional singing ("professione del cantante") with the intonation of the voice ("l'intonazione della voce"), by which he meant both singing in tune and the manner of commencing a note in good style ("la buona maniera"). Some performers, he relates, begin a phrase not on the written note but on the third below, while others start on the composer's note itself and deliver it as a crescendo, believing this to be a good manner of putting forth the voice with grace ("dicendosi questa essere la buona maniera per mettere la voce con grazia"). Although under-third beginnings had become quite common, Caccini felt that singers often dwelt far too long on the third below, instead of scarcely suggesting it. His comment may refer to Giovanni Battista Bovicelli, who in 1594 stated that "when the first note [the under-third] is held longer, and the second is quicker [that is, the note which fills in the third], the greater the grace one gives to the voice"/"quanto più si tiene la prima nota, e la seconda è più veloce, si dà anco maggior gratia alla voce"; 11). Nevertheless, despite his reservations about this practice, Caccini had himself notated a number of under-thirds in *Le nuove musiche*. Still, of the two practices in general use, he preferred that vocalists begin with a crescendo, but he also advised singers to employ a great deal of variety, as long as whatever novelty they introduced achieved the goal of moving the affections of listeners. The method he found the most affective, however, involved commencing first notes with a decrescendo immediately followed by an *esclamazione*. Caccini believed that *esclamazioni* were the principal means of stirring the passions, and he defined the technique as "nothing more than the relaxed voice being strengthened somewhat"/"esclamazione propriamente altro non è, che nel lassare della voce rinforzarla alquanto." He then explained why he considered the coupling of a decrescendo with an *esclamazione* to be the ideal way of initiating a phrase. If singers delivered the first note with a crescendo instead of a decrescendo, the following *esclamazione* would sound strained and coarse ("sforzata e cruda"), primarily because vocalists would be forced to crescendo even more if they wished to deliver the exclamation properly. *Esclamazioni* did not suit every type of music, however, notably dance songs and airy pieces, but in appropriate music, Caccini expected this form of *grazia* to occur on minims (half notes) and dotted semiminims (quarter notes) that descend, especially when the following note is short, as this makes the grace more affective. Singers should deliver semibreves (whole notes), on the other hand, with a crescendo and decrescendo instead of an *esclamazione*. These longer notes gave performers ample time to execute a more protracted rise and fall of the voice, but in the examples illustrating his text Caccini actually prescribed *esclamazioni* on notes ranging in value from minims to semibreves.

Furthermore, in his illustration of the variety singers could achieve through different forms of *esclamazione*, Caccini recommends performing the first note shown in Example 4.4 with a gradual decrescendo on the dotted minim (half note), followed by a somewhat more spirited swell of the voice on the falling semiminim (quarter note), before a much livelier *esclamazione* is introduced on the word "deh." He describes this second *esclamazione* as much livelier ("più viva"), because the melody leaps downward. Yet in addition to these procedures, the example demonstrates how vocalists can make a passage written in one way more graceful by performing it in another manner. He draws the reader's attention to the second syllable of "languire," suggesting that the music would become considerably more graceful if singers delivered the equally notated *crome* (eighth notes) with a dot on the second note of the group.

EXAMPLE 4.4 *Variety in* esclamazioni *and grace achieved through an unequal note pattern*

Caccini next turns his attention to the *trillo* and the *gruppo*. He suggests vocalists learn to execute both of these fundamental elements of passionate singing in the manner indicated in Example 4.5; that is, performers should restrike each note with the throat on the vowel *à*, accelerating from the slower notes to the quicker ones. Although Caccini indicates abrupt changes of rhythm from one note value to the next, many singers today find a smoother acceleration more satisfactory.

EXAMPLE 4.5 Trillo *and* gruppo

The subsequent examples of exquisiteness in singing ("squisitezza") that he includes encompass several principles of *affetto cantando*, particularly uneven note patterns, the *ribattuta di gola*, and three types of *cascate*. Caccini shows singers various ways they might grace passages by making equally written notes uneven through the noble negligence of rhythm (Example 4.6), and then he illustrates the addition of the *trillo* to this nobly negligent style (Example 4.7). Next he writes out the *ribattuta di gola* or the restriking of the throat, without explaining how to perform it (Example 4.8), and he finishes the series of examples with single ("scempia") and double ("doppia") falls ("cascate"), as well as the place for taking breath within those *cascate* ("ricorre il fiato"; Example 4.9).

EXAMPLE 4.6 *Uneven note patterns*

EXAMPLE 4.7 Trilli *added to the uneven patterns*

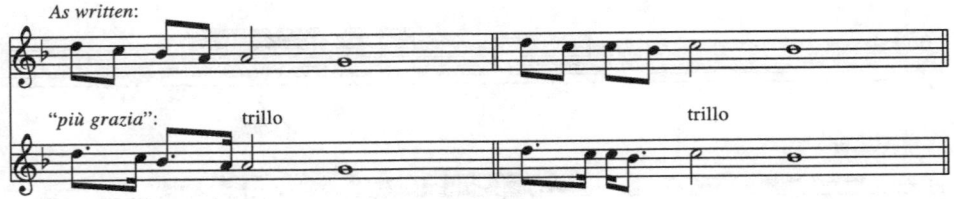

EXAMPLE 4.8 Ribattuta di gola

EXAMPLE 4.9 Cascate

With the essential ingredients of *affetto cantando* firmly in place, Caccini proceeds to give a number of further illustrations so that singers may, as he says, train themselves in all the most affective passages ("with practice of them [the following examples] and the others [given above, singers] will be able to train themselves in all the most affective passages"/"tutti passi affettuosissimi con la pratica de'quali altri potrà esercitarsi in loro"; Example 4.10). These passages include uneven note patterns, *cascate* (4.10b, h), *gruppi* (4.10e, g), *trilli* of several types (4.10c, d, f, g), and the *ribattuta di gola* in the midst of other figures (4.10d).

EXAMPLE 4.10 *Caccini's examples of the most affective passages*

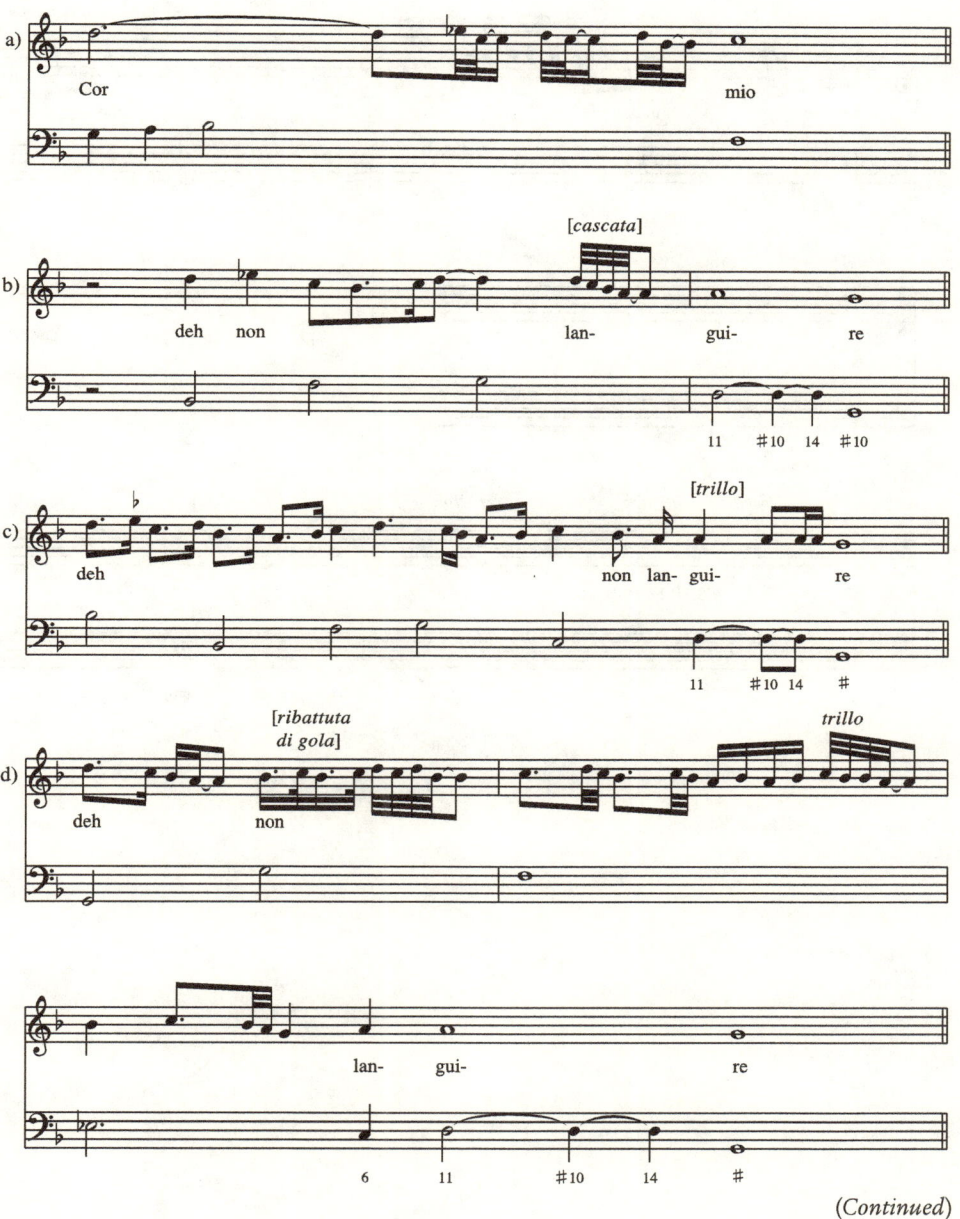

(Continued)

EXAMPLE 4.10 *(Continued)*

Caccini concludes his discussion of passionate singing with a brief mention of voice register. He suggests that each vocalist, especially when accompanied by a chitarrone or other stringed instrument, should choose "a tone [pitch level] in which one could sing in a full and natural voice, so as to avoid the feigned voice"/"un tuono, nel quale possa cantare in voce piena, e naturale per isfuggire le voci finte."

At the end of his music examples, Caccini demonstrates how he would apply the various principles of passionate singing to one of his songs, making sure to mark the appropriate place for each device (Example 4.11). The text of the song, adapted from a poem by Gabriello Chiabrera, deals with the torment of a person who has been reduced to ashes in the eyes of a beloved one, and Caccini begins the song with the interjection "deh" treated by means of *epizeuxis* (the immediate restatement of a word or two). He delivers the first "deh" with a decrescendo and then utters the repetition of the interjection through a spirited *esclamazione,* thus paralleling the type of increased vehemence orators normally gave repeated words. In fact, he recommends expressing every "deh" in the song with an *esclamazione,* and this underlines the important, and common, role musical exclamations played in the delivery of vehement interjections. Caccini also indicates where singers should apply *sprezzatura* (mm. 8–9) and where they should broaden the tempo ("con misura più larga"; mm. 12–13). These changes of pace certainly reflect the nature of the words, for in measures 8–9 the divine breezes wander here and there, and in measures 12–13 the broadening of the tempo well suits the notion of the protagonist dying a little. Beyond these directions, Caccini marks the places singers should perform the *trillo,* the first in measure 9 on a semibreve (whole note) and the second at the end of the song, where the *trillo* should last for a half "battuta," that is, for a half tactus or measure (perhaps he means singers should begin the ornament half way through the dotted semibreve [whole note] over which he wrote "tr").

Text and translation:

Deh dove son fuggiti	Ah, where have they fled,
Deh dove son spariti	ah, where have they vanished,
Gl'occhi de quali ai rai[3]	the eyes in which I have shone.
Io son cener omai[?]	Am I now reduced to ashes?
Aure divine ch'errate	Divine breezes, which mistakenly
Peregrine in questa part'e in quella	wander in this part and in that,
Deh recate novella dell'alma luce loro	ah bring news of their soul's light,
Aure ch'io me ne moro	breezes in which I will die a little.

Caccini's terms:

"scemar di voce," decrescendo

"esclamazione spiritosa," spirited *esclamazione*

"esclamazione più viva," livelier *esclamazione*

"senza misura quasi favellando in armonia con la suddetta sprezzatura," without measure [i.e., regular rhythm], as if speaking in tones, with the aforesaid negligence

"con misura più larga," with measure, more broadly

"esclamazione rinforzata," *esclamazione,* strengthened

"trillo per una mezza battuta," trill for a half tactus [i.e., half the measure]

EXAMPLE 4.11 *Caccini, "Deh dove son fuggiti"*

(Continued)

EXAMPLE 4.11 (*Continued*)

Clearly, this song does not contain *passaggi*, yet we can learn how he added divisions, as well as *grazia*, to his music through a comparison of "Ardi cor mio" from *Le nuove musiche* with a simplified version included in the manuscript Brussels, Bibliothèque du Conservatoire Royal, 704 (Example 4.12). Caccini employs rhythmic *sprezzatura* in several places (mm. 1, 2, 4, 8, and 12), and his *passaggi* range from simple decorative patterns (mm. 3, 4, 7, and 8) to complex divisions (mm. 5–6, 11). He also inserts the *ribattuta di gola* at the beginning of measure 13 and a single *cascata* in the second half of that measure. Although not marked, singers might wish to introduce *trilli* on the last note of measure 4 and the first note of measure 14, similar locations to those Caccini had marked elsewhere (see, in particular, Examples 4.7 and 4.11 above).

Text and translation:

Ardi cor mio	Burn my heart,
Che non fu vista mai	for never was seen
Fiamma di piu bei rai	a flame with more beautiful rays.

Ardi cor mio	Burn my heart,
Che'l foco che t'incende	for the fire that inflames you
Piu chiaro splende	shines more brightly
De'rai del biondo dio	than the rays of the blonde god.
Ardi cor mio	Burn my heart.

EXAMPLE 4.12 *Caccini, "Ardi cor mio"*

(*Continued*)

EXAMPLE 4.12 (*Continued*)

CLAUDIO MONTEVERDI, "BACI SOAVI E CARI"

As I have shown in numerous sections of this book, singers can inadvertently take performance well outside sixteenth-century practices by applying modern concepts to the music of earlier cultures. In fact, how we interpret the documentary debris of history ultimately determines the context(s) we impose on specific works, particularly with regard to performing style. When we sift through the documents that come down to us, we inevitably bring certain concepts to the fore and either place others in the background or ignore them altogether. This organizational process leads, consciously or unconsciously, to the selective creation of a context, and the conclusions we draw about the structure of the music we wish to perform succeed or fail according to not only the strength of the premises we adduce in support of those conclusions but also the appropriateness of the context from which we derived the premises in the first place.

I choose Claudio Monteverdi's "Baci soavi e cari" (*Madrigali a cinque voci . . . libro primo*, 1587) as my case study for part song because at least one commentator, Gary Tomlinson (1987: 40), in selecting the madrigal for particularly harsh criticism, describes it as a work that demonstrates the young composer's limited text-setting capabilities. With expressions such as "youthful *imitatio*" and "youthful eclecticism," Tomlinson locates the madrigal at the lowest point on a continuum of maturity, because Monteverdi's incorporation of an affective style of composition was not as subtle as Tomlinson asserts it became in the Second Book (1987: 33, 41). However, from within the context I have chosen to employ, the madrigal emerges as a successful work rather than unsuccessful, for Monteverdi, even at the age of nineteen, had a much subtler understanding of musical-rhetorical principles than Tomlinson imagines.

Tomlinson's complaints about "Baci soavi e cari" focus on five main defects (1987: 40). First, the poem's syntax is long-winded at best, contorted and obscure at worst (the strophe runs to a "sprawling" thirteen lines). Second, Monteverdi only partially projected this syntax in his music. Third, the composer's musical response to the first period (lines 1–6) seems somewhat schematic. Monteverdi accommodated lines 4–5 through a partially transposed repetition of lines 1–2 and managed to convey a sense of syntactic completion through a long affective peroration (conclusion) on line 6 that leads to a full cadence. Fourth, Monteverdi hardly understood the poet's central period at all. He split it down the middle with a full cadence at the end of line 8 and an overly long exclamation at the beginning of line 9. As a result, he reduced the already difficult syntax of lines 7–10 to nonsense. In addition to these four points, the only premises adduced to support the conclusion that the rhetorical gestures of texts like this one do not inspire complementary musical structures, Tomlinson complains of the clumsy simultaneous diminished fourth (in the vertical sonority, D–F♯–B♭) Monteverdi introduced to compensate for the "bland" way he set the first statement of the words "la mia vita finire"/"end my life" (line 12).

The poem itself, however, the first stanza of a *canzone* by Giambattista Guarini, is not long-winded, contorted, and obscure, for it actually presents a remarkably clear structure for the young composer to follow (compare my translation with that by Tomlinson; I have taken the text of Guarini's poem from Monteverdi 1587, but capitalization, punctuation, and spacing of lines have been supplied editorially):

Text and translation:

Guarini's poem:	Tomlinson's translation:	My translation:
Baci soavi e cari,	Sweet and dear kisses,	Kisses suave and dear,
cibi della mia vita,	sustenance of my life,	food of my life,
ch'or m'involate hor mi rendete il core:	which now steal away,	which now steal away
	now give back my heart,	now give back my heart:
4 per voi, convien ch'impari	for your sake I must learn	through you, I must learn
come un'alma rapita	how a stolen heart	how a ravished soul
non senta il duol di mort'e pur si more.	feels no pain of dying and yet dies.	feels not the pain of death and yet it dies.
7 Quant'ha di dolce amore,	All that is sweet in love,	How much sweetness has love,
perche sempr'io vi baci:	whenever I kiss you,	because I always kiss you:
o dolcissime rose	oh sweetest roses,	oh sweetest roses
in voi tutto ripose.	resides in you.	in you everything rests.
11 Et s'io potessi à i vostri dolci baci,	And if I could, with your sweet kisses,	And if I could with your sweet kisses,
la mia vita finire,	end my life—	end my life,
o che dolce morire.	oh what a sweet death!	oh what sweet dying.

Guarini mixes end-stopped and enjambed lines and arranges the strophe in three periods, each period comprising a distinct thought. The poem begins with two parallel metrical structures that address the "baci" (both consisting of a pair of seven-syllable lines followed by an eleven-syllable line). Then four seven-syllable lines, divided in half by the interjection "O," precede a conclusion of three lines designed to summarize the thoughts on kisses and the sweet torment they bring.

The syntax of these periods becomes readily apparent when the cadence structure Monteverdi applies to the poem is used as a guide, for he certainly aligned his musical cadences with the resting points of the text. In G-Dorian, the mode in which Monteverdi composed "Baci soavi e cari," these cadences are:

Primary: G, D

Secondary: B♭

Transitory: F, A

Monteverdi, like other composers before him, aligned poetic and musical syntax, and his cadential plan for "Baci soavi e cari" elucidates Guarini's syntax, for he employs cadentially stopped lines to produce the musical equivalent of the pauses a speaker would apply in delivering the poem (an asterisk denotes a cadence reinforced by either a falling fifth or a rising fourth in the lowest sounding voice):

	Baci soavi e cari,	D, imperfect (m. 3)
	cibi della mia vita,	G, avoided, imperfect * (m. 5)
	ch'or m'involate hor mi	
	rendete il core:	B♭, avoided, imperfect * (m. 9)
4	per voi, convien ch'impari	A, imperfect (m. 12)
	come un'alma rapita	D, avoided, imperfect * (m. 14)
	non senta il duol di mort'e	
	pur si more, e pur si more.	D, avoided, imperfect * (m. 26)
7	Quant'ha di dolce amore,	D, imperfect (m. 29)
	perche sempr'io vi baci:	G, avoided, imperfect * (m. 32)
	o dolcissime rose	A, by leap in the *basso*, imperfect (m. 35)
	in voi tutto ripose.	D, imperfect * (m. 37)
11	Et s'io potessi à i vostri	
	dolci baci,	B♭, avoided, imperfect * (m. 41)
	la mia vita finire,	rests on D, quasi-cadentially (m. 45)
	o che dolce morire,	D, avoided, imperfect * (m. 49)
	o che dolce morire.	G, avoided, imperfect * (m. 54)
	Et s'io potessi à i vostri	
	dolci baci,	B♭, avoided, imperfect * (m. 57)
	la mia vita finire,	rests on D, quasi-cadentially (m. 61)
	o che dolce morire,	D, avoided, imperfect * (m. 65)
	o che dolce morire.	G, imperfect * (m. 70)

Throughout the madrigal, Monteverdi selects primary, secondary, and transitory cadence notes as his places of rest and regularly avoids the cadence at middle distinctions of the argument (Example 4.13). Avoided cadences weaken the effect of a *clausula*, giving the expectation that more will be spoken on the subject, and when composers set this type of stop to a note other than the final of the mode, they suspend the sense of a sentence in such a way that the ideas that follow ought presently to succeed.

EXAMPLE 4.13 *"Baci soavi e cari"*

Ba- ci so- a- vi e ca- ri, ci- bi del- la mia vi- ta, ch'or

Ba- ci so- a- vi e ca- ri, ci- bi del- la mia vi- ta,

Ba- ci so- a- vi e ca- ri, ci- bi del- la mia vi- ta,

Ba- ci so- a- vi e ca- ri, ci- bi del- la mia vi- ta,

m'in- vo- la- te hor mi ren- de- te il co- re:

ch'or m'in- vo- la- te hor mi ren- de- te il co- re: per

ch'or m'in- vo- la- te hor mi ren- de- te il co- re: per

ch'or m'in- vo- la- te hor mi ren- de- te il co- re: per

per

non

voi con- vien ch'im- pa- ri co- me un al- ma ra- pi- ta

voi con- vien ch'im- pa- ri co- me un al- ma ra- pi- ta

voi con- vien ch'im- pa- ri co- me un al- ma ra- pi- ta

voi con- vien ch'im- pa- ri co- me un al- ma ra- pi- ta

sen- ta il duol di mor- t'e pur

e pur si mo- re

non sen- ta il duol di mor-

non sen- ta il duol di mor-

non sen- ta il duol

(Continued)

EXAMPLE 4.13 (*Continued*)

30

per- che sem- pr'io vi ba- ci: O dol- cis- si- me

che sem- pr'io vi ba- ci: O dol- cis- si- me

che sem- pr'io vi ba- ci: O dol- cis- si- me

che sem- pr'io vi ba- ci: O dol- cis- si- me

O dol- cis- si- me

35

ro- se in voi tut- to ri- po- se. Et s'io po- tes- si à i vo- stri dol-

ro- se in voi tut- to ri- po- se. Et s'io po- tes- si à i vo- stri dol-

ro- se in voi tut- to ri- po- se. Et s'io po- tes- si à i vo- stri dol-

ro- se in voi tut- to ri- po- se. Et s'io po- tes- si à i vo- stri dol-

ro- se in voi tut- to ri- po- se.

(Continued)

EXAMPLE 4.13 *(Continued)*

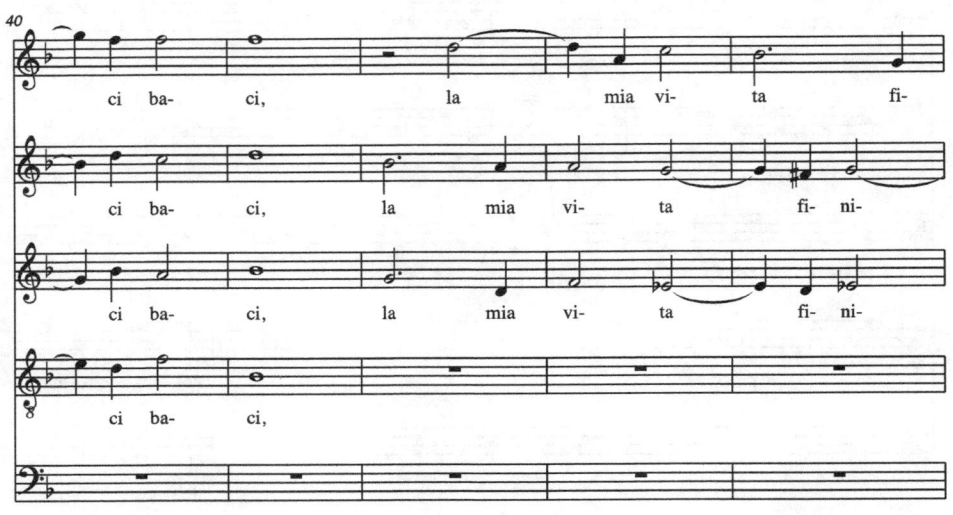

dol- ce mo- ri- re. Et s'io po-

dol- ce mo- ri- re. Et s'io po-

dol- ce mo- ri- re. Et s'io po-

dol- ce mo- ri- re. Et s'io po-

dol- ce mo- ri- re.

tes- si à i vo- stri dol- ci ba- ci, la mia vi-

tes- si à i vo- stri dol- ci ba- ci, la mia vi- ta

tes- si à i vo- stri dol- ci ba- ci, la mia vi-

tes- si à i vo- stri dol- ci ba- ci, la mia vi- ta

la mia vi- ta

(*Continued*)

EXAMPLE 4.13 (*Continued*)

Monteverdi's syntax, in addition to reinforcing the structure established by Guarini, transports the poem from the world of the written word to the realm of musical oration. He treats the opening word, "baci," as a *propositio* (when orators state in a "few wordes the summe of that matter, whereof we presently intend to speake"; Peacham the Elder 1577: fol. S2v) and uses rests in all the voices to separate the proposition he wishes listeners to consider from the description of the "baci" that follows. He then furthers the oratorical structure of the initial period by marking the natural break in the thought at the end of line 3 with a *clausula* on the secondary cadence note B♭ (Example 4.13, m. 9).

This cadence mirrors the colon implied in the text and leads the listener to expect much more to be spoken on the subject. Guarini enjambs the next two lines (4 and 5), and at the end of the fourth line, the music cadences briefly on the transitory resting point, A, the pause implied by this *clausula* paralleling the momentary stop a sixteenth-century speaker probably would have introduced after the word "impari." Short interruptions of the sound in places like this arrest the attention of listeners and help speakers and singers distinguish one idea from another. These techniques typify rhetorical and musical practices of the late sixteenth century, yet Monteverdi's setting of this opening period goes beyond the typical, for in measures 9–14 he cleverly alerts the listener to the parallelism of the text's metrical structure through a transposed repetition of the first five measures of the piece. But this time he has modified the material somewhat and presents it in the lowest four voices.

In the final line of the period, Monteverdi emphasizes the passionate language of the text (the pain of death) in a particularly affective way. He slows the rhythm to draw attention to the words and applies the musical-rhetorical figure *hypotyposis* to enhance the persuasiveness of the text. The application of *hypotyposis* helped composers elevate musical language from the commonplace, and in measures 14–20 Monteverdi took advantage of two features of the modal system to set the text eloquently. He treats B and E as notes of permutation so that these pitches could oscillate between their natural and flat forms (permutation means that a note could be sung as either *fa* or *mi*). This oscillation produces nonharmonic relations between B*mi*, B*fa*, E*mi*, and E*fa*, and his subsemitonal approach to the structural foundation of the mode, G, causes further dissonance between that F*mi* and F*fa*/C*fa*. These dissonant tensions permeate the section and portray the pain of death vividly. But beyond *hypotyposis*, the introduction of the rhetorical figure *epizeuxis* at the end of the line amplifies the torment kisses bring this ravished soul (the repetition of "e pur si more"). Monteverdi, it would seem, manages to do more than merely convey a sense of syntactic completion in this verse, for he appears to have designed his setting to project the ruling passion of the text musically. The period closes with a cadence on one of the structural foundations of the mode, D (m. 26), and because this *clausula* falls on the *repercussio* (the reciting note of the mode), listeners realize that although the text of the period has come to a full and perfect close the story is not yet finished.

Monteverdi's treatment of the middle period also makes Guarini's syntax plainly evident. But, as mentioned above, Tomlinson believes that Monteverdi split this period down the middle with a full cadence at the end of line 8 and an overly long exclamation at the beginning of line 9, thus reducing the already difficult syntax to nonsense. In this problematic interpretation, Tomlinson tries to connect the first and last lines syntactically ("Quant'ha di dolce amore . . . in voi tutto ripose"/"All that is sweet in love . . .

resides in you"), and this leads him to translate the period in a way that turns Guarini's rather straightforward syntax into something that certainly could be considered difficult and contorted:

Guarini:	*Tomlinson's translation*:
Quant'ha di dolce amore,	All that is sweet in love,
perche sempr'io vi baci:	whenever I kiss you,
o dolcissime rose	oh sweetest roses,
in voi tutto ripose.	resides in you.

A more literal translation of these verses might very well capture the actual disposition of the period. Guarini seems to have composed a bipartite structure in which the sense of the second half of the sentence extends and completes the thought of the first half:

> How much sweetness has love,
> because I always kiss you:
> oh sweetest roses
> in you everything rests.

I doubt that Monteverdi viewed the sense of the text in Tomlinson's way, for he unquestionably divides the sentence in half with an avoided, imperfect cadence on G (m. 32), a cadence that, to use Zarlino's words, marks a middle distinction of the argument. One might even be tempted to interpret this *clausula* as the musical equivalent of the colon implied in the text, for although Monteverdi constructed this cadence on the final of the mode, he weakened its strength, like that of most *clausulae* at middle distinctions, through the avoidance of the cadence note in one of the two controlling voices.

The second half of the period begins with the exclamatory interjection "O" set homophonically to a semibreve (whole note; m. 33), and the abrupt oscillation to a vertical sonority built on F, which accompanies this emotional outburst, provides a striking nonharmonic contrast to the strong subsemitonal pull (F♯) that led to the preceding cadence on G, the structural foundation of the mode. Composers often set interjections, such as "O," "deh," and "ahi," to longer note values so that performers could demonstrate the sudden and great moving of the vital and lively powers these interjections represent (Hart 1551: 160). Speakers normally deliver exclamations with a louder voice (Hart 1551: 160; Butler 1633: 61), and when the similarities between spoken and sung exclamations are revealed, Monteverdi's musical setting of the interjection "O" does not seem unusual, especially if we view late sixteenth-century musical notation as a schematic representation of sound reducing expression to a set of symbols that at best merely approximate the unwritten nuances that constitute a performing style (whether heard in a composer's head or realized from the score in actual performance). From this point of view, singers can make performing practices implicit in Monteverdi's notational symbols manifest only when they apply customs in vogue during the latter part of the sixteenth century to the notation.

Indeed, two of these customs, Caccini's *esclamazione* and the *crescere e scemare della voce* (see the discussion of these aspects of delivery in the previous section) may help explain why Monteverdi chose to set the interjection "O" to a semibreve (whole note). Caccini, who had been composing pieces that employed these two manners of delivery since the early or mid-1580s, maintains that longer notes, particularly minims (half notes) and dotted crotchets (quarter notes), may benefit from an *esclamazione* and that semibreves will move the affections more if singers deliver them with a crescendo and decrescendo. When composers set these interjections to longer notes, singers have the opportunity to utter exclamatory outbursts persuasively; that is, they have ample time to perform either an *esclamazione* or a crescendo and decrescendo. Moreover, Caccini's manner of delivering interjections, such as "deh" (ah) and "ahi" (alas), gives a sense of forward motion to long notes and aligns singing with speaking. Orators commonly uttered exclamations by beginning the passage sharply, raising the loudness of the particle of exclamation, and ending it in a lower volume (Hart 1551: 160; Butler 1633: 61). In coupling the interjection "O" to a semibreve at the beginning of a musical phrase, Monteverdi simply follows normal compositional practice, and his approach in this passage hardly may be construed as a sign of inexperience. In fact, his setting signals performers to deliver the passage in a way similar to speakers—raise the loudness of the particle of exclamation through either an *esclamazione* or a crescendo and decrescendo and moderate the dynamics toward the end (the Consort of Musicke, 1996, take this approach in their recording of the madrigal, where the singers deliver the interjection by crescendoing through the semibreve).

Singers may enhance the persuasive effect of this amorous exclamation further if they apply another aspect of late sixteenth-century performing practice to "Baci soavi e cari." Nicola Vicentino (1555: IV, 42, fols. 94r–v) suggested that since composers wrote musical works on various subjects and fantasias, singers should use diverse ways of singing to imitate the composition. As mentioned earlier (Part 3, "Figures and Passionate Ornaments Made Manifest"), in the Vicentinian world of performance, performers would sing *piano e forte* and *presto e tardo* to conform to the ideas of the composer and to impress upon listeners the passions of the words and harmony. I have already discussed principles of dynamics in relation to the middle period of "Baci soavi e cari," but the role of tempo modification in lines 7–10 is best viewed from the context of the madrigal as a whole.

Throughout "Baci soavi e cari," Monteverdi set the lines either homophonically in a canzonetta-like style or contrapuntally, and the various fantasias he crafted to convey the passions of the text would have alerted singers of his day to the diverse tempos needed to project the affections eloquently. The passion embodied in each fantasia of this madrigal prevails until another musical stimulus, usually introduced after a distinction of the argument (a resting point), arouses a different affection, and singers skilled in discovering these passions and demonstrating them musically probably would have recognized the opportunities Monteverdi's impassioned setting afforded them. Vicentino (1555: IV, 42, fol. 94v) contends that singers should alter the tempo, as well as the dynamics, frequently in accordance with the passions of the words and harmony, and although we cannot determine the precise way sixteenth-century singers would have put Vicentino's principles into practice, I apply his general directives to "Baci soavi e cari" in order to show how knowledge of sixteenth-century tempo flexibility enriches our contextual understanding of compositional structure.

Singers might deliver the opening line of the poem ("Baci soavi e cari"/"Kisses suave and dear") slowly so that listeners have the opportunity to reflect on the *propositio* and its first descriptor. The second and third lines ("cibi della mia vita, ch'or m'involate or mi rendete il core"/"food of my life, which now steal away, now give back my heart"), which further qualify the "baci," could be delivered more quickly, whereas the fourth and fifth lines ("per voi, convien ch'impari come un'alma rapita"/"through you, I must learn how a ravished soul") might return to the opening slower tempo to underscore the parallel nature of the musical structure. The final line of the first period ("non senta il duol di mort'e pur si more"/"feels not the pain of death and yet it dies") could retain this tempo, because the slower rhythm Monteverdi employs in this contrapuntal section would allow singers to exhibit the nonharmonic tensions of the passage prominently. The performers probably should deliver the return to homophonic writing at the beginning of the second period ("Quant'ha di dolce amore"/"How much sweetness has love"), along with the contrapuntal texture of the next line ("perche sempr'io vi baci"/"because I always kiss you"), somewhat more quickly than the previous lines, and they could sing the exclamatory outburst that follows ("o dolcissime rose"/"oh sweetest roses") with the sort of emphatic declamation it seems to require. They might retain this slower tempo through the last line of the period ("in voi tutto riposе"/"in you everything rests"), and the initial line of the final period ("Et s'io potessi à i vostri dolci baci"/"And if I could with your sweet kisses") could receive a brighter tempo, before the singers display the sentiments of the next line ("la mia vita finire"/"end my life") with a slower tempo. They could maintain this slower pace for the exclamation in the following line ("o che dolce morire"/"oh what sweet dying"), and a further slowing of the tempo would draw attention to the repetition of the exclamation. At this point,

Monteverdi repeats the entire final period, and because he musically elides the first three of its lines, the quicker tempo that might be applied to the initial line of the repetition seems appropriate for all three. But a slower pace for the *epizeuxis* that closes the madrigal would emphasize the conclusion to the poem.

Undoubtedly, when singers place lines 7–10, especially the exclamatory outburst, "O dolcissime rose"/"Oh sweetest roses," within an overall plan for tempo modification, the problems Tomlinson identifies in the period disappear completely. No longer can a modern commentator accuse Monteverdi of foolishly splitting the period down the middle with an overly long exclamation, for the compositional structure the composer chose encourages performers to use, in Vicentino's words (1555: IV, 42, fol. 94r), diverse ways of singing to demonstrate the passions of the words and harmony powerfully. Similarly, Tomlinson's criticism of the "clumsy" dissonance Monteverdi introduced in the middle of the next period may be countered if we place the offending interval in a different context.

Simultaneous diminished fourths/augmented fifths of the type Monteverdi employs (in the *concentus*, D–F♯–B♭; m. 44) had always been a normal by-product of the linear thinking that governed sixteenth-century polyphony. Each voice part in a composition of this era follows its own inner logic, and because the voices proceed somewhat independently of one another, they generate the types of nonharmonic relations that Renaissance musicians expected to hear (for a broad discussion of this issue, see Toft 1992). As noted in the Appendix ("The Addition of Sharps and Flats"), Juan Bermudo, writing in 1555 (V, 32, fol. 139r), explains how these dissonances occur: "because singers have accustomed the ear to hearing it [the diminished fourth] in one voice [that is, linearly in a single voice part], they use it [the vertical diminished fourth, C♯–F, between voice parts] in composition, if it is prepared first"/"y como los cantores tengan hecho el oydo, oyendo lo en una boz: lo usan en composicion, si primero se prepara"] (Example 4.14; Toft 1992: 28–29, 79 discusses this practice).[4] Bermudo prepares the dissonance by embedding it in one of those *re-ut-re* (D–C–D) melodic progressions that singers commonly render with a half step, and a sixteenth-century performer, following the inner logic of the progression, would sing D C D as D C♯ D whether or not the composer or copyist notated the semitone and whether or not dissonance would be incurred. The diminished fourth occurs, then, as a by-product of singers being trained to hear what suits their own voice parts. Analogously, Monteverdi notates the *re-ut-re* (G–F–G) progression in "Baci soavi e cari" with a half step (G F♯ G; m. 44), thus creating a vertical diminished fourth with B♭, and he maintains the F♯ in the sonority until the end of the line, where the text comes to rest, in the lowest sounding voice, on the *repercussio* D (m. 45). In the late sixteenth century, musicians frequently raised the third above these structurally important notes (as noted in the Appendix, "The

Addition of Sharps and Flats"), and Monteverdi follows custom. Moreover, his setting of the words "la mia vita finire"/"end my life," far from being bland, provides a poignant transition to the exclamatory outburst, "O che dolce morire"/"Oh what sweet dying." The nonharmonic relation between the *altus* and *cantus*, created by the leap up to F*fa* (F♮) in the *cantus* (m. 45), heightens the effect of the interjection, and the melodic lines Monteverdi fashioned for the first statement of the outburst (high pitch lowered at the cadence; mm. 45–49) mirror the spoken delivery of exclamations—begin sharply and end in a lower volume.

EXAMPLE 4.14 *Diminished fourth; Bermudo 1555: V, 32, fol. 139r*

Monteverdi's skillful manipulation of both musical and rhetorical devices augments the persuasiveness of Guarini's poem, and my explanation of how Monteverdi created a vehicle through which singers could move listeners powerfully draws on a range of concepts from modal theory, rhetoric, and traditions of performance that thickens the contextual discussion of "Baci soavi e cari." Obviously, this approach points not to the limitations of Monteverdi's abilities as a young composer but to the limitations of meaning that any given context imposes on our understanding of what a musical poet had in mind.

***

Passionate ayres and part songs represent some of the loftiest and most affective musical orations from the sixteenth century. These works contain the sorts of auricular and sententious devices that give music efficacy or the power to move listeners. With figures, singers persuade both copiously and vehemently, sung discourse achieving its greatest persuasiveness and hence its highest style when adorned with figures that at once both delight the ear and stir the mind. Audiences from the time, similarly disciplined in the art of rhetoric, would have appreciated these matters and taken pleasure from a presentation that, through the combination of intellectual prowess and vehement delivery, moved the affections "wonderfully" (Peacham the Elder 1577: fol. P3v). Moreover, the skillful handling of the techniques of *elocutio* by Dowland, Caccini, and Monteverdi to effect an imitation of human actions and passions demonstrates their mastery of affective persuasion. Today, a knowledge of the rhetorical basis of passionate ayres and part songs enables modern performers to re-create the late Renaissance style of eloquent delivery from within known tenets of the time. By recovering the principles with which singers from the era probably were thoroughly familiar, we can bridge the gap that exists between historical documents, the artifacts of their culture, and actual modern performance. We now can begin to develop an intuitive understanding of their music and of approaches to performing it with passionate voices.

NOTES

2. Caccini specifically mentions the songs "Dovrò dunque morire," "Perfidissimo volto," and "Vedrò'l mio sol," published in *Le nuove musiche*, as dating from that time (1602: "A i lettori"). For further information, see Hitchcock (2009): 4, n. 14.

3. Caccini's text at this point reads "quali er rai." I have altered it to "quali ai rai" to bring the phrase into line with the version of the poem in Chiabrera (1615).

4. The diminished fourth/augmented fifth often occurs at *clausulae* (see Toft 1992: 65), and the dissonance B♭–F♯ is found in the intabulations of two of Josquin Desprez's motets, "Pater noster" (*prima pars*: mm. 29, 77, 91, 98, and 119, Francesco da Milano; and *secunda pars*: mm. 4, 10, 19, Francesco da Milano) and "Praeter rerum seriem" (*prima pars*: m. 43, Albert de Rippe; and *secunda pars*: m. 51, Albert de Rippe). For transcriptions of these intabulations, see Toft (1983): ii, 145–205.

Appendix

UNDERSTANDING LEARNED COMPOSITIONS

Sixteenth-century musicians thought about the structure of music differently than we do today, for they based their discussions of intervals, scales, and musical syntax on hexachords, modes, and rhetoric (particularly grammatical considerations), and in order for us to perform their music more from within sixteenth-century culture, we might wish to follow Gioseffo Zarlino's advice mentioned in the Introduction and strive to acquire "a complete knowledge of all manner of things concerning music"/"cognitione perfetta delle cose della Musica" (1558: 345–46). In other words, if we try to understand compositional procedures from a sixteenth-century perspective and become aware of what the musical poet, that is, the composer, had in mind (Vicentino 1555: IV, 42, fol. 94v), we will be less likely to impose a modern (tonal) view of musical organization, and the performing conventions associated with that view, on modal works. As part of our preparation for performance, then, we probably should familiarize ourselves with the terms and concepts that shaped the musical sensibilities of Renaissance singers.

Gamut

Theorists called the ordinary range of notes available to musicians the *gamut*. This musical space extended from G at the bottom of the modern bass clef to e'' at the top of the treble clef (Example A.1). The word *gamut* came from a combination of the letter name for the lowest-sounding note of the system, *gamma*, and the solmization syllable attached to it, *ut*.[1]

EXAMPLE A.1 *The* gamut

Pitch	Letter name	Solmization syllables/Hexachords						
e″	ee							la
d″	dd						la	sol
c″	cc						sol	fa
b♮′	♮♮							mi
b♭′	♭♭						fa	
a′	aa					la	mi	re
g′	g					sol	re	ut
f′	f					fa	ut	
e′	e				la	mi		
d′	d			la	sol	re		
c′	c			sol	fa	ut		
b♮	♮				mi			
b♭	♭			fa				
a	a		la	mi	re			
g	G		sol	re	ut			
f	F		fa	ut				
e	E	la	mi					
d	D	sol	re					
c	C	fa	ut					
B	B	mi						
A	A	re						
G	Γ	ut						

As the chart shows, the note B could be sung either as a B♮, that is, *b durum* or *b quadrado* (the hard or square "b"), or as B♭, that is, *b mollis* or *b rotondo* (the soft or round "b"). Musicians identified the octave placement of pitches in the *gamut* by the syllables associated with them; for instance, *c* carried the designation C*faut* (reading horizontally across the chart in Example A.1), whereas *c′* was labeled C*solfaut* and *c″*, C*solfa*.

Hexachords

Singers found their way around melodies based in the *gamut* through a series of three interlocked hexachords, each hexachord comprising six notes carrying the solmization syllables *ut re mi fa sol la*. These syllables had been derived from the words that began successive lines of the hymn *Ut queant laxis,* and the initial notes of the melodic phrases accompanying these lines rose by step from C to A:

Pitch	Hymn Text	
C	Ut	queant laxis
D	Re-	sonare fibris
E	Mi-	ra gestorum
F	Fa-	muli tuorum
G	Sol-	ve pollute
A	La-	bii reatum, Sancte Johannes

[That thy servants may freely sing forth the wonders of thy deeds, remove all stain of guilt from their unclean lips, Saint John.]

These notes, when collected together, produced the interval relationship tone-tone-semitone-tone-tone, and in the sixteenth century, this fixed pattern could begin on either *c, f,* or *g.* Theorists called the *f* hexachord soft, because it employed *b mollis* to create the required interval structure, but when the pattern began on *g,* a hard hexachord resulted from the inclusion of *b durum.* Since the *c* hexachord did not contain either form of *b,* theorists labeled it natural (Example A.2).[2] Within every hexachord, then, singers solmized (sang) the central half step as *mi-fa,* and when performers had to sight-sing a melody that extended beyond six notes, they simply mutated (their term) from one hexachord to another. In order to move between hexachords, they began singing any of the notes available for mutation (pitches carrying two or three solmization syllables) with one syllable but left that note thinking of it as a syllable in another hexachord (Example A.3).

EXAMPLE A.2 *Hexachords*

EXAMPLE A.3 *Mutation from one hexachord to another; Verdelot, "Madonna il tuo bel viso,"* mm. *16–19*

Modes

Theorists further organized the musical space available to composers through a series of scales called tones or modes. Although the precise origins of the modes remain somewhat obscure, the modal system known to sixteenth-century musicians had been well documented by contemporary theorists. Most writers discussed a scheme comprising eight scales, numbered 1 to 8,[3] and classified these scales not only by the pitch on which they centered (the *finalis*) but also as to whether the range or *ambitus* of the scales occurred entirely above the *finalis* (the authentic form of the mode) or surrounded it from the fourth below to the fifth above (the plagal form):

General Classification	Central Pitch (*finalis*)	Names of the Eight Modes: Authentic Form	Plagal Form
Protus	*d*	1. Dorian, *d-d*	2. Hypodorian, *a-a*
Deuterus	*e*	3. Phrygian, *e-e*	4. Hypophrygian, *b-b*
Tritus	*f*	5. Lydian, *f-f*	6. Hypolydian, *c-c*
Tetrardus	*g*	7. Mixolydian, *g-g*	8. Hypomixolydian, *d-d*

Several factors determined the hierarchical importance of the pitches within each mode. Example A.4 summarizes a number of sixteenth-century conventions. Theorists divided the modal octave into two segments that helped define the mode's character, one segment outlining the interval of a fifth and the other a fourth, and they further classified these two intervals according to their internal structure, calling each pattern of tones and semitone a species. They recognized four species of fifth,

1. Tone, semitone, tone, tone (*re mi fa sol la*)
2. Semitone, tone, tone, tone (*mi fa sol re mi*)
3. Tone, tone, tone, semitone (*fa sol re mi fa*)
4. Tone, tone, semitone, tone (*ut re mi fa sol*)

and three species of fourth,

1. Tone, semitone, tone (*re mi fa sol*)
2. Semitone, tone, tone (*mi fa sol la*)
3. Tone, tone, semitone (*ut re mi fa*)

The notes bounding the species of fifth and fourth, together with the *repercussio*, the pitch on which singers traditionally recited psalm text, were regarded as the structural foundations of the modes. Example A.4 shows the species that characterize each modal scale, the repercussion note (the upper pitch of the repercussion interval), and the principal and secondary cadence notes. Knowledge of these elements of modal scales allows us to understand some of the basic features of compositional structure so that we can begin to discover appropriate ways of organizing the music into easily discernible units for listeners. By understanding which modes a composer chose to use in a piece, singers can easily determine the cadential points and the hierarchy of pauses they imply.

EXAMPLE A.4 *The modal system*

PROTUS

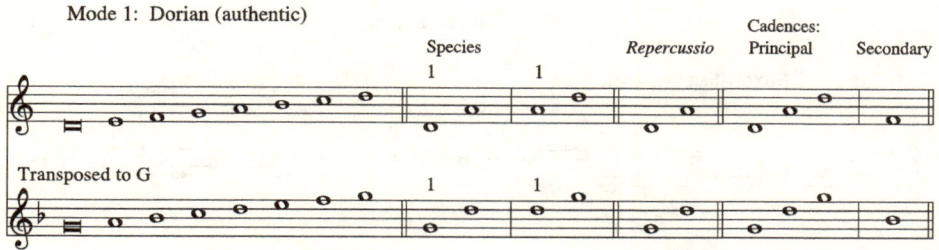

DEUTERUS

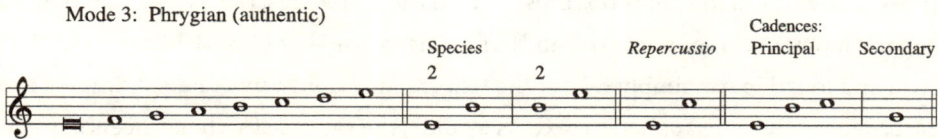

(Continued)

EXAMPLE A.4 (*Continued*)

TRITUS

Mode 5: Lydian (authentic)

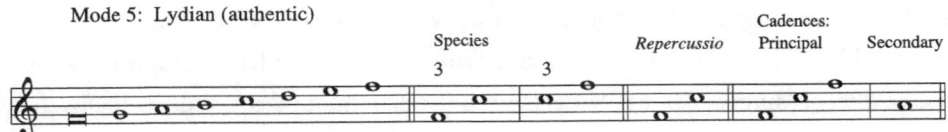

Mode 6: Hypolydian (plagal)

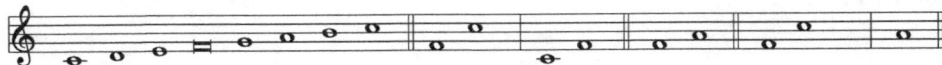

TETRARDUS

Mode 7: Mixolydian (authentic)

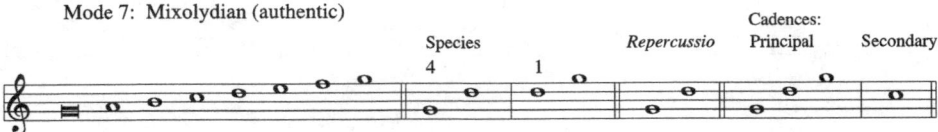

Mode 8: Hypomixolydian (plagal)

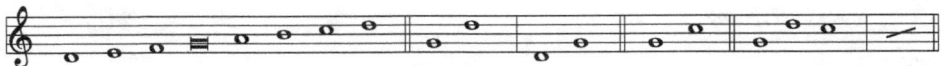

Cadences

Theorists defined a cadence (*cadenza* in Italian; *cadentia* or *clausula* in Latin) as a resting point in which two voices, one descending by step and the other rising by step, proceed to an octave or unison. Example A.5 shows the basic formulation of *clausulae* in two-, three-, and four-part textures. Within these voicings, the two parts moving by step to a moment of repose control and define the cadential motion, while the additional third and fourth parts simply fill out the texture in various ways. Indeed, when we use the cadence structure applied to texts as a guide, the syntax of sixteenth-century vocal music becomes readily apparent, for during the period composers routinely aligned musical cadences with resting points in poetry.

EXAMPLE A.5 *Cadences*

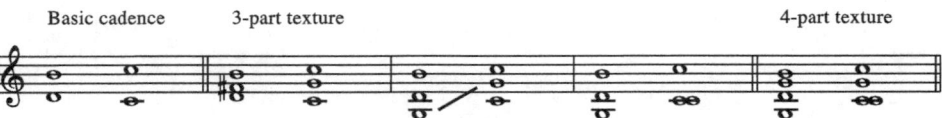

In 1517, Andreas Ornithoparchus (100, 204), citing Johannes Tinctoris as his authority, defined a *clausula* in two ways: as a musical phrase that ends in either rest or perfection, or as the conjunction of the various voices in perfect intervals. This basic definition was known throughout the century, and by the mid-1500s, certain theorists, such as Stefano Vanneo (1533: fol. 93v), Giovanni del Lago (1540: 39–43), and particularly Gioseffo Zarlino (1558: 221–26), provided more elaborate discussions of the term (pertinent excerpts from these and other authors appear in Harrán 1986: 388–97). These theorists equated cadences to the punctuation used in writing and oratory. Zarlino, for example, followed well-established tradition and drew upon his knowledge of grammatical punctuation to formulate a theory of musical *cadenze*.[4] He defined the cadence as an action the voices perform together that denotes either a general repose of the harmony or the perfection of the sense of the words on which the piece is composed. He expanded this definition by describing cadences as equivalent to the *punto* (punctuation) of oration, calling them the *punto* of musical composition. Zarlino went on to equate these resting points to the pauses one makes in the argument of an oration, not only at a middle distinction (resting point) but also at a final one, so that listeners may momentarily reflect on what they have just heard. In conclusion, he stated that cadences had been invented for designating the perfection of the parts of a larger composition and for marking the end of perfect sentences in the text. In these latter places, composers should use an absolute or perfect cadence on an octave or unison (Example A.6a), but for middle distinctions of the harmony and text, that is, when sentences have not reached final perfection, one should employ an imperfect or improper cadence on a third, fifth, sixth, or other similar consonance (Example A.6b). Zarlino called this avoiding the cadence. Composers could further lessen the cadential effect of an avoided cadence if one of the two voices proceeding to a perfect cadence turned elsewhere instead (Example A.6c). Along these lines, Loys Bourgeois, writing in 1550 (60–61), described another method of avoiding the cadence. *Clausulae* solmized *la sol la, sol fa sol*, and *re ut re* also could occur in the interrupted form *la sol, sol fa*, and *re ut*, and through this procedure, one of the two voice parts creating the cadence drops out before the listener hears the ultimate sonority (Example A.6d). But in addition to these customs, Juan Bermudo (1555: V, 32, fols. 139r–v) discussed a situation in which the effect of a cadence could be feigned, and he called this type of cadence a *clausula disimulada*. Bermudo considered the cadence shown in Example A.6e to be feigned, because the cadence note C, to which the *altus* normally would have progressed, was provided by the *tenor*, allowing the *altus* to leap to E. In other words, a different voice proceeded to the cadence note instead of the expected one. Moreover, composers could also weaken the effect of a *clausula* by having one or both voices leap to the cadence note, and numerous examples of this approach to a resting point exist (see Example A.6f for one such cadence).[5]

EXAMPLE A.6 *Types of cadences*

Composers further intertwined musical and textual syntax by aligning pauses in the text with the primary, secondary, and transitory resting points of a mode (a convenient summary of the information on primary, secondary, and transitory cadences may be found in *New Grove*, s.v. "Mode"). Theorists defined primary *clausulae* as those in which the cadence notes constitute the main structural foundations of a mode. They derived these resting points from the notes bounding the species of fourths and fifths (which included the *finalis*) and from the repercussion notes (Example A.4). Secondary cadences may be inserted without disturbing the mode but did not form part of the mode's structural foundations (Example A.4). Transitory *clausulae*, however, occur on cadence notes foreign to the mode, and in 1588, Pietro Pontio (fols. 94ff.) identified the following as appropriate locations for transitory moments of repose:

Modes 1, 2:	g, c
Modes 3, 4:	g, b♮
Mode 5:	d, g
Mode 6:	d, g
Mode 7:	c, f, a, e
Mode 8:	f, a

But beyond these compositional considerations, musicians had two basic methods of approaching cadence notes, one producing a stronger effect than the other. Depending on the nature of the part writing and the conclusiveness they wished to convey, performers might proceed to a resting point (1) from the closest imperfect interval, the stronger of the two methods, either subsemitonally (the voice rising by step to the cadence note proceeds by semitone) or suprasemitonally (the voice descending by step to the cadence note approaches by semitone; see the next section "The Addition of Sharps and Flats" for a fuller discussion of these practices); or (2) from an unaltered imperfect interval, that is, subtonally (the voice rising by step to the cadence note proceeds by whole tone), a less conclusive close (Example A.7).

EXAMPLE A.7 *Approaches to cadence notes*

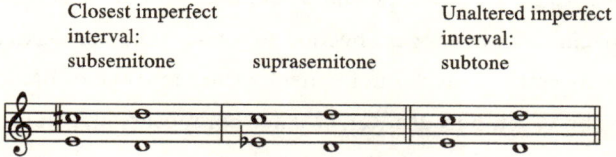

Closest imperfect
interval:
subsemitone   suprasemitone

Unaltered imperfect
interval:
subtone

As this discussion of cadences demonstrates, both composers and performers had various ways of weakening the effects of the *clausulae* available to them, but they also had several means of intensifying cadences. They could add dissonant suspensions, ornamental figuration, or subsemitonal approaches to the cadence note (if they did not occur naturally in the music), or any combination of these, and composers might increase a *clausula's* conclusiveness by having the lowest sounding voice descend a fifth or rise a fourth.

Without a doubt, sixteenth-century musicians considered cadences the punctuation of music. Through *clausulae* they made the sense of the poem obvious and comprehensible. Composers aligned poetic and musical syntax, and their cadential plans reinforced poetic structure, for they punctuated lines with cadences to produce the musical equivalent of the various pauses a speaker would apply in delivering a poem.

Transposition, Scales of *b mollis* and *b durum*, Notes of Permutation

Modal structures could be transposed to different pitch levels, and Example A.8 (*protus* mode) shows one of the common transpositions. Composers regularly placed the interval pattern for Dorian on G, and this necessitated the inclusion of B♭ in the scale. But instead of writing the sign *b mollis* before every B in a piece, musicians placed the flat sign at the beginning of the staff, where it became a signature (see the lower staff of Example A.8). In the sixteenth century, signatures alerted performers to the presence of the underlying scales of either *b mollis* (indicated by the flat on B) or *b durum* (no flat in the signature), scalar systems quite separate from the various patterns of intervals that defined modes.

EXAMPLE A.8 *Transposed Dorian*

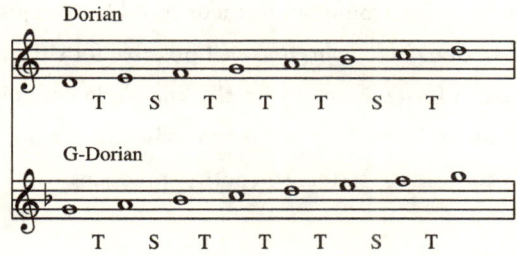

Dorian

T   S   T   T   T   S   T

G-Dorian

T   S   T   T   T   S   T

These two scales had a degree of flexibility built into them. In *b durum*, for example, theorists considered the pitch B to be a note of permutation, for it could be sung as *fa* (B♭), as well as *mi* (B♮), especially when singers needed to avoid linear or vertical tritones with F.[6] Sixteenth-century musicians did not consider the exchange of B*fa* for B*mi* to violate modal integrity, however, because Renaissance composers maintained the identity of a mode by other means, such as, species and cadences. The regular oscillation between B♮ and B♭, then, should be viewed as an important part of modal procedure that helped shape the sense of mode in polyphonic music. Example A.9 shows not only the set of three interlocked hexachords used in the scale of *b durum* but also the two permutations available to composers and singers. Two areas of oscillation are inherent in this hexachord system, one, B/B♭, derived from the B*mi*-B*fa* duality of the note of permutation; and the other, E/E♭, resulting from the application of the *fa supra la* (*fa* above *la*) convention to the soft hexachord (that is, when melodies progressed no farther than one step beyond *la*, performers frequently sang this extension to the hexachord as *fa*, that is, as a semitone above *la*; further discussion of this procedure can be found in the next section "The Addition of Sharps and Flats"). B♭ is thus part of the system, and this presents performers with the possibility of extemporaneously adding a suprasemitonal B♭–A motion at cadences on A.

EXAMPLE A.9 *Notes of permutation in the scale of* b durum

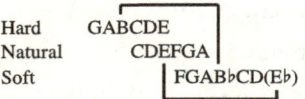

Hard	GABCDE
Natural	CDEFGA
Soft	FGAB♭CD(E♭)

Similarly, the hexachord system inherent in the scale of *b mollis* contains two areas of oscillation, one, E/E♭, derived from the E*mi*-E*fa* duality of the note of permutation and the other, A/A♭, resulting from the application of the *fa supra la* convention to the fictive hexachord on B♭, the fictive hexachord being necessary to create the note of permutation, E♭ (Example A.10). Thus E♭ becomes an implicit part of the *cantus mollis* scale, and A♭ an extension to the outer boundaries of the hexachord order. Within modes built on the *cantus mollis* scale, then, one would expect to encounter E♭s, and the appearance of A♭s, although extending the system to its natural limits, would not be inconceivable. And just like B♭ in the *b durum* scale, the availability of E♭ in *b mollis* makes it possible for singers to approach cadences on D suprasemitonally, E♭–D. Armed with the knowledge of how Renaissance musicians employed oscillation to shape the music listeners heard, performers today can re-create vocal lines so as to conform to sixteenth-century practices.

EXAMPLE A.10 *Notes of permutation in the scale of* b mollis

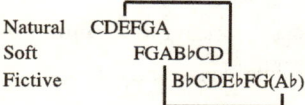

Natural   CDEFGA
Soft   FGAB♭CD
Fictive   B♭CDE♭FG(A♭)

Modal Mixtures

Composers often chose to write a piece in a single mode,[7] but when they wished to combine modes, they had two basic ways of intermingling one mode with another. If they followed a *mixtus* procedure, both the authentic and plagal forms appeared in the piece, and in four-part polyphony, this could be considered the norm, for composers regularly set the *superius* and *tenor* voices in the authentic form of a mode and the *altus* and *bassus* voices in the plagal form, simply because the ranges of singers fell quite naturally into either authentic or plagal. For instance, in Dorian mode, treble voices occupied the authentic range (d'–d"), whereas alto voices suited the plagal (a–a'). Similarly, tenor voices fell into the authentic range (d–d'), while basses occupied the plagal (A–a). If, however, composers employed a *conmixtus* approach, they combined two completely different modes in a single piece, and they routinely made the change of mode obvious to the listener not only by dwelling on the species characteristic of the new mode but also by frequenting the resting points associated with that mode.

Mimetic Procedures[8]

Two broad categories of mimetic procedures, *fuga* and *imitatione*, fall under the heading *anaphora*, a figure from rhetoric involving the repetition of the same word or words at the beginning of successive sentences or poetic lines. In the early seventeenth century, Joachim Burmeister (1606: 65) used the word *anaphora* to designate what Johannes Nucius later called *repetitio* (1613: fol. G2v) and what modern writers usually label as a "point of imitation." Charles Butler (1636: 71) defined a point as "a certain number and order of observable Notes in any one Parte, iterated in the same or in divers Partes."

Composers constructed an *anaphora*, or what might also be called a mimetic point, as either a *fuga* or an *imitatione*, Gioseffo Zarlino discussing both of these techniques at length in *Le istitutioni harmoniche* (1558: 212–20). Zarlino described *fuga* as the literal repetition of the solmization syllables of the *guida* (guide or leading voice) by the other voices and *imitatione* as a structure in which this repetition was not exact (Example A.11). According to Zarlino, these mimetic procedures could be either *legato* or *sciolta*, that is, either strict or free. In strict writing, the composer duplicated an entire melody in another voice, but in free writing the following voice proceeded independently after a while. Depending on the context, singers had the option, then, of completing the creative process the composer had begun by realizing a mimetic passage either as an *imitatione* or as a *fuga*; that is, performers could repeat the solmization syllables exactly in each part (*fuga*) or they could modify them when the *thema* is restated in the other voices (*imitatione*), in which case a major 3rd (*ut-mi*) might become a minor 3rd (*re-fa*).

EXAMPLE A.11 Mimesis

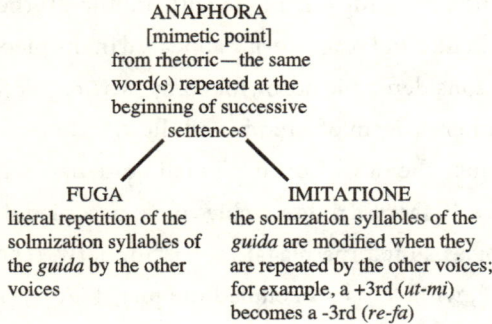

ANAPHORA
[mimetic point]
from rhetoric—the same
word(s) repeated at the
beginning of successive
sentences

FUGA
literal repetition of the solmization syllables of the *guida* by the other voices

IMITATIONE
the solmzation syllables of the *guida* are modified when they are repeated by the other voices; for example, a +3rd (*ut-mi*) becomes a -3rd (*re-fa*)

Supplementum

Composers in the sixteenth century frequently brought pieces to a close through a section called a *supplementum* or *cauda* (Burmeister 1606: 53; Nucius 1613: fol. G3v; see also Bartel 1997: 344–46). In these closing passages, one or two voices hold fast while the others continue polyphonically to bring the music gradually to its final resting point. This procedure abounds in the period, and the passage shown in Example A.12 typifies the practice.

EXAMPLE A.12 Supplementum; *Arcadelt, "Madonna s'io v'offendo," mm. 34–39*

Fantasia, Improvisation, Musical Memory, and the Characteristics of Intervals

During the sixteenth century, the term *fantasia* referred to more than the musical genre that bears the same name, for it also denoted a short thematic cell on which compositions or sections of compositions were based (Example A.13).[9] Composers could join any number of these fantasias together to form a larger work, or they could base an entire piece on an elaboration or expansion of a single *thema* (theme; see, for example, the "Fantasies de Joskin" and Claudin de Sermisy's "Missa ad placitum" discussed in Butler 1974: 602–5). When they created pieces from various musical subjects (each subject being a different fantasia), composers embedded a series of distinct affections in their music, every section requiring individual treatment by performers. Sir Thomas More reminds us that "the fassion of the melodye dothe so represente the meaning of the thing, that it doth wonderfullye move, stirre, pearce, and enflame the hearers myndes"/"ita rei sensum quendam melodiae forma repraesentat, ut animos auditorum mirum in modum afficiat, penetret, incendat" (1516: 420; trans. 1559: 182–83), and Nicola Vicentino (1555: IV, 42, fol. 94r) further suggests that because singers needed to be aware of what the musical poet (composer) had in mind, they had to use diverse ways of delivering these fantasia-based passages so that their style of performance would match each new passion as it arose. Richard Hooker (1597: 75) describes just how quickly affections could change in a piece of music:

> Musicall harmonie whether by instrument or by voyce [is] . . . a thing which delighteth all ages and beseemeth all states; a thing as seasonable in griefe as in joy; as decent being added unto actions of greatest waight and solemnitie, as being used when men most sequester themselves from action. The reason hereof is an admirable facilitie which musique hath to expresse and represent to the minde more inwardly then any other sensible meane the very standing rising and falling, the very steps and inflections everyway, the turnes and varieties of all passions whereunto the minde is subject: yea so to imitate them, that whether it resemble unto us the same state wherein our mindes alreadie are, or a cleane contrarie, we are not more contentedly by the one confirmed, then changed and led away by the other.

The key to understanding the intention of the composer, then, lay in determining the precise nature of each fantasia so that the affection embodied in it could be presented to listeners persuasively.

EXAMPLE A.13 *Francesco Canova da Milano, Fantasia 30, mm. 1–4 (taken from Ness 1970)*

The great *improvisatori* of the sixteenth century no doubt stored large numbers of these thematic cells in their memory as reservoirs of material for improvisatory purposes, and some of the mystery surrounding the genius of spontaneous creativity disappears when we realize how the art of memory functioned in the musical sense (Yates 1966 discusses the rhetorical memory process, and Butler 1974 demonstrates how musicians applied this process to the fantasia). Claudius Sebastiani (1563) recommended that students commit to memory as much material as possible, "at least the *loci* [places where improvisatory formulae are stored in the memory], whether fugae [mimetic points] or the more suitable fantasias [short thematic fragments]"/"ad minus locos sive Fugas aut Fantasias magis idoneas" (quoted in Butler 1974: 609). Sebastiani's comment parallels one of the main goals of the orator: "indeed, the first concern ought to be that we prepare for ourselves a most copious stock of good words and figures"/"prima enim cura esse debet, ut quam copiosissimam suppellectilem bonorum verborum ac figurarum nobis paremus" (Melanthonis 1850: 722). Once memorized, performers could recall and elaborate these fantasias at will to create music extemporaneously. In fact, Pontus de Tyard (1555: 192) linked the rhetorical memory process to the way in which the lutenist Francesco Canova da Milano began one of his impromptu performances: "the tables being cleared [after a banquet], he took one, and as if tuning his strings, sat near the end of the table to seek out a fantasia"/"les tables levées il en prent un, et comme pour tater les accors, se met pres d'un bout de la table à rechercher une fantasie." In other words, while Francesco acted as if he were readying his instrument for performance, he quickly surveyed the various fantasias stored in his memory and selected one for delivery; or as Tyard described the method, Francesco sought out a fantasia.

Modern performers probably should be aware of the basic concepts associated with the term *fantasia* and take care to discover what passion each *thema* in a composition represented. Nicola Vicentino suggested one way of achieving this end, and in his treatise he described the affective characteristics of various intervals (Kaufmann 1966: 148–50 summarizes the information in chart form). His most revealing comment in this regard concerned the minor third, a very weak and sad interval that, if it ascends slowly, has the nature of a man when he is tired ("di sua natura, laquale è molto debole, et ha del mesto . . . quando ascenderà con il moto tardo; havrà della natura d'un huomo quando è stracco;" 1555: II, 14, fol. 33v). Hence, in performing a fantasia beginning with this motion, modern performers might wish to reflect the tired nature of slowly rising minor thirds in the tempo they adopt (as seen in Example A.13). The passion embodied in the *thema* would prevail until some new stimulus, such as a different fantasia, required them to adapt their manner of performance to it. The introduction of a new *thema*, however, did not always imply a change of character, for composers often chose to maintain the previous affect, especially when the end of one section overlapped with the beginning of the next, a procedure that would probably prevent performers from altering the tempo on the first statement of a new subject.

THE ADDITION OF SHARPS AND FLATS

One of the major problems confronting performers of sixteenth-century vocal music concerns the ambiguity of pitch notation in the sources that come down to us. For the most part, printers and copyists did not notate the signs *b durum* (sharp) and *b mollis* (flat) on the pages they produced, and consequently, certain important details never got written down. Composers, printers, and copyists expected singers to be familiar with the principles governing the application of these signs and to make the appropriate alterations at the time of performance. Thus, the final shaping of the music in both harmonic and melodic content fell to performers, and in order for us to complete the composer's creative process, we must recover the aural traditions sixteenth-century vocal notation only partly records by reconstructing the practices governing the addition of sharps and flats from the documents that survive, particularly theoretical treatises and intabulations of part songs for lute, vihuela, guitar, and keyboard. Treatises establish the theoretical framework within which singers operated, and tablatures, because they specify all pitches precisely, provide modern performers with an unprecedented view of how some of the greatest musicians of the era added sharps and flats to vocal sources. Tablatures demonstrate that more than one way of solmizing specific passages existed, and intabulations illustrate not only the range of practices known in the sixteenth century but also the flexible way musicians applied theoretical principles, often with little regard for consistency of application. In fact, if we abandon modern notions of consistency and uniformity and embrace sixteenth-century diversity in a real fashion, we might begin to sound less like foreigners in their musical culture(s).

The Flemish singer Ghiselin Danckerts (c. 1510–after 1565), in the well-documented dispute between two singers in the Roman church of S. Lorenzo in Damaso, provided evidence of the divergent approaches Renaissance musicians took to resolving the problems associated with ambiguous pitch notation (Lockwood 1965). Since, as this dispute aptly reveals, even the singers in one chapel could not agree on what course to follow, the contrasting interpretations encountered in intabulations should come as no surprise. The flexibility of the theoretical framework within which sixteenth-century performers operated made this diversity inevitable. But were Renaissance instrumentalists actually aware of the theoretical precepts of their own time, and if they were, did they know how to apply them in the vocal works they intabulated? That many lutenists and keyboard players understood modal theory and the principles of solmization can hardly be doubted, for biographical information on instrumentalists active in Italy, Spain, Germany, and England confirms that a number of players found employment as singers and that some lutenists even taught singing or held the position of maestro di capella (for further discussion of this topic, see Toft 1992: 41–45). For example, the lutenist Jean Matelart was appointed in Rome c. 1565 as maestro di capella at S. Lorenzo in Damaso (*New Grove* 11: 818), and in the 1540s, the vihuelist Luis de Narvaez taught singing to the children in the chapel of Phillip II of Spain (Anglés 1965: 104–5, 109, 113). Moreover, in 1550, one Cantelmo alias Andrejolo Giov. Geronimo di Napoli, *musico*, undertook to teach a young student to play the *viola da mano*, to sing with art, and to read and write (Pope 1961: 375, n. 21), and a number of lutenists at the court of Mantua in the late fifteenth and early sixteenth centuries also functioned as singers (Prizer 1980). The same appears to be true in Germany in the latter half of the sixteenth century, for at least seven lutenists worked as court or cathedral singers.[10] And in England, several town waytes in Norwich sang at the cathedral, the actor William Kempe (1600: 17) characterizing their abilities as among the best in the land: "theyr voices be admirable, everie one of them able to serve in any Cathedrall Church in Christendoome for Quiristers."[11]

In addition, numerous sixteenth-century instruction books for student instrumentalists teach and stress the importance of acquiring a knowledge of modal theory, solmization, and mensural notation, particularly those by Hans Gerle (1532), Juan Bermudo (1555), Thomas de Sancta Maria (1565), and Vincenzo Galilei (1568). But perhaps most importantly, instrumentalists strove to produce an accurate transcription and adopted the singer's linear approach when intabulating vocal music. The standard practice, as described by Adrian Le Roy in his *A briefe and plaine Instruction* (1574), called for lutenists to cipher one part at a time, adding whatever sharps and flats they deemed necessary. As lutenists intabulated the other voices, they adjusted the sharps and flats of the previously ciphered parts to accommodate the new voice. In the *superius* of Example A.14, for instance, Le Roy applied the *fa supra la* convention (see below for discussion), avoiding the melodic tritone between F and B, but on intabulating the *tenor* part he decided that this voice needed a B*mi* and changed the *superius* from B♭ to B♮. For Le Roy, the requirements of the *tenor* obviously took precedence over the desire to avoid the tritone in the *superius*. Singers of the period could have experienced the same problem when sight reading the chanson, as the performer of the *superius* part may well have felt the need to introduce B♭, while the *tenor* was compelled to sing B♮. If the dissonant octave that resulted proved distasteful, they would have to find a resolution to the conflict, and fortunately for us today, Le Roy acted as the maître de chapelle and produced a workable solution to the passage.

EXAMPLE A.14 *Linear approach to intabulating vocal parts; Le Roy 1574, "Si le bien," mm. 65–67*

We can probably safely assume, then, that many instrumentalists understood solmization and other aspects of contemporary theoretical teaching. The theorist Pietro Aaron even consulted the Italian lutenist Marco Dall'Aquila (c. 1480–after 1538) on a question of music theory (*New Grove* 5: 162), and another writer, Giovanni Spataro, commented on the skill with which some instrumentalists incorporated sharps and flats:

I say, therefore, that good players of instruments do play songs artfully through a certain practice, not as they are simply composed and written by the unlearned composers, but play them as they should be signed: and similarly do experienced singers: many times they sing the harmony [that is, the music] better than it had been composed and signed by the composers. [Florio 1611 translates "concento" as concordance, harmony, or tunable accord.]

Dico adonca che li boni pulsatori de li instrumenti facti per arte per certa sua practica sonano li canti non come simplicemente sono composti et scripti da li indocti compositori ma li sonano come debeno esser signati: et similemente fano li periti cantori: molte volte cantano li concenti meglio che non sono stati compositi: et signati da li compositori. (MS. Vatican Lat 5318, fol. 144v; cited in Berger 1987: 164)

Instrumentalists certainly seem to have worked within the same theoretical framework as singers, and since many of the sharps and flats encountered in intabulations have a direct bearing on vocal practices, or at least so Spataro implies in the passage just cited, I place the discussion of extempore pitch alteration in a broad documentary context rooted in customs that existed at a time when the music was part of a living tradition. By combining information derived from theoretical treatises with principles extracted from intabulations, we can base our own performances on the work of musicians more familiar with the customs of their own geographical area than any of us today ever could hope to be. Many daring practices, particularly with regard to dissonance treatment, had become the norm in the sixteenth century, and if we place these practices on a continuum extending from the conservative to the liberal, we can establish the boundaries of the style, as well as the range of options available within those boundaries.

The information that follows summarizes the sixteenth-century customs associated with the addition of sharps and flats. In my view, we probably should avoid elevating generic theoretical principles to "rules" that must be observed, for the literal application of "rules" distorts the sound of the music to such an extent that *frottole*, madrigals, chansons, and other part songs can lose their distinctive Renaissance flavor. Individual taste played an important role in determining specific procedures, and both theoretical sources and intabulations confirm that sixteenth-century style, particularly with regard to dissonance treatment, was broad. Indeed, if we want our performances to mirror those of the sixteenth century, we might wish to generate our aural image of Renaissance polyphony from those documents that preserve the practices of performing musicians.

General Principles

Cadences

Theorists recommended approaching cadence notes from the closest imperfect interval. Thomas de Sancta Maria (1565: I, 24, fol. 63v) established terminology to describe the two methods of creating this sonority. Cadences could be either *remisso* or *sostenido*, and in the *remisso* or "relaxed" form, one voice employed a subtone and the other a suprasemitone, but in the *sostenido* or "sharped" cadence, singers used a subsemitone and a supratone. As shown in Example A.15, the *remisso* form already approached the cadence note from the closest imperfect interval, but in a *sostenido* close the voice parts frequently lacked the semitonal motion to the cadence note, so performers had to supply it by adding a sharp. But, as Juan Bermudo maintained (1555: IV, 48, fol. 88r), when the addition of a sharp proved impossible (generally because dissonance would result), musicians had the option of lowering the descending note instead (Example A.15).

EXAMPLE A.15 Remisso *and* sostenido *cadences*

However, despite Bermudo's suggestion, a number of musicians chose to incur dissonance at *clausulae*, especially when the strong subsemitonal pull to the cadence note received priority over theoretical precepts that, on the surface, seemed to prohibit vertical and linear tritones (see the discussion of dissonance below). Both *remisso* and *sostenido* cadences occur in Giovanni Maria da Crema's intabulation of Arcadelt's "Lasciar il velo," and in Example A.16, Crema treated the *clausula* on D in measures 12–13 in *remisso* fashion, primarily because he needed to remove the tritone between B♭ and E in the *bassus*. But at a similar cadence in measures 40–41, the part writing allowed him to opt for a *sostenido* approach, even though the introduction of the sharp created dissonance between the *superius* and the *altus/tenor*.

Beyond these two methods of approach, a few authors refer to another practice that appears to have been universal. The theorists Aaron, Bermudo, and Sancta Maria advocate raising the third when it occurs above a cadence note, Aaron maintaining that the custom had become so common by 1529 that experienced singers had no need for a notated sign:

EXAMPLE A.16 *Remisso and sostenido cadences; Arcadelt, "Lasciar il velo," mm. 11–13, 39–41 (in this and the following examples, sharps and flats derived from tabulatures are shown above the staves)*

Crema, *Intabolatura*, 1546

Although this sign [the sharp for raised thirds], then, is less needed by learned and experienced singers, the sign [on the solmization syllable *sol* in Aaron's example] is given because perhaps an inexperienced and unintelligent singer could not give a perfect delivery of this position or syllable [without it].

Ben che tal segno appresso gli dotti & pratichi cantori manco è di bisogno: ma sol si pone perche forse il mal pratico & non intelligente cantore, non darebbe pronuntia perfetta a tal positione overa syllaba. (II, 20, fol. Kv)

Aaron incorporated the raised third because he felt that a minor interval above the bass would sound unpleasant. The addition of the sharp, then, helped to make a sweeter sound, and although intabulators frequently prized this sweetness, they by no means universally adopted the raised third. Nonetheless, Example A.17a shows the typical alteration employed above cadence notes (D in this case), and Example A.17b demonstrates that this sound had indeed become so common that some intabulators also raised thirds in noncadential passages (compare Bianchini's 1546 interpretation of the opening measure in the example with Phalèse's in 1547b).

Noncadential Progressions to an Octave or Unison

Quite apart from cadences, however, singers could approach any two voice parts proceeding to an octave or unison from the closest imperfect interval. Example A.18

EXAMPLE A.17 *Raised thirds: (a) above a cadence note; Arcadelt, "Il ciel che rado," mm. 17–19; (b) in noncadential passages; Sermisy, "Il me souffit," mm. 14–17*

(a)

Bakfark, *Intabulatura*, 1553

(b)

Left   Bianchini, *Intabolatura*, 1546
Right   Phalèse, *Des chansons reduictz*, 1547

illustrates this procedure in a noncadential progression to G between the *altus* and *bassus* in Philippe Verdelot's "Quanto sia liet'il giorno" (1536).

Sol-fa-sol Progressions

Singers also supplied unnotated semitones in noncadential melodic progressions sol-mized *re ut re, sol fa sol,* and *la sol la,* mainly because these progressions looked and

EXAMPLE A.18 *Noncadential subsemitones; Verdelot, "Quanto sia liet'il giorno," mm. 30–31*

Verdelot, *Intavolatura*, 1536

sounded like cadences, even though the text did not come to a resting point (Sancta Maria 1565: I, 25, fol. 74v). Example A.19 shows the *tenor* and *bassus* voices of Verdelot's "Quanto sia liet'il giorno" proceeding to an octave on D in measure 16, and in two of the three intabulations the instrumentalists raised the *tenor*'s C in the *la-sol-la* progression. In addition, the passage further illustrates the strong subsemitonal pull performers felt in noncadential passages when one of the voices proceeded by step to the *finalis* of the mode (G in transposed Dorian; see the *altus*, mm. 16–17).

EXAMPLE A.19 La sol la *rendered semitonally; Verdelot "Quanto sia liet'il giorno," mm. 15–17*

Left   Verdelot, *Intavolatura*, 1536
Center   Crema, *Intabolatura*, 1546
Right   Fuenllana, *Orphenica lyra*, 1554

Vertical Dissonance

MI CONTRA FA   The most common dictum associated with vertical dissonance concerns the prohibition of sounding *mi* against *fa* (*mi contra fa*). Theorists normally stated this precept as a warning to singers who might mistakenly solmize a *mi* in one part and a *fa* in another, thus producing a forbidden interval, particularly the tritone or dissonant octave. For instance, Example A.20 (m. 4) contains *mi contra fa* between the B*mi* sounded by both the *altus* and the *bassus* and the *tenor*'s F*fa*, which the intabulator removed by rendering both B♮s as B*fa*. Numerous theorists, however, after explicitly prohibiting *mi contra fa*, immediately qualify their position by discussing frequent exceptions to the rule. Zarlino's comments typify the situation (1558: 169):

> one must never place the syllable *mi* against *fa* in perfect consonances . . . however, one should point out that at times one uses the diminished fifth in counterpoint in place of the perfect fifth, similarly the tritone in place of the perfect fourth, [both of] which make good effects.

> si dovesse mai porre la voce del Mi contra quella del Fa, nelle consonanze perfette . . . Si debbe però avertire, che alle volte si pone la Semidiapente ne i Contrapunti in luogo della Diapente; similmente il Tritono in luogo della Diatesseron, che fanno buoni effetti.

Example A.20 illustrates the "good effect" *mi* against *fa* can make during the approach to the cadence note G (m. 5; the sharp has been supplied editorially).

EXAMPLE A.20 Mi contra fa *removed (m. 4) and introduced (m. 5); Arcadelt, "Ahime,"* mm. 4–6

Phalèse, *Des chansons & motetz reduictz*, 1547

Bermudo (1555: V, 32, fol. 139r), writing at about the same time as Zarlino, explained why singers needed this degree of latitude in the correction of vertical dissonance:

> as a result of the way singers have trained their ears, [that is,] to hear what [is] in one voice, it [and here Bermudo refers to the diminished fourth C♯-F] is used in composition, if it is prepared first.

> y como los cantores tengan hecho el oydo, oyendo lo en una boz: lo usan en composicion, si primero se prepara.

The vertical dissonances that emerge from how "singers have trained their ears" almost invariably result from the voice parts' following their own inner logic in which one voice, sounding *mi*, clashes with another, sounding *fa*. All these clashes, the by-products of the vocal lines' moving somewhat independently of one another, form an integral part of sixteenth-century style, and according to Bermudo, permissible vertical dissonance can occur on the unstressed parts of a measure, in passing (especially in rapid passages), and at either feigned cadences or *clausulae* involving suspension figures (as shown in Example A.20).

One dissonance Bermudo (1555: V, 32, fol. 140r) does not condone, however, is *mi contra fa* in an octave, for it causes too much displeasure. But not all theorists agreed with him. Francisco Correa de Arauxo (1626: fol. 81v), citing the composers Josquin and Gombert and the theorist Francisco de Montanos (1592) as his authorities, discussed a dissonance in which an intense note sounded against a relaxed one ("punto intenso contra remisso"): "in many of them [compositions], there is no sign for *b durum*; nevertheless, reason demands it and the force [of the music] requires that it be there"/"en muchos de ellos no ay nota bequadrado, pero no obsta que la razon la pide, y la fuerça obliga a que la aya." Correa observed these dissonant octaves in a number of sixteenth-century compositions but found that in some of these works, the sign necessary to create the dissonance had been omitted, even though reason demanded it and the force of the music required that it be there. He cited Gombert's "Ay me qui vouldra" as an example of this omission and referred to Antonio de Cabezón's keyboard intabulation of it (1578) as a publication in which the passage had been interpreted correctly (Example A.21).

NONHARMONIC RELATIONS   Theorists also prohibited vertical dissonance that occurred as nonharmonic or false relations. Zarlino defined these relations in 1558 (179, 181) and prohibited them in two-part compositions:

EXAMPLE A.21 *Dissonant octave; Gombert, "Ay me qui vouldra," mm. 42–43*

Cabezón, *Obras de Música*, 1578

one should know that when it is said that the parts of a composition do not have a harmonic relation between the voices [that is, between two voices], it is the same as saying that the parts are separated from one another by an augmented or diminished octave or by a diminished fifth or tritone, or by other similar [intervals]. . . . These intervals, then, which are not permitted in melody should be avoided in [two-part polyphonic] song, inasmuch as they are distasteful as regards the relations between the parts.

Onde si debbe sapere, che tanto è dire, che le parti della cantilena non habbiano tra loro relatione harmonica nelle loro voci, quanto a dire, che le parti siano vicine, o lontane l'una dall'altra per una Diapason superflua, o per una Semidiapason; overamente per una Semidiapente, o per un Tritono, o altre simili. . . . Questi intervalli adunque, che nel modulare non si ammettono, si debbeno schivare di porti nelle cantilene di maniera, che si odino per relationi tra le parti.

But

in compositions for more voices, I believe that such respect [that is, the avoidance of nonharmonic relations] is not so necessary . . . yet such relations in music, along with some other intervals of similar sound, give little pleasure by themselves but make wonderful effects when accompanied by others [that is, by other types of intervals].

> nelle compositioni di più voci, parmi che tal rispetto non sia tanto necessario ... cosi ancora cotali Relationi nella Musica; & alcuni altri intervalli vi sono, che da per sè danno poca dilettatione: ma accompagnati con altri fanno mirabili effetti.

In other words, singers regularly retained tritones, and they even employed octave false relations. Examples of tritone and octave nonharmonic relations abound in the intabu-lations (Example A.22a), and although instances of simultaneous false octaves can certainly be found, they are not common (Example A.22b).

EXAMPLE A.22 *Nonharmonic relations: (a) tritone; Arcadelt, "Bella Fioretta," m. 52 and "Quand'io penso," mm. 9–12; (b) simultaneous false octave; Arcadelt, "Io mi pensai," mm. 11–12*

(a)

Fuenllana, *Orphenica lyra*, 1554

Francesco, *Intabolatura*, 1547

(b)

a- mar voi m'in- chi-

chi- na- ch'ad

voi ch'ad

-ne ad a- mar voi

Fuenllana, *Orphenica lyra*, 1554

Melodic Dissonance

The theorists' treatment of melodic dissonance follows a pattern similar to that of vertical dissonance; that is, they emphatically prohibit the use of certain intervals yet demonstrate how musicians may use these forbidden intervals in composition. Zarlino (1558: 237), for example, declared that melodic dissonance should be eliminated, even if the composer had not so indicated:

> It is true that in melodic [motion] one finds some intervals, such as the fourth, fifth, and octave, in which the singer must place a chromatic note (even though it had not been marked by the composer) so that the motion of the parts will be properly disposed. Nor must the composer mark it [the chromatic note], because it is superfluous, for these [dissonant] intervals really should not be sung.

> È ben vero, che nelle modulationi si trovano alcuni intervalli, come sono quelli di Quarta, di Quinta, & di Ottava, ne i quali il Cantore dè porre la chorda chromatica, ancora che non sia stata segnata dal Compositore; accioche la modulatione delle parti sia drittamente ordinata. Ne il Compositore la debbe porre: perche è superfluo: essendo che non si dè cantare veramente se non quelli intervalli. [See Example A.23a for one such offending interval in the *tenor* part of Claudin de Sermisy's "Joyssance".]

But Zarlino (236) also stated that composers could occasionally use one of these intervals melodically (he specifically mentions the diminished fifth) when it suited the meaning of the words (compare Example A.23a, where the lutenist removed the direct tritone in the *tenor*, with A.23b, where the intabulator retained the *altus*'s tritone between E and B♭, presumably because the note D intervenes to mitigate the obviousness of the dissonance).

EXAMPLE A.23 *Melodic dissonance: (a) tritone removed; Sermisy, "Joyssance," mm. 10–13; (b) tritone retained (altus, mm. 10–11); Arcadelt, "Il ciel de rado," mm. 8–11*

(a)

Phalèse, *Des chansons reduictz*, 1546

(b)

Bakfark, *Intabulatura*, 1553

One particular convention, known throughout the sixteenth century, that some theorists discussed in relation to melodic tritones was eventually codified by Michael Praetorius (1619: III, 3, 31) into the familiar phrase "one note ascending above *la* always is sung as *fa*"/"unicâ notulâ ascendente super la, semper canendum esse fa" (Example A.24a). But Ornithoparchus (1517: I, 5, 21) had already established this *fa-supra-la* convention, stated in a different form, for chant:

Whensoever a Song ascends from *Dsolre* to *Alamire* by a fift, mediately or immediately, and further onely to a second [ascends], you must sing *fa* in *bfa♮mi* in every *Tone* [mode], till the song do againe touch *Dsolre*, whether it be marked or no.

Quoties cantus ascendit ex Dsolre ad alamire per quintam mediate vel immediate, et ultra tantum ad secundam, cantandam est fa in bfa♮mi in omni tono, quo ad cantus iterum dsolre tetigerit, sive signet sive non.

Although Ornithoparchus did not supply a musical example to demonstrate this principle, his description fits the illustration in Praetorius's treatise perfectly (Example A.24a). Moreover, the principle also applies to compositions employing the soft hexachord:

Also when the song ascends no higher than *bfabmi* [B] or *Elami* in *bmollis* [that is, in the *bmollis* scale] then one always should sing *fa* in these places.

Item quando cantus non altius ascendit quam in befabemi, sive in Elami bemollari, tum semper oportet in hic canere fa. (Coclico 1552, fol. Dr; Example A.24b)

EXAMPLE A.24 Fa supra la *(Praetorius 1619: III, 3, 31)*

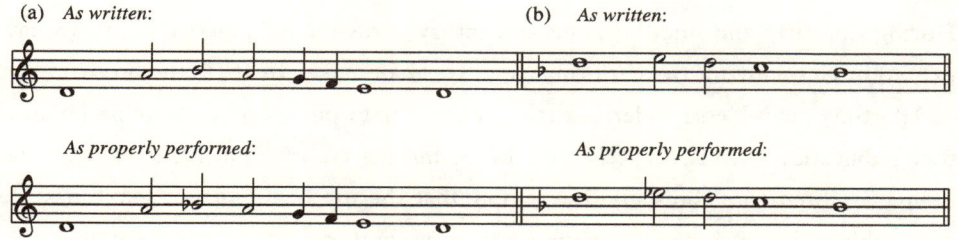

(a) *As written:*   (b) *As written:*

As properly performed: *As properly performed:*

Other theorists, such as Martin Agricola (1533: IV, fol. Bvr) and Hermann Finck (1556: I, fol. Fr), imply that this convention should be adopted as the normal practice in polyphony unless the sign ♮ or ♯ is written beside the note in question.

Characteristically, however, theorists mention exceptions to the precept. The most common of these occurs when the two notes of the tritone are so widely separated that the dissonance would not be heard anyway (Ornithoparchus/Dowland 1517/1609: I, 5, 21 and 135).

Mimesis

In mimetic passages, singers had to decide whether to render an *anaphora* as an *imitazione* or a *fuga*, that is, whether or not to repeat the solmization syllables exactly. Example A.25

presents a mimetic point from Arcadelt's "Vostra fui," which Diego Pisador (1552) treats as an *imitazione* instead of a *fuga* (Arcadelt pairs the voices *tenor-superius* and *bassus-altus*; this latter pair would require an E♭ for the *mimesis* to become a *fuga*).

EXAMPLE A.25 *Mimesis; Arcadelt, "Vostra fui," mm. 18–22*

Pisador, *Libro di musica*, 1552

THE GERMAN CUSTOM

During the early and middle sixteenth century, a distinctive practice seems to have existed in Germany for the performance of German music. In 1555, the brothers Paul and Bartholomeus Hessen referred to this practice in the preface to the tenor part book of their publication *Viel feiner lieblicher stücklein Spanischer, Welscher, Englischer, Französischer composition und tenz* (Breslau). They imply that the use of unnotated semitones was acceptable in the music of other countries but was contrary to custom in German music:

> the little cross, which frequently is marked [in the Hessens' edition], signifies the semitone [and is] so contrary to customary German music. With it [the little cross], [one] would show the custom of your country to much pleasant sweetness, where they [the little crosses] would be placed properly. Also you would have noticed some imperfect places, but because such people in your country so compose, and for the most part are not regarded as wrong, [they, the little crosses] are also not designated for German compositions. We have not wanted to change [anything] in order to retain its proper nature and that [you] be left with the proverb "Each country has its own custom and manner."

die vielfaltigen bezeichneten kreutzlein/bedeuten die Semitonien/so wider den gebrauch deutscher Musica befunden/wirdt darmit ihres landes gebrauch angezeiget/zu fiel angenemer lieblicheit/wo sie recht gemacht werden. Auch werden an etlichen orten vitia gespürt/weil aber solches bein [= beim] ihrer nation also componiert und zum theil nit fur unrecht geacht/Auch nicht fur deutsche compositz ausgeben/haben wir nichts endern wollen/damit ihr art und das sprichwort bleibe und erhalten/Jedes land furt seinen eignen brauch und weise.

The notational practices of both *Viel feiner lieblicher stücklein* and the Hessens' other publication from the same year, *Etlicher gutter Teutscher und Polnischer tenz*, substantiate these remarks. Indeed, the foreign dances in *Viel feiner lieblicher stücklein* contain many notated sharps, whereas only 5 of the 155 German/Polish dances in their second volume mark the *kreutzlein*. The tablatures of Hans Gerle, a Nürnberg musician, who between 1532 and 1546 intabulated both German and foreign vocal music, further illustrate the nationalistic practices described by the Hessens and demonstrate that musicians also applied the practice to vocal music.

The normal use of semitones, as described above, must have been well known throughout Europe, and Gerle's intabulations certainly confirm that a distinct practice existed in Germany for German music, with texts in the vernacular, written by native composers. As one would expect, however, Gerle does not fully substantiate the position taken by the Hessens, and his use of semitones falls into three broad categories: those pieces approaching all the cadence notes by the subtone, those approaching all the cadence notes by the subsemitone, and those containing a mixture of the two procedures.

For the first two categories, no textual or musical reasons suggest why Gerle chose to render one text with subsemitonal *clausulae* and another with subtonal cadences, and on occasion he even varied his treatment of *clausulae* when he intabulated the same piece twice. This remains one of the most fascinating aspects of Renaissance performing practice: the flexibility that pervaded the application of unnotated sharps. In Ludwig Senfl's "Patientiam muess ich han," for instance, Gerle designated a G♮ in the intabulation for viols but gave a G♯ in the version for lute (Example A.26a). This sort of freedom permeates sixteenth-century sources, especially when more than one German performer intabulated a given work, and Example A.26b shows a passage in which Gerle notated subtones, but both the lutenist Sebastian Ochsenkun (1558) and an anonymous intabulator stipulated subsemitones. Obviously, a variety of practices existed in Germany, and the Hessens' statements reflect just one facet of those customs.

Within the third category, Gerle seems to have organized his cadential procedure in a logical manner for at least some works; that is, *clausulae* at the end of large sections carry subsemitones, but internal cadences carry subtones. His plan can be seen most clearly in Senfl's "O Herr, ich rüef dein'n Namen an" (Example A.27).

EXAMPLE A.26 *Subtone and subsemitone at cadence: (a) Senfl, "Patientiam muess ich han,"*
mm. 20–21; (b) Senfl, "Mein selbs bin ich," mm. 19–21

(a)

Gerle, *Musica Teusch*, 1532

(b)

Left   Gerle, *Musica Teusch*, 1532 (for viols)
Right   Ochsenkun, *Tabulaturbuch*, 1558
Anon., Munich Ms. 1512

One might presume that the vertical constraints present in measures 24, 29, and 44 explain why Gerle chose not to incorporate subsemitones at these points, but other *clausulae* within the work do not contain such restrictions (mm. 5, 11, 39, and 48), yet Gerle rendered these with subtones as well. He did not, of course, limit this method of treating *clausulae* to German music, and the recovery of Gerle's fascinating strategy for organizing cadential procedures in foreign music reveals another side of sixteenth-century German fashion that enables us to re-create the variety of practices existing in Germany.

EXAMPLE A.27 *Senfl, "O Herr, ich rüef dein'n Namen an;" Hans Gerle,* Musica und Tabulatur, *1546 (for viols)*

O   Herr,   ich rüef   dein'n Na-   men
Schau   wie   der Türk   so grau-   sam

O   Herr,   ich   rüef   dein'n Na-   men
Schau   wie   der   Türk   so grau-   sam

O   Herr,   ich   rüef   dein'n Na-   men
Schau   wie   der   Türk   so grau-   sam

O   Herr,   ich   rüef   dein'n Na-   men an
Schau   wie   der   Türk   so grau-   sam wüet't

an,   dann   mir   sunst   nie-   mand hel-
wüet't   da-   vor   uns   lie-   ber   Herr

an   dann mir   sunst   nie-   mand hel-
wüet't   da-   vor   uns   lie-   ber   Herr

an   dann   mir   sunst   nie-   mand hel-
wüet't   da-   vor   uns   lie-   ber   Herr

dein'n Na- men   an   dann   mir   sunst   nie-   mand hel-
so grau- sam   wüet't   da-   vor   uns   lie-   ber   Herr

(Continued)

EXAMPLE A.27 (*Continued*)

fen kann in die- sen stren- gen Zei-
be - hüet und hilf uns ihn be- strei-

fen kann in die- sen stren- gen Zei-
be - hüet und hilf uns ihn be-

fen kann in die- sen stren-
be - hüet und hilf uns ihn

fen kann in die- sen stren- gen Zei-
be - hüet und hilf uns ihn be- strei-

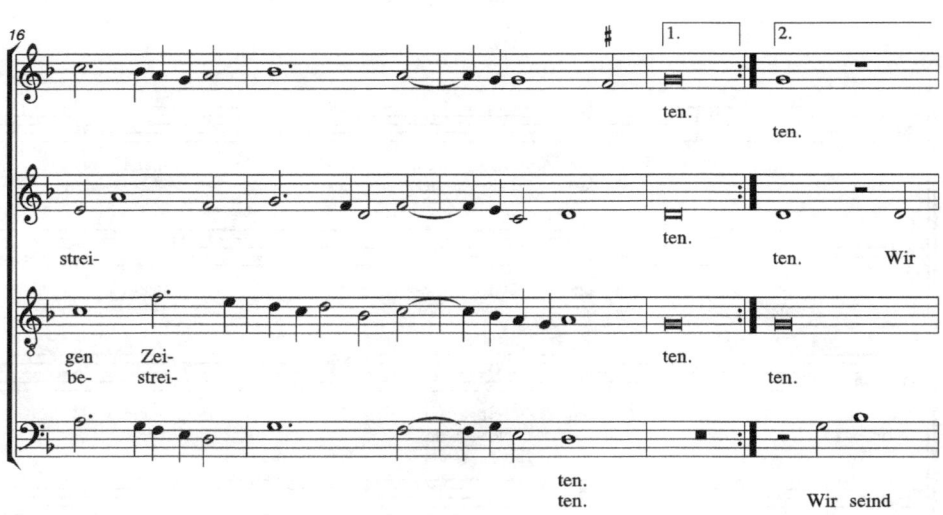

ten.
ten.

strei- ten.
ten. Wir

gen Zei- ten.
be- strei- ten.

ten.
ten.
Wir seind

20

Wir seind sunst ganz und gar ver-

seind sunst ganz und gar ver-

Wir seind sunst ganz und gar ver-

sunst ganz und gar ver- lor'n ver-

25

lor'n. Ob wir schon ha- ben dei- nen

lor'n. Ob wir schon ha- ben dei nen Zorn dei- nen

lor'n. Ob wir schon ha- ben dei- nen

lor'n. Ob wir schon ha- ben dei- nen

(Continued)

EXAMPLE A.27 (*Continued*)

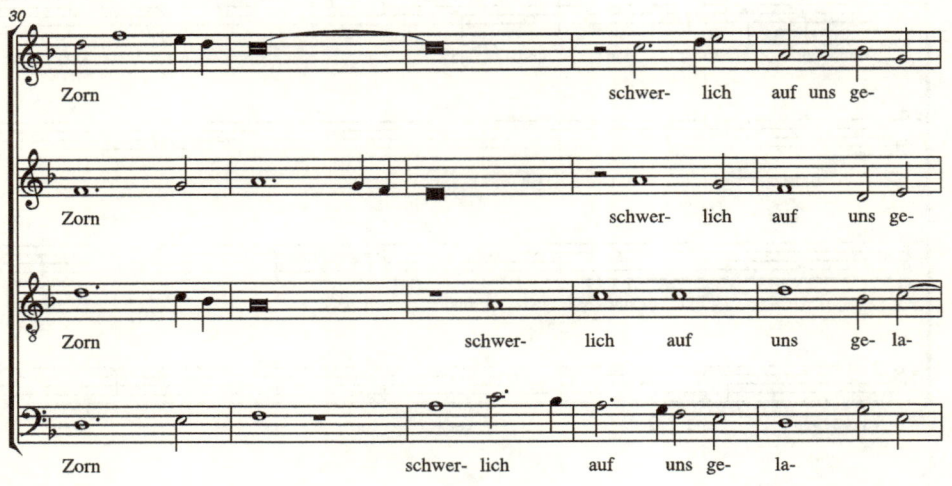

Zorn ... schwer- lich auf uns ge-

Zorn ... schwer- lich auf uns ge-

Zorn ... schwer- lich auf uns ge- la-

Zorn ... schwer- lich auf uns ge- la-

la- den so denk doch das wir sein ge- tauft

la- den so denk doch das wir sein ge-

den so denk doch das wir sein ge-

den so denk doch das wir sein ge-

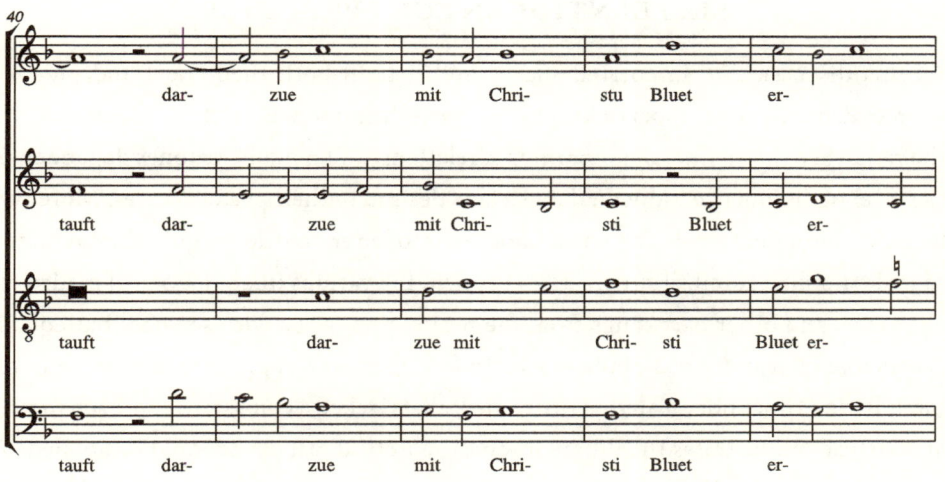

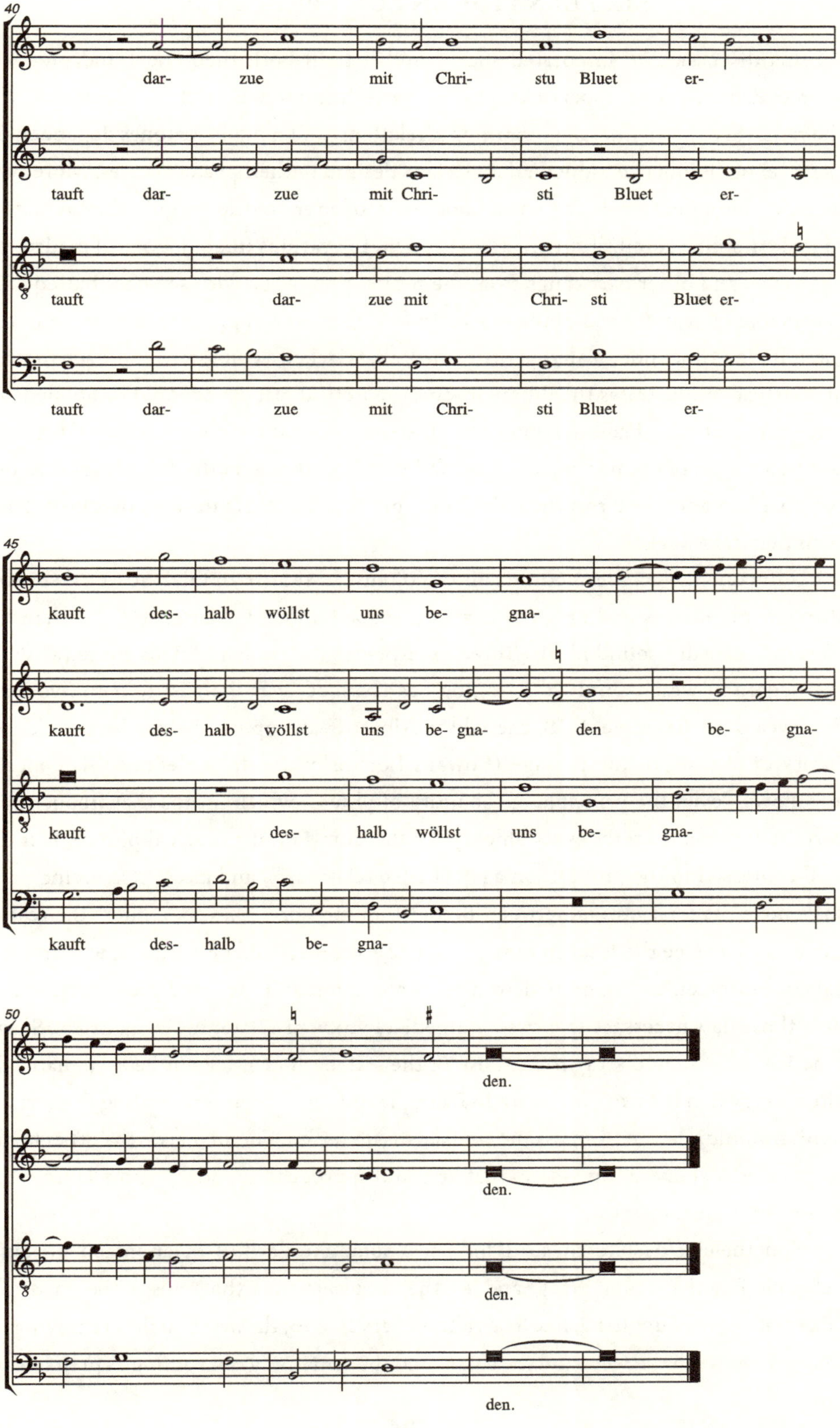
40
dar- zue mit Chri- stu Bluet er-
tauft dar- zue mit Chri- sti Bluet er-
tauft dar- zue mit Chri- sti Bluet er-
tauft dar- zue mit Chri- sti Bluet er-
45
kauft des- halb wöllst uns be- gna-
kauft des- halb wöllst uns be- gna- den be- gna-
kauft des- halb wöllst uns be- gna-
kauft des- halb be- gna-
50
den.
den.
den.
den.

SIXTEENTH-CENTURY PRACTICE

As this discussion of unnotated sharps and flats in both theoretical and practical sources demonstrates, upper or lower voice parts did not preclude the subsemitone, and the removal of *mi contra fa*, nonharmonic relations, and melodic tritones depended on the level of dissonance individual musicians desired in their performances. Moreover, because the act of translating vocal notation into letter notation required intabulators to make implicit solmization practices explicit, the various intabulations of madrigals, chansons, and other part songs from the period present us with separate but equally acceptable interpretations of the music. In fact, the array of practices exhibited in the intabulations does not mean that instrumentalists lacked a consistent approach to their art; instead, it illustrates the different ways theoretical principles could be applied. To force one method of solmization onto all sixteenth-century musicians would distort our perception of the period, and if we fail to reflect the breadth of their tastes in our own performances, we run the risk of interpreting the music in ways that lie outside their musical values.

Unfortunately, modern editors all too often add sharps and flats to vocal sources through an understanding of the music shaped more by current taste than by sixteenth-century sound ideals. Three excerpts from Arcadelt's "Bella Fioretta" show the degree to which aural conditioning has changed over the past four to five hundred years. In Example A.28, the editor Albert Seay applies the modern notion of "unity of phrase" to the passage (Edward Lowinsky, 1964: ix, defines this concept as follows: "even the principle of the unity of phrase, which means that frequently a certain accidental exercises its efficacy for the duration of a musical phrase, is fairly well expressed in the prohibition against false relations"), and after introducing a flat to remove the *mi contra fa* between B♭ and E in measure 30, Seay renders the rest of the Es as flats (see the *tenor* in mm. 31 and 32). Yet Miguel de Fuenllana, who in typical sixteenth-century fashion viewed pitch alteration as a localized procedure, added only those flats necessary to correct immediate problems. Later in the madrigal, Seay's practices continue to stray from those of the sixteenth century, for he systematically alters every E in the excerpt shown in Example A.29 to E♭, thus eradicating the sorts of nonharmonic relations Renaissance musicians preferred. Fuenllana, on the other hand, introduced just one E♭ (m. 44) so that he could approach the cadence note D from the closest imperfect interval.

Nonetheless, despite these differences, some similarities of approach do exist between Fuenllana and Seay, and in the *supplementum* that closes the madrigal (Example A.30) Fuenllana, like Seay, alters every E to E♭, the first two flats removing *mi contra fa* between the *tenor* and the *bassus* and the remaining ones acting as preparation

EXAMPLE A.28 *Arcadelt, "Bella Fioretta," mm. 29–33*

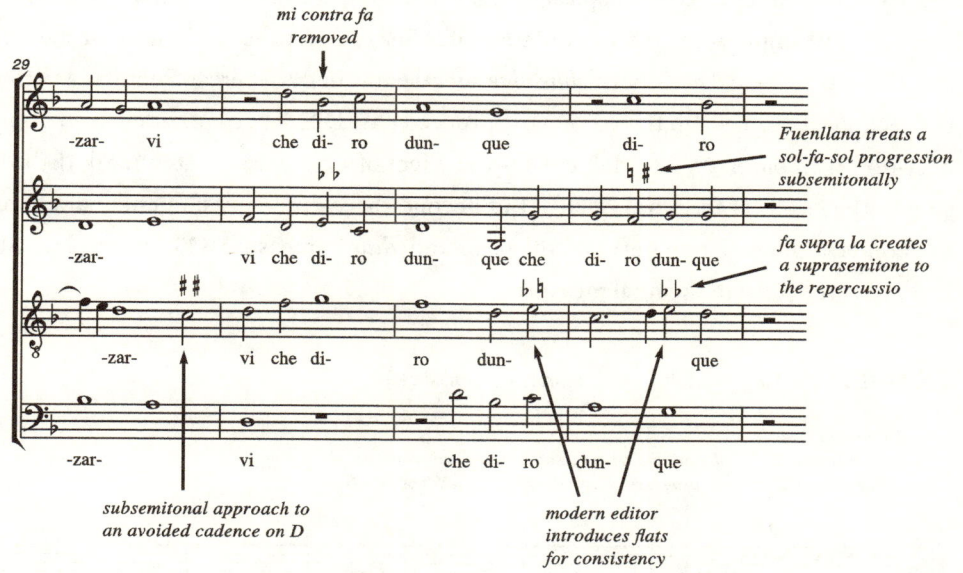

Left Seay, *Arcadelt, Opera omnia,* 1970
Right Fuenllana, *Orphenica lyra,* 1554

EXAMPLE A.29 *Arcadelt, "Bella Fioretta," mm. 42–45*

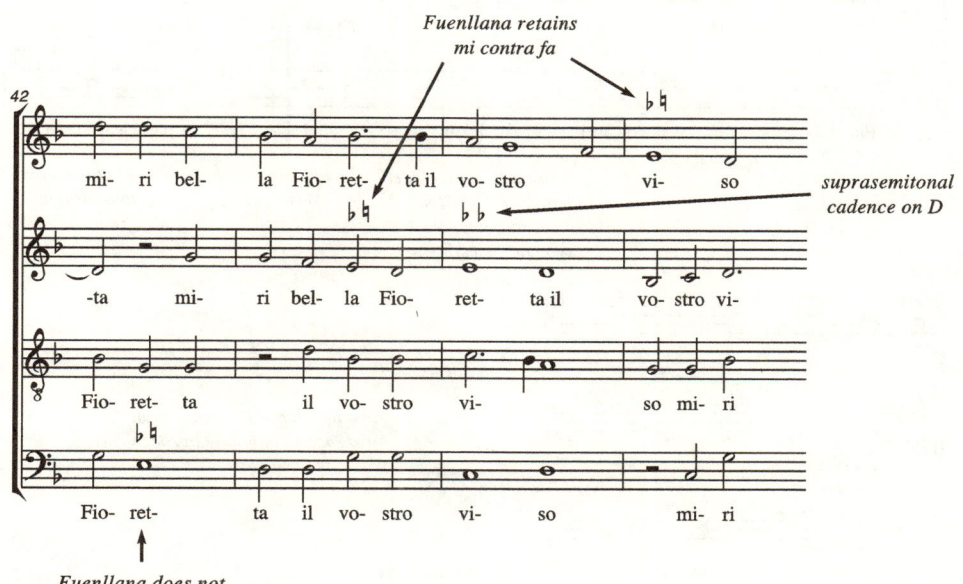

Left Seay, *Arcadelt, Opera omnia,* 1970
Right Fuenllana, *Orphenica lyra,* 1554

for the suprasemitonal avoided cadence on D that ends the piece. However, the cadence in measure 50 leading to the *supplementum*, when compared to the similar one in measure 44 of Example A.29, further differentiates Seay's practices from those of the sixteenth century. Seay treats both *clausulae* suprasemitonally, whereas Fuenllana varies the second cadence when the voice parts proceed past D to a perfect cadence on G (in m. 44 of Example A.29, Arcadelt creates the effect of a cadence on D to mark the full stop in the *bassus* at the word "viso"). But beyond these differences, Fuenllana retains the nonharmonic relation between the *tenor* and *altus* in measure 52 of Example A.30 and raises the third in the final measure.

EXAMPLE A.30 *Arcadelt, "Bella Fioretta," mm. 48–54*

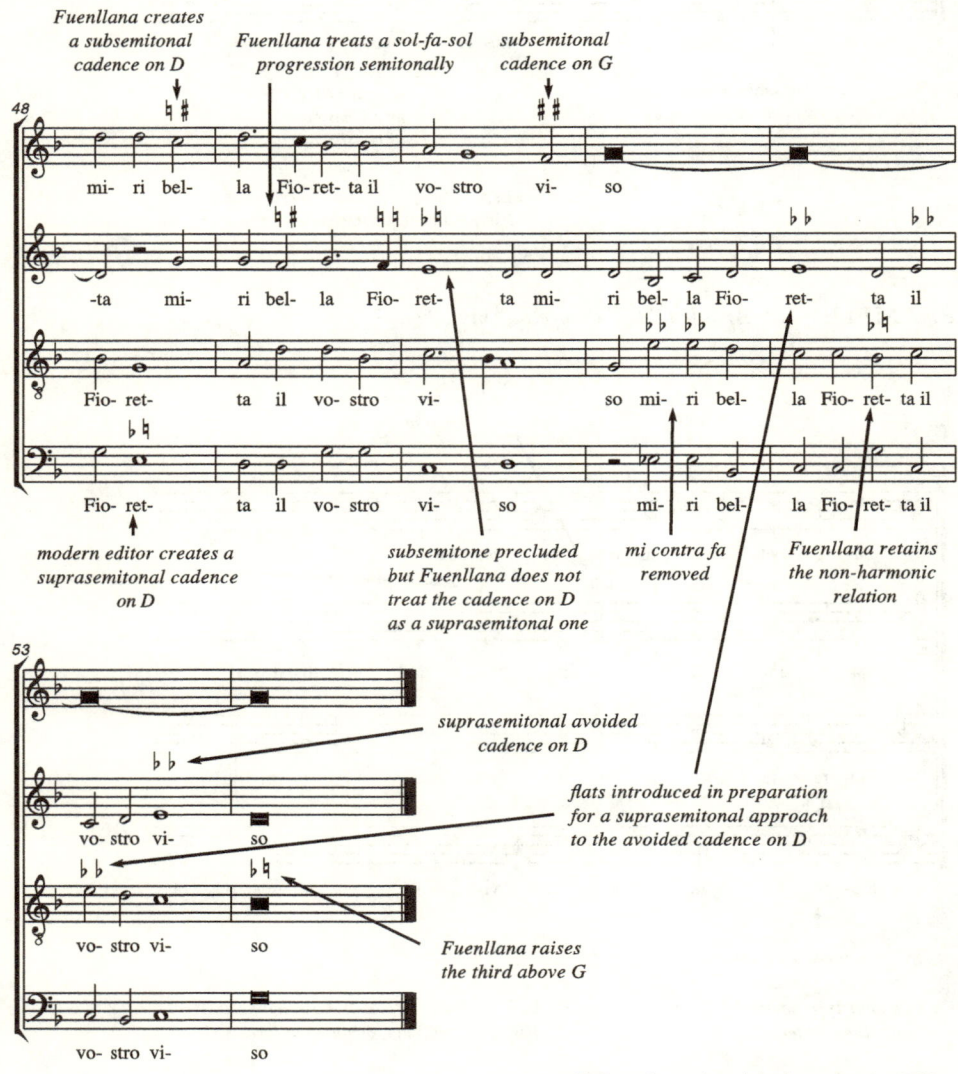

Left   Seay, *Arcadelt, Opera omnia*, 1970
Right   Fuenllana, *Orphenica lyra*, 1554

Contrasting applications of sharps and flats, then, can produce dramatically different readings of a work. Seay's modern interpretation of "Bella Fioretta" clearly does not emulate sixteenth-century models particularly well, for some of his alterations, which are often overly cautious, actually run counter to sixteenth-century customs. But, of course, musicians of the time could and did take conservative approaches to the addition of sharps and flats, and perhaps this aspect of Renaissance musical culture can best be illustrated by comparing intabulations of a single madrigal. Example A.31 presents three versions of Verdelot's "Quanto sia liet'il giorno" produced by midcentury musicians whose tastes ranged from conservative to liberal. Although these performers interpreted a number of passages identically, their readings diverge significantly enough at times to reveal the true range of practices that existed in the middle of the century.

Text and translation:

Quanto sia liet'il giorno	How joyous is the day
Nel qual le cose antiche	on which ancient things
Son hor da voi dimostre, e celebrate	are now by you revealed, and celebrated.
Si vede perch'intorno	Indeed it can be seen because on every side
Tutte le genti amiche	all friendly people
Si son in questa parte radunate	have in this place gathered.
Noi che la nostr'etate	We, who spend our lives
Ne boschi, e nelle selve consumiamo	in woods, and in forests,
Venuti anchor qui siamo	have also come here.
Io nimpha et noi pastori	I, a nymph, and we, shepherds,
Et giam cantando insieme i nostri amori.	and ever singing together about our loves.

Giovanni Maria da Crema's intabulation represents the conservative end of the spectrum, while Fuenllana's version and the one in Verdelot's own *Intavolatura* (1536), for which Adrian Willaert personally edited the lute parts, are much more daring in their application of sharps and flats. All three musicians approach cadences on the *finalis* G subsemitonally (mm. 10, 20, 33–34, and 38–39), and they tend to treat *la-sol-la* progressions semitonally when they involve the *finalis* (mm. 1, 3, 11, and 13). In addition, they prefer raised thirds above cadence notes, especially above D (mm. 22 and 25) and G (the composer includes the third above G only at the final cadence in mm. 40–41). But when their practices diverge, the character of the music can be either affected minimally, as in the *la-sol-la* progressions in measures 3, 6, 13, and 16, where only Crema

EXAMPLE A.31 *Sharps and flats in Verdelot's "Quanto sia liet'il giorno"*

Left   Verdelot, *Intavolatura*, 1536
Center Crema, *Intabolatura*, 1546
Right   Fuenllana, *Orphenica lyra*, 1554

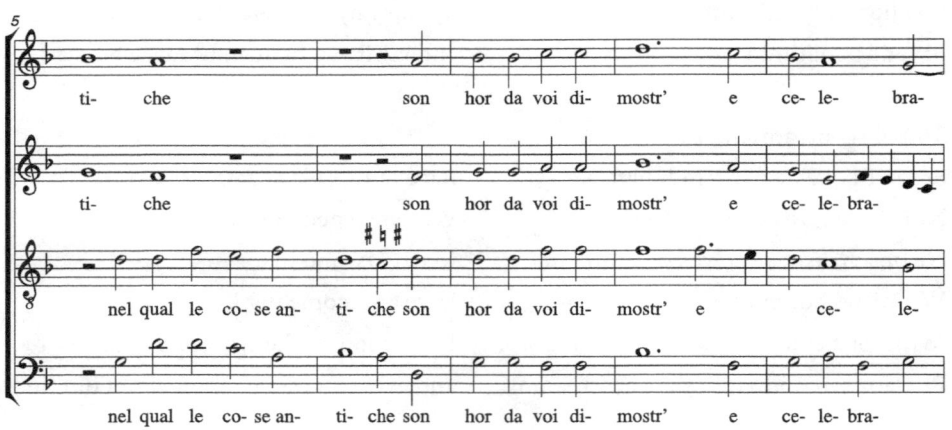

te si ve- de perch' in- tor- no tut- te le gent' a-

te si ve- de perch' in- tor- no tut- te le gent' a-

bra- te si ve- de perch' in- tor- no

te si ve- de perch' in- tor- no

mi- che si son' in que- sta par- te ra- du- na-

mi- che si son' in que- sta par- te ra- du- na-

tut- te le gent' a- mi- che si son' in que- sta par- te ra- du-

tut- te le gent' a- mi- che si son' in que- sta par- te ra- du- na-

(Continued)

EXAMPLE A.31 (*Continued*)

te noi che la nostr' e- ta- te nei bo- schi et nel- le sel- ve con- su-

te noi che la nostr' e- ta- te nei bo- schi et nel- le sel- ve con- su-

na- te noi che la nostr' e- ta- te nei bo- schi et nel- le sel- ve con- su-

te noi che la nostr' e- ta- te nei bo- schi et nel- le sel- ve con- su-

mia- mo ve- nut' an- chor qui sia- mo io nym- pha et

mia- mo ve- nut' an- chor qui sia- mo e noi pa- sto- ri et

mia- mo ve- nut' an- chor qui sia- mo e noi pa- sto- ri et

mia- mo ve- nut' an- chor qui sia- mo e noi pa- sto- ri et

Note: 'x' indicates note omitted

giam can- tan- do in- sie- me i no- stri a- mo- ri et
giam can- tan- do in- sie- me i no- stri a- mo- ri et
giam can- tan- do in- sie- me i no- stri a- mo- ri et
gima can- tan do in- sie- me i no- stri a- mo- ri et

giam can- tan- do in- sie- me i no- stri a- mo-
giam can- tan- do in- sie- me i no- stri a-
giam can- tan- do in- sie- me i no- stri a-
giam can- tan- do in- sie- me i no- stri a- mo- ri

ri
mo- ri
mo- ri
i no- stri a- mo- ri

omits the semitone; or transformed fundamentally, as in measures 23–25, 28–29, and 39–41.

In the first of these transformational passages, all three musicians raise the third above D in measure 22, and both Verdelot and Fuenllana retain this sonority in the next measure. The presence of this F♯ prompted Verdelot to alter the *superius*'s B♭ to B♮, the other two performers maintaining B♭, and in the drive to the *clausula* on D in measure 25 Verdelot and Fuenllana approach the cadence note suprasemitonally from E♭, while Crema retains the E♮ in the *bassus* and adds a sharp to the *altus*'s C. But even more striking effects occur in the other two passages. In measures 28–29, Verdelot and Fuenllana, unlike Crema, create a structure in which the vertical sonority moves in parallel motion. Example A.32 shows the flavor of parallelism each musician prefers. Similarly, in the *supplementum* (mm. 39–41), all three performers raise every one of the *tenor*'s Bs in preparation for the raised third above the final G, but only Verdelot and Fuenllana lower the *altus*'s Es to create a suprasemitonal approach to the *repercussio* D.

But beyond these colorful readings of the text, Crema's intabulation demonstrates the flexibility with which musicians treated repeated material. In the approach to the identical *clausulae* on G in measures 33–34 and 38–39, Crema renders the first one as a *sostenido* cadence, retaining the E♮ in the *bassus* and raising both Fs in the *superius*, and the second as a *remisso* cadence, with an alteration to just the second F. The practice

EXAMPLE A.32 *Parallel motion; Verdelot, "Quanto sia liet'il giorno," mm. 28–29*

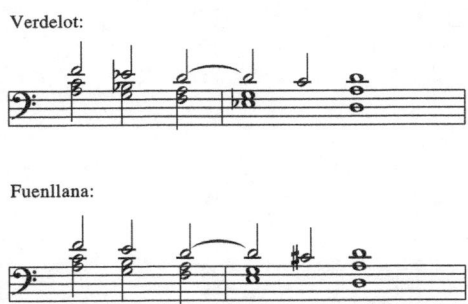

of introducing chromaticism within a single voice part was common in the sixteenth century (see Toft 1992: 56–62 for further examples of this practice), and Crema's decision to reserve the subsemitone for the penultimate note in only one of the cadences illustrates not a lack of consistency on his part but the type of variety Renaissance musicians prized in their performances.

NOTES

1. Solmization, a method of sight singing, uses hexachords to establish the intervallic relationships between notes (see below for a discussion of hexachords); for example, to sing a perfect fourth, one could employ, depending on the context, the syllables *ut-fa, re-sol,* or *mi-la.*

2. Theorists constructed hexachords on other notes but called these hexachords fictive, because one or more of their pitches lay outside the normal system of *musica vera* (true or real music based on the ordinary notes of the *gamut*). Fictive hexachords contained *musica ficta* (feigned, fictitious, or false music), and in a hexachord built on B♭ (B♭ C D E♭ F G), E♭ fell outside the *vera* pitches of the *gamut*, whereas B♭ was part of the normal system.

3. In the middle of the century, the theorist Heinrich Glarean (1547) advocated a twelve-mode system. The four extra modes centered on A and C, and Glarean called them Aeolian/Hypoaeloian and Ionian/Hypoionian respectively. Ionian came from the transposed Lydian mode, which by Glarean's time regularly included *b mollis*, and Aeolian from Dorian transposed to A. However, many writers in the later sixteenth century continued to discuss the traditional eight-mode system, and musicians never adopted Glarean's suggestions universally. The transposition of modes is addressed below.

4. The discussion of musical cadences in grammatical terms is, of course, much older than Lago, Vanneo, and Zarlino. Medieval treatises establish the connection (see Crane 1960: 29–78; Jonsson and Treitler 1983: 1–23; and Bower 1989: 133–45), and Zarlino probably knew the writings of Lago (1540: 39–43). The following is a summary of Zarlino (1558: 221–26). The purposes of punctuation, particularly in relation to performance, are discussed much more fully in Part 3, "All the Senses Satisfied."

5. Francis Bacon (1627: 38) referred to the avoidance of a cadence as the musical equivalent of the rhetorical figure *praeter expectatum* ("contrary to expectation"). Although he did not provide a technical explanation, he suggested that "Sliding from the Close or Cadence" gave listeners the pleasure of "Being deceived."

6. In this section, I am following the concept of hexachords outlined in Ornithoparchus (1517: 19–20, 134–35), Lanfranco (1533: 12ff., 26ff.), and Cretz (1553: fols. B5v–6r). Lanfranco discusses notes of permutation.

7. I disagree with Harold Powers' contention that Renaissance musicians did not make pre-compositional decisions to compose pieces in given modes (see Powers 1981, 1992a, 1992b), for a number of sixteenth-century theorists certainly contradict his claim. See especially Ornithoparchus (1517: 46, 156), Vicentino (1555: III, 15, fols. 47v–48v, trans. Maniates 1996: 149–51, esp. 149), Zarlino (1558: 329–32, 337–39, trans. Cohen 1983: 76–81, esp. 81 and 92–94, esp. 92), Sancta Maria (1565: fols. 60r–71r, trans. Howell and Hultberg 1991: 163–203, esp. 163, 179), and Montanos (1592, trans. Urquhart 1969: 118–75, esp. 126, 142, 146).

8. The word *imitation* (*imitatione* in Italian) had a specific meaning in the sixteenth century (see below for a discussion of *imitatione*), and for this reason I choose not to use it as a generic term for what might better be labeled by the Greek word for imitation, *mimesis.*

9. A most illuminating discussion of this facet of the fantasia appears in Butler (1974: 602–15), and some of the following discussion is based on Butler's article.

10. Amos (1975) lists the following lutenists as singers: Nikolaus Balamanuto, at the court of Innsbruck 1564–1580; Tiberius Balamanuto, at the Tirolian court 1582–1593; Julio Crema, at the court of Innsbruck 1581–1585; Hans von Metz, Kapellmeister c. 1540, at the Hofkapelle in Stuttgart; Johann Stobäus, at the ducal chapel of Konigsberg in 1601, and Kantor of the cathedral of Konigsberg in 1602; Giovanni Vuolpa, at the court of Innsbruck in 1582; and Christoph Westermeier, at the court of Hechingen in 1577.

11. Janssen (1978) appendix 2 lists these waytes as choristers in the cathedral: Richard Graves, 1584–85; Arthur Jackson, 1590–1609; Peter Sandlyn, 1607; Peter Spratt, Sr., 1574–75; and Anthony Wilson, 1574–75.

Glossary

accento—accent; also ornament (the plural form, *accenti*, can mean ornamentation)

affections—see passions

affetto—affection or passion

affetto cantando—passionate singing

ambitus—the range of a mode

anabasis—an ascending melody used to depict the sense of the words (Bartel 1997: 179–80)

anadiplosis—a figure in which the last word of one clause becomes the first word of the next (Peacham the Elder 1577: fol. J3r)

anaphora—a figure in which the same word is iterated at the beginning of successive sentences (Fraunce 1588: ch. 19)

anastrophe—a figure containing a preposterous ordering of words that runs contrary to normal speaking (Sherry 1550: 31)

antithesis—a figure that "is a proper coupling togeather of contraries, and it is eyther in wordes that be contrary, or in contrary sentences" (Peacham the Elder 1577: fol. R1r)

aposiopesis—a figure denoting abrupt terminations: "when through some affection, as of feare, anger, sorrow, bashfulnesse, and such like, we breake of[f] our speech, before it be all ended" (Peacham the Elder 1577: fol. N1v)

articulus—a figure that separates "words & clauses one from another, either by distinguishing the sound [with commas], or by separating the sense" (Peacham the Elder 1593: 56) *auricular* figures—those whose purpose simply was to delight the ear: "not onely the whole body of a tale in a poeme or historie may be made in such sort pleasant and agreable to the eare, but also every clause by it selfe, and every single word carried in a clause, may have their pleasant sweetnesse apart" (Puttenham 1589: 134)

authentic—signifies that the range of the mode is from the final to the octave above (Dorian, Phrygian, Lydian, and Mixolydian)

auxesis—a figure involving an ascent by degrees to the top of some matter as "when we make our saying grow and increase by an orderly placing of our words, making the latter word always exceede the former, in force of signifycation . . . In this fygure, order must be dilligently observed, that the stronger may follow the weaker, and the worthyer the lesse worthy" (Peacham the Elder 1577: fol. Q2v)

b durum—sharp

b mollis—flat

b quadrado—sharp

b rotondo—flat

cadence—a resting point in music equivalent to punctuation in language in which two voices, one descending by step and the other rising by step, proceed to an octave or unison

> types: *perfect*—all voices form perfect consonances with the cadence note
>
> > *imperfect*—a third or sixth is heard in the concentus at the cadence note, that is, in a voice other than the two that control the cadence
> >
> > *avoided*—the two voices controlling the cadence appear to be proceeding to a perfect cadence but one of them turns elsewhere instead
> >
> > *interrupted*—one or more voices drop out at the cadence
> >
> > *feigned*—another voice proceeds to the cadence note instead of the expected one
> >
> > *by leap*—one or both voices leap to a cadence note
>
> approaches: subsemitone—the voice rising by step to the cadence note approaches by a semitone
>
> > *subtone*—the voice rising by step to the cadence note approaches by a whole tone
> >
> > *suprasemitone*—the voice descending by step to the cadence note approaches by a semitone

cadentia—cadence

cadenza—cadence

catabasis—a descending melody used to depict the sense of the words (Bartel 1997: 214–15)

cauda—see *supplementum*

clausula—cadence

clausula disimulada—a different voice proceeds to the cadence note instead of the expected one

climax (gradatio)—rhetoric: a figure in which "the worde, whiche endeth the sentence goyng before, doeth begin the nexte" (Wilson 1553: 405–6)

> music: the stepwise repetition of a melodic fragment (Bartel 1997: 220–25); I adapt early seventeenth-century definitions of the term to suit the song repertoire, using *climax* for single repetitions and *gradatio* for extensions of the figure beyond one restatement

colon—the punctuation mark ":" or the segment of a sentence preceding the colon (it often consists of one or more commas)

comes—the following voice in a mimetic passage

comma—the punctuation mark "," or the segment of a sentence preceding the comma

concentus—the vertical combination of notes sounding together

conmixtus—two different modes intermingled in one piece

dialogism—a figure "where *two Persons* are brought in as 'twere *Dialoguing* one another, one of 'em moving the *Question* and t'other making the *Answer,* you must change your *voyce* by turns, as if *two Men* were really a talking together" (Le Faucheur 1657: 135)

distinctions—punctuation: comma, semicolon, colon, period, question mark, exclamation mark, parentheses (round brackets)

ditti—the words of the song

divisions—figural patterns that embellish several or many notes by dividing longer notes into shorter ones

dux—guida, the leading voice in a mimetic passage

ecphonesis—a figure "when through affection either of anger, sorrow, gladnesse, marveyling, feare, or any such lyke, we breake out in voyce with an exclamation, & outcry to expresse the passions of our minde, after this manner. O lamentable estate, O cursed misery, O wicked impudency, O joy incomparable, O rare and singuler bewty" (Peacham the Elder 1577: fol.K4r)

eloquence—"where any matter or act done or to be done is expressed in wordes, cleane, propise, ornate, and comely, wherof sentences be so aptly compact, that they by a vertue inexplicable, do draw unto them the mindes and consent of the hearers, beynge therewith either persuaded, meved, or to delectacion induced" (Elyot 1546: fol. 40v)

emphasis—a figure whose purpose is to "inforce the sence of any thing by a word of more than ordinary efficacie" (Puttenham 1589: 153); also the stress a speaker places on an important word or idea in a sentence *enargia*—a class of figures that "satisfie & delight th'eare onely by a goodly outward shew set upon the matter with wordes, and speaches smothly and tunably running" (Puttenham 1589: 119)

energia—a class of figures that worked inwardly to stir the mind "by certaine intendments or sence of such wordes & speaches" (Puttenham 1589: 119)

epanalepsis—a figure in which a sentence begins and ends with the same word (Peacham the Elder 1593: 46)

epimone—a figure involving the regular repetitions of one phrase at equal distance because that phrase "beareth the whole burden of the song" (Puttenham 1589: 188)

epistrophe—a figure in which the same word is iterated at the end of successive sentences (Hoskins 1599: 127)

epizeuxis—a figure involving the immediate restatement of a word or two for greater vehemence (Peacham the Elder 1577: fol. J3r)

esclamazione—a certain strengthening of the relaxed voice; one of the expressive devices in Caccini's *affetto cantando* (Caccini 1602: "A i lettori")

exordium—the beginning of an oration that serves to prepare the audience to listen with interest (Sonnino 1968: 243)

exornation—the adornment or beautification of language through the application of rhetorical figures

fa—refers to the solmization syllable, or may mean flat; for example, B*fa* = B♭

fantasia—the musical genre or the short thematic cell on which compositions or sections of compositions are based

fa supra la—an abbreviation for the Latin phrase "unicâ notulâ ascendente supra la, semper canendum essa fa"/"one note ascending above *la* always is sung as *fa*" (Praetorius 1619: III, 3, 31)

figure—a form of speech artfully varied from common usage (Quintilian: IX, 352–55), or "a certaine lively or good grace set upon wordes, speaches and sentences to some purpose and not in vaine, giving them ornament or efficacie by many maner of alterations in shape, in sounde, and also in sence, sometime by way of surplusage, sometime by defect, sometime by disorder, or mutation, & also by putting into our speaches more pithe and substance, subtilitie, quicknesse, efficacie or moderation, in this or that sort tuning and tempring them, by amplification, abridgement, opening, closing, enforcing, meekening or otherwise disposing them to the best purpose" (Puttenham 1589: 133)

finalis—the final of a mode

fuga—*mimesis* involving the literal repetition of the solmization syllables of the *guida* by the other voices *gamut*—the entire theoretical range of notes available to composers from G on the bottom line of the modern bass clef to e″ in the top space of the modern treble clef

graces—small melodic figures, frequently of no more than a few notes, embellishing single notes

gradatio—see *climax* (music)

guida—the leading voice in a mimetic passage

heterolepsis—a leap from a consonant note to a dissonant one (Bartel 1997: 293–94)

hexachord—a series of six notes carrying the solmization syllables *ut-re-mi-fa-sol-la* and always containing the interval relationship tone-tone-semitone-tone-tone between the notes; in the scales of *b durum* (pieces with no signature) and *b mollis* (pieces with B♭ in the signature), hexachords are built on the notes G, C, and F and are labeled respectively hard, natural, and soft; hexachords may be constructed on other notes, in which case they are called fictive (because these hexachords lie outside the normal system)

hypotyposis—rhetoric: a large group of figures that are directed toward lively description or counterfeit representation (Puttenham 1589: 199)

    music: a generic term for any musical device that serves to illustrate the text in a literal fashion (Bartel 1997: 307–11)

hypozeuxis—a figure in which the language is adorned by supplying the same word in more than one clause (Puttenham 1589: 138–39)

imitatione—*mimesis* in which the solmization syllables of the *guida* are modified when they are repeated by the other voices; for example, the interval of a major third in the *guida* (solmized *ut-mi*) may become a minor third in the *comes* (solmized *re-fa*)

kreutzlein—sharp

ligature—a notational custom in which two or more notes are joined together to form one compound symbol; shown in modern transcriptions through a bracket over the notes that were ligated together in the original document

melisma—a group of several (or more) notes sung to a single text syllable

member—the segment of the sentence enclosed by two punctuation marks

mi—refers to the solmization syllable, or may mean sharp; for example, C*mi* = C♯

mi contra fa—*mi* against *fa*, the simultaneous sounding of *mi* in one voice and *fa* in another; this produces dissonant relationships, the most common being B (*mi*) against F (*fa*) and E (*mi*) against B♭ (*fa*)

mimesis—generic term for all imitative compositional techniques

mixtus—the authentic and plagal forms of a mode intermingled in one piece

mode—an octave scale beginning on D (Protus), E (Deuterus), F (Tritus), or G (Tetrardus) *musica ficta*—feigned, fictitious, or false music that lies outside the ordinary notes of the *gamut*

musica vera—true or real music based on the ordinary notes of the *gamut*

mutation—the changing of one solmization syllable into another in order to sing a melody, the range of which extends beyond a single hexachord

mutatio toni—an abrupt change in *concentus* for expressive purposes (Bartel 1997: 334–39)

nonharmonic relation—false relation, nonsimultaneous

palillogia—rhetoric: a figure that serves to add weight to the idea expressed in the text by emphasizing a particular aspect of its meaning, as "when the word repeated hath another signification" (Peacham the Elder 1577: fol. J2v, Diaphora); music: a figure involving the repetition of a melodic fragment at the same pitch (Bartel 1997: 342–44)

paronomasia—a figure in which "a word is changed in signification by changing of a letter or sillable" (Fraunce 1588: ch. 24)

parrhesia—rhetoric: the use of pungent language to reprehend the hearers for some fault (*Rhetorica*: IV, 348–55); music: the *mi-fa* clash of the false relation or other dissonances between parts (Bartel 1997: 352–56)

passaggi—see divisions

passions—"none other thyng, but a stirryng, or forcyng of the mynde, either to desier, or elles to detest, and lothe any thyng, more vehemently then by nature we are commonly wonte to doe" (Wilson 1553: 266); passions are caused by certain internal acts or operations of the soul that stir in the mind and alter the humors of the body; they are things such as love, pain, ire, joy, fear, hope, flight, hatred, etc. (Wright 1604: 8, 33–34)

pathopoeia—rhetoric: the generic term for two categories of rhetorical devices that move the minds of listeners to indignation, anger, fear, envy, hatred, hope, gladness, mirth, laughter, sorrow, or sadness; the first type is called imagination and embraces "sharp figures" that stir the sorts of vehement affections that one finds in tragedy, that is, matters that are great, cruel, horrible, marvelous, pleasant, etc.; the second type is called commiseration, through which the orator brings listeners to tears or moves them to pity or forgiveness (Sherry 1550: 68; Peacham the Elder 1577: fol. P3r); music: chromaticism (Bartel 1997: 359–62)

period—the punctuation mark "." or the accumulated segments of a sentence preceding that punctuation mark

permutation—the change of one note for another in modal/hexachordal systems; for example, B could be sung as either *mi* or *fa*, and this produced the frequent oscillation between B*mi* (B♮) and B*fa* (B♭) found in modal music plagal—signifies that the range of the mode surrounds the final, that is, from the fourth below to the fifth above (Hypodorian, Hypophrygian, Hypolydian, and Hypomixolydian)

point—"a certain number and order of observable Notes in anyone Parte, iterated in the same or in divers Partes" (Butler 1636: 71)

praeter expectatum—contrary to expectation; the avoiding of a cadence (Bacon 1627: 38)

prolongatio—the extension of a dissonance beyond the normal expectation (Bartel 1997: 371–72)

propositio—when orators state in a "few wordes the summe of that matter, whereof we presently intend to speake" (Peacham the Elder 1577: fol. S2v)

prosopopoeia—"a fayning of any person, when in our speach we represent the person of anie, and make it [that person] speake as though he were there present" (Fraunce 1588: fol. G2r); the orator personifies the inner thoughts and affections of an absent person, making that person actually seem to appear before the eyes of the hearer (Quintilian: IX, 390–91; Peacham the Elder 1577: fol. O2r–v)

punto intenso contra remisso—an intense (sharped) note sounding against a relaxed (lowered) note; this produces dissonant octaves and unisons, for example, C against C♯ (Correa de Arauxo 1626: fol. 81v)

remisso—relaxed or lowered

repercussio—the reciting note of a mode; in Dorian on D this note is A, but in Hypodorian on D it is F

rhetoric—"the science, wherby is taughte an artificiall fourme of spekyng, wherin is the power to perswade, move, and delyte" (Elyot 1546: fol. 41v); traditionally, the art of rhetoric was divided into five areas: *inventio, dispositio, elocutio* or *decoratio, memoria,* and *pronunciatio; inventio* entailed finding the subject matter, and in *dispositio,* the material was ordered or arranged to serve the writer's purposes; once the material was arranged, *elocutio* involved amplifying and decorating the poetry with fine words and sentences; the discourse then was memorized (*memoria*) and delivered, *pronunciatio* being concerned with the techniques of delivery orators employed to move the passions of listeners

ribattuta di gola—the rhythmic re-striking of the throat in a dotted pattern (Caccini 1602: "A i lettori")

schemes—a class of figures that remove language from the common custom by creating highly artificial patterns of speech (for example, repetitions of all sorts; Peacham the Elder 1577: fol. E1v)

sensable figures—figures that stir the mind by altering conceit or sense (Puttenham 1589: 133, 148)

sententious figures—figures designed "all at once to beautifie and geve sence and sententiousnes to the whole language at large" (stirring the mind while delighting the ear;
   Puttenham 1589: 163)

solfa—solmization

solmization—a method of sight singing using hexachords to establish the interval relationships between notes; for example, to sing a perfect fourth one could employ,
   depending on the context, the syllables *ut-fa*, *re-sol*, or *mi-la*

sostenido—sharped

species—the modal octave is divided into two parts, one consisting of the interval of
   a fifth and the other of a fourth; these two intervals may be classified according to
   their structure, each pattern of intervals being called a species; there are four species of fifth (1 *re mi fa sol la*, 2 *mi fa sol re mi*, 3 *fa sol re mi fa*, 4 *ut re mi fa sol*) and three
   species of fourth (1 *re mi fa sol*, 2 *mi fa sol la*, 3 *ut re mi fa*); species help define the
   character of a mode

sprezzatura—the noble negligence of rhythm; one of the expressive devices in Caccini's
   affetto cantando (Caccini 1614: "Alcuni avvertimenti")

subjection—a figure in which several questions are asked and answers are given to all
   of them (Le Faucheur 1657: 144)

subsemitone—the semitone below

subtone—the whole tone below

supplementum—to draw a piece to a close, one or two voices hold fast while the others
   continue polyphonically (Burmeister 1606: 53; Nucius 1613: fol. G3v)

suprasemitone—the semitone above

supratone—the whole tone above

symploche—a figure that occurs "when one and the selfe [same] word doth begin and
   end many verses in sute" (Puttenham 1589: 166)

synathroismos—a figure that involves "a multiplication or heaping togeather of manye
   wordes, sygnifyinge dyvers thinges of like nature" (Peacham the Elder 1577:
   fol. Q2r)

syncopatio catechrestica—an irregular resolution of a suspension (Bartel 1997: 401)

syncope—a suspension (Bartel 1997: 396–405)

synonymia—rhetoric: a figure designed to make the sense stronger and more obvious
   by using words that differ from the preceding ones in form or sound but mean the
   same (Sherry 1550: 49; Peacham the Elder 1577: fol. P4r; Puttenham 1589: 179);
   music: the repetition of a melodic fragment at a different pitch level (but not one
   step higher or lower; Bartel 1997: 407, Mattheson)

thema—the musical subject or melodic cell on which a composition or a section of a
   composition is based

tritonus—tritone

tropes—a class of figures that serve to alter the signification of a word or words from the normal meaning to something not proper but quite close (for example, metaphor; Peacham the Elder 1577: fol. B1v)

zeugma—a figure in which a single word serves more than one clause; if the common servitor appears in the first clause of a series, it is called *prozeugma* (Puttenham 1589: 136–37)

References

Aaron, Pietro. 1529. *Toscanello in musica*. Venice: Bernardino & Matheo de Vitali. Facs. Bologna: Forni, 1969.

Abramov-van Rijk, Elena. 2009. *Parlar cantando: The Practice of Reciting Verses in Italy from 1300 to 1600*. Bern: Peter Lang.

Agricola, Martin. 1533. *Musica choralis deudsch*. Wittenberg: Georg Rhau.

Ahle, Johann G. 1697. *Musikalisches Sommer-Gespräche*. Mühlhausen: Pauli & Brückner.

Amos, Charles Nelson. 1975. Lute Practice and Lutenists in Germany between 1500 and 1750. Ph.D. diss., University of Iowa.

Anglés, Higinio. 1965. *La música en la Corte de Carlos V*. Monumentos de la música española, vol. 2. Barcelona: Instituto Espanol de Musicologia.

Ascham, Roger. 1545. *Toxophilus, The schole of shootinge*. London: Edouardi Whytchurch. Facs. Amsterdam: Theatrum Orbis Terrarum, 1969.

Bacon, Francis. 1627. *Sylva sylvarum*. London: William Lee.

Bakfark, Valentin. 1553. *Intabulatura*. Lyon: Moderne.

Barnett, Dene. 1987. *The Art of Gesture: The Practices and Principles of 18th-Century Acting*. Heidelberg: C. Winter.

Bartel, Dietrich. 1997. *Musica poetica: Musical-Rhetorical Figures in German Baroque Music*. Lincoln: University of Nebraska Press.

Barton, John. 1634. *The Art of Rhetorick Concisely and Compleatly Handled*. London: Nicolas Alsop.

Bassano, Giovanni. 1585. *Ricercate, passaggi et cadentie*. Venice: Vincenzi & Amadino.

Bassano, Giovanni. 1591. *Motetti, madrigali et canzoni francese*. Venice: Vincenti. Lost, manuscript copy in the hand of Friedrich Chrysander in Staats- und Universitätsbibliothek Hamburg, MS MB 2488.

Berger, Karol. 1987. *Musica ficta*. Cambridge: Cambridge University Press.

Bermudo, Juan. 1555. *Declaración de instrumentos musicales*. Osuna: Juan de Leon. Facs., Kassel: Bärenreiter, 1957.

Bernhard, Christoph. c. 1657. *Tractatus compositionis augmentatus*. In *Die Kompositionslehre Heinrich Schützens in der Fassung seines Schülers Christoph Bernhard*. Ed. Joseph M. Müller-Blattau. Kassel: Bärenreiter, 1963.

Bianchini, Dominico. 1546. *Intabolatura de lauto . . . Libro primo*. Venice: Gardane.

Bodleian Library, Oxford, MS Tenbury 1018, c. 1615.

Bodleian Library, Oxford, MS Tenbury 1019, c. 1615.

Bossinensis, Franciscus. 1509. *Tenori e contrabassi intabulati col sopran in canto figurato . . . Libro primo* Venice: Petrucci.

Bossinensis, Franciscus. 1511. *Tenori e contrabassi intabulati col sopran in canto figurato . . . Libro secundo* Venice: Petrucci.

Bourgeois, Loys. 1550. *Le droict chemin de musique*. Geneva: Jena Gérard. Facs., Kilkenny: Boethius Press, 1982.

Bovicelli, Giovanni Battista. 1594. *Regole, passaggi di musica, madrigali, e motetti passeggiati*. Venice: Vincenti.

Bower, Calvin M. 1989. The Grammatical Model of Musical Understanding in the Middle Ages. In *Hermeneutics and Medieval Culture*, ed. Patrick J. Gallacher and Helen Damico, pp. 133–45. Albany: State University of New York Press.

Brinsley, John. 1612. *Ludus literarius: or, The Grammar Schoole*. London: Thomas Man.

Brinsley, John. 1622. *A Consolation for our Grammar Schooles*. London: Thomas Man.

British Library, MS Add. 15117, c. 1614–16.

British Library, Ms Add. 24665 (Giles Earle's songbook), 1615–20.

British Library, MS Add. 29481, c. 1620–30.

British Library, MS Add. 31403 (Edward Bevin), after 1625.

British Library, MS Egerton 2971 (Robertus Downes' songbook), between 1610 and 1622.

Brown, Clive. 1999. *Classical and Romantic Performing Practice, 1750–1900*. Oxford: Oxford University Press.

Brown, Howard. 1973–74. Embellishment in Early Sixteenth-Century Italian Intabulations. *Proceedings of the Royal Musical Association* 100: 49–83.

Brown, Howard. 1982. Emulation, Competition, and Homage: Imitation and Theories of Imitation in the Renaissance. *Journal of the American Musicological Society* 35: 1–48.

Brussels. Bibliothèque du Conservatoire Royal de Musique, MS 27088, undated.

Bulwer, John. 1644. *Chirologia: or the Naturall Language of the Hand . . . Chironomia: or the Art of Manuall Rhetorike*. London: T. Harper. Ed. James W. Cleary. Carbondale: Southern Illinois University Press, 1974.

Burmeister, Joachim. 1606. *Musica poetica*. Rostock: Stephan Myliander. Facs., Kassel: Bärenreiter, 1955.

Butler, Charles. 1633. *The English Grammar*. Oxford: William Turner.

Butler, Charles. 1636. *The Principles of Musik*. London: John Haviland. Facs., Amsterdam: Theatrum Orbis Terrarum, 1970.

Butler, Gregory G. 1974. The Fantasia as Musical Image. *Musical Quarterly* 60: 602–15.

Butler, Gregory G. 1980. Music and Rhetoric in Early Seventeenth-Century English Sources. *Musical Quarterly* 66: 53–64.

Byrd, William. 1588. *Psalmes, sonets, & songs of sadnes and pietie*. London: Thomas East.

Cabezón, Antonio de. 1578. *Obras de música*. Madrid: Francisco Sanchez.

Caccini, Giulio. 1602. *Le nuove musiche*. Florence: Marescotti. Ed. H. Wiley Hitchcock. Madison, Wisc.: A-R Editions, 2009.

Caccini, Giulio. 1614. *Nuove musiche e nuova maniera di scriverle*. Florence: Pignoni. Ed. H. Wiley Hitchcock. Madison, Wisc.: A-R Editions, 1978.

Cambridge. Fitzwilliam Museum, MS Mu 782 (formerly 52.D.25), c. 1618–early 1620s.

Cambridge. King's College, Rowe MS 2 (Francis Turpyn's songbook), c. 1610–1615.

Campion, Thomas. c. 1613/1. *Two Bookes of Ayres, The First*. London: Tho. Snodham.

Campion, Thomas. c. 1613/2. *Two Bookes of Ayres, The Second*. London: Tho. Snodham.

Campion, Thomas. 1613/3. *A Relation of the late Royall Entertainment . . . at Cawsome-House*. London: John Budge.

Campion, Thomas. 1614. *The Description of a Maske . . . At the Mariage of the Right Honourable the Earl of Somerset*. London: Laurence Lisle.

Campion, Thomas. c. 1618/3. *The Third and Fourth Booke of Ayres*. London: Thomas Snodham.

Campion, Thomas. c. 1618/4. *The Third and Fourth Booke of Ayres*. London: Thomas Snodham.

Casa, Girolamo dalla. 1584. *Il vero modo di diminuir*. Venice: Gardano.

Castiglione, Baldassare. 1588. *The Courtier* [polyglot edition of *Il libro del cortegiano*]. London: John Wolfe. First published as *Il libro del cortegiano*. Venice: Aldo Romano & Andra d'Asola, 1528.

Cavalieri, Emilio de'. 1600. *Rappresentatione di anima, et di corpo*. Rome: N. Mutij. Facs. Farnsborough: Gregg, 1967.

Chiabrera, Gabriello. 1615. *Polifemo geloso, favoletta da rappresentarsi cantando*. Florence: Zanobi Pignoni.

Christ Church Library, Oxford, MS 87 (Elizabeth Davenant's songbook), c. 1624.

Christ Church Library, Oxford, MS 439, c. 1610–1620 or c. 1620–1630.

Clement, Francis. 1587. *The Petie Schole*. London: Thomas Vautrollier. Facs., Leeds: Scolar Press, 1967.

Coclico, Adrian Petit. 1552. *Compendium musices*. Nürnberg: Johann Berg & Ulrich Neuber. Facs., Kassel: Bärenreiter, 1954.

Collingwood, Robin G. 1961. *The Idea of History*. London: Oxford University Press.

Conforto, Giovanni Luca. 1593. *Breve et facile maniera d'essercitarsi ad ogni scolaro*. Rome: n.p..

The Consort of Musicke. 1996. *Monteverdi, Il primo libro de madrigali, 1587*. Virgin Veritas, 7243 5 45143 2 6.

Coprario, John. 1606. *Funeral Teares*. London: John Windet.

Coprario, John. 1613. *Songs of Mourning*. London: John Browne.

Correa de Arauxo, Francisco. 1626. *Facultad orgánica*. Alcala: A. Arnao. Facs. Geneva: Minkoff, 1981.

Crane, Frederick. 1960. A Study of Theoretical Writings on Musical Form to ca. 1460. Ph.D. diss., University of Iowa.

Crema, Giovanni Maria da. 1546. *Intabolatura de lauto*. Venice: Gardane.

Cretz, Ioannem. 1553. *Compendiosa introductio in choralem musicam*. Augsburg: Philippus Ulhardus.

Crocioni, Giovanni. 1938. *L'Alidoro o dei primordi del melodramma*. Bologna: Luigi Parma.

Crutchfield, Will. 1989. Some Thoughts on Reconstructing Singing Styles of the Past. *Journal of the Conductor's Guild* 10: 111–20.

Danyel, John. 1606. *Songs for the Lute, Viol and Voice*. London: T. E.

Dobson, Eric J. 1968. *English Pronunciation 1500–1700*, 2nd ed., 2 vols. Oxford: Clarendon Press.

Doughtie, Edward. 1970. *Lyrics from English Airs 1596–1622*. Cambridge, Mass.: Harvard University Press.

Dowland, John. 1597. *The First Booke of Songes or Ayres*. London: Peter Short (subsequent editions in 1600, 1603, 1606, and 1613).

Dowland, John. 1600. *The Second Booke of Songs or Ayres*. London: Thomas Este.

Dowland, John. 1603. *The Third and Last Booke of Songs or Aires*. London: Thomas Adams.

Dowland, John. 1609. *Andreas Ornithoparcus His Micrologus, or Introduction*. London: Thomas Adams.

Dowland, John. 1612. *A Pilgrimes Solace*. London: M. L., J. B., and T. S.

Dowland, Robert. 1610. *A Musicall Banquet*. London: Thomas Adams.

Dublin. Trinity College, MS F.5.13, c. 1615 or before 1618–20.

Elders, Willem. 1981. Guillaume Dufay as Musical Orator. *Tijdschrift van de Vereniging voor Nederlandse Muziekgeschiedenis* 31: 1–15.

Elyot, Thomas. 1546. *The Boke Named the Governour*. London: Thomae Bertheleti.

Erig, Richard. 1979. *Italienische Diminutionen*. Zurich: Amadeus.

Ferrabosco, Alfonso. 1609. *Ayres*. London: T. Snodham.

Finck, Hermann. 1556. *Practica musica*. Wittenberg: Georg Rhau. Facs., Bologna: Forni, 1969.

Florio, John. 1611. *Queen Anna's New World of Words, or Dictionarie of the Italian and English Tongues*. London: Melch. Bradwood.

Ford, Thomas. 1607. *Musicke of Sundrie Kindes*. London: John Windet.

Francesco da Milano. 1547. *Intabolatura de lauto*. Venice: Gardane.

Fraunce, Abraham. 1588. *The Arcadian Rhetorike*. London: Thomas Orwin.

Freitas, Roger. 2002. Towards a Verdian Ideal of Singing: Emancipation from Modern Orthodoxy. *Journal of the Royal Musical Association* 127: 226–57.

Frottole, Libro primo. 1504. Venice: Petrucci.

Fuenllana, Miguel de. 1554. *Orphenica lyra*. Seville: Martin de Montesdoca.

Galilei, Vincenzo. 1568. *Fronimo dialogo*. Venice: Girolamo Scotto.

Galliculus, Johannes. 1538. *Libellus de compositione cantus*. Wittenberg: Georg Rhau.

Ganassi, Silvestro di. 1535. *Opera intitulata Fontegara.* Venice: Ganassi.

Gerle, Hans. 1532. *Musica Teusch.* Nürnberg: Formschneyder.

Gerle, Hans. 1546. *Musica und tabulatur.* Nürnberg: Formschneyder.

Giustiniani, Vincenzo. c. 1628. *Discorso sopra la musica.* Lucca: Archivio di Stato, MS O. 49. Ed. Angelo Solerti, *Le origini del melodramma.* Torino: Fratelli Bocca, 1903. Repr., Hildesheim: Georg Olms, 1969.

Glarean, Heinrich. 1547. *Dodecachordon.* Basel: Heinrich Petri. Facs., New York: Broude, 1967.

Granger, Thomas. 1616. *Syntagma Grammaticum* London: T. Dawson. Facs., Menston: Scolar Press, 1971.

Greene, John. 1615. *A Refutation of the Apology for Actors.* London: W. White.

Harrán, Don. 1986. *Word-Tone Relations in Musical Thought from Antiquity to the Seventeenth Century.* Neuhausen-Stuttgart: Hänssler-Verlag.

Hart, John. 1551. The Opening of the Unreasonable Writing of our Inglish Toung, 1551 (British Library, Royal MS 17.C.VII). Ed. in Bror Danielsson, *John Hart's Works of English Orthography and Pronunciation,* Stockholm Studies in English 5. Stockholm: Almquist & Wiksell, 1955.

Hart, John. 1569. *An Orthographie.* London: W. Serres. Facs., Menston: Scolar Press, 1969.

Hertford, Earl of. 1591. *The Honorable Entertainement gieven to the Queenes Maiestie in Progresse, at Elvetham in Hampshire, by the right Honorable the Earle of Hertford 1591.* London: John Wolfe.

Hessen, Paul, and Bartholomeus Hessen. 1555a. *Eticher gutter Teutscher und Polnischer tenz.* Breslau: Crispinum Scharffenberg.

Hessen, Paul, and Bartholomeus Hessen. 1555b. *Viel feiner lieblicher stücklein Spanischer, Welscher, Englischer, Französischer composition und tenz.* Breslau: Crispinum Scharffenberg.

Heywood, Thomas. 1612. *An Apology for Actors.* London: Nicholas Okes. Facs., New York: Garland, 1973.

Hitchcock, H. Wiley. 2009. *Giulio Caccini, Le Nuove Musiche.* Madison, Wisc.: A-R Editions.

Hobbes, Thomas. 1637. *A Briefe of the Art of Rhetorique.* London: Tho. Cotes. In *The Rhetorics of Thomas Hobbes and Bernard Lamy,* ed. John T. Harwood. Carbondale: Southern Illinois University Press, 1986.

Hooker, Richard. 1597. *Of the Lawes of Ecclesiasticall Politie, The fift Booke.* London: John Windet. Facs., Amsterdam: Theatrum Orbis Terrarum, 1971.

Hoskins, John. 1599. *Direccōns for Speech and Style.* In *The Life, Letters, and Writings of John Hoskyns 1566–1638,* ed. Louise B. Osborn. Hamden: Archon Books, 1973.

Janssen, Carole Ann. 1978. The Waytes of Norwich in Medieval and Renaissance Civic Pageantry. Ph.D. diss., University of New Brunswick.

Jones, Robert. 1600. *The First Booke of Songes or Ayres.* London: Peter Short.

Jones, Robert. 1601. *The Second Booke of Songs or Ayres.* London: P. S.

Jones, Robert. 1605. *Ultimum Vale.* London: John Windet.

Jones, Robert. 1609. *A Musicall Dreame.* London: John Windet.

Jonsson, Ritva, and Leo Treitler. 1983. Medieval Music and Language: A Reconsideration of the Relationship. In *Studies in the History of Music* 1, pp. 1–23. New York: Broude.

Joseph, Sister Miriam. 1947. *Shakespeare's Use of the Arts of Language.* New York: Columbia University Press.

Kassel. Murhard'sche Bibliothek der Stadt Kassel und Landesbibliothek, MS 4o Mus. 91/1–5, undated.

Kaufmann, Henry W. 1966. *The Life and Works of Nicola Vicentino (1511–c. 1576).* N.p.: American Institute of Musicology.

Kempe, William. 1588. *The Education of Children in Learning.* London: Thomas Orwin.

Kempe, William. 1600. *Kemp's Nine Daies Wonder.* London: E. A. Ed. Alexander Dyce, London: Camden Society, 1840.

Lago, Giovanni del. 1540. *Breve introduttione di musica misurata.* Venice: Brandino & Ottaviano Scotto. Facs., Bologna: Forni, 1969.

Lanfranco, Giovanni Maria. 1533. *Scintille di musica.* Brescia: Ludovico Britannico. Facs., Bologna: Forni, 1970.

Lanham, Richard. 1968. *A Handlist of Rhetorical Terms.* Berkeley: University of California Press.

LeCoat, Gerard. 1975. *The Rhetoric of the Arts, 1550–1650*. Bern: Herbert Lang.

Le Faucheur, Michel. 1657. *Traitté de l'action de l'orateur ou de la prononciation et du geste*. Paris: Augustin Courbé. Trans. *An Essay upon the Action of an Orator, as to his Pronunciation and Gesture*. London: Nich. Cox, undated.

Leipzig. Universitätsbibliothek, Thomaskirche, MS 49 (1–4), undated.

Le Roy, Adrian. 1574. *A briefe and plaine Instruction*. London: J. Kyngston for J. Robothome.

Liber secundus cantionum sacrarum. 1554. Louvain: Phalèse.

Lily, William. 1567. *Brevissima institutio*. London: Reginaldium Vuolfium. Facs., New York: Scholars' Facsimiles & Reprints, 1945.

Lockwood, Lewis. 1965. A Dispute on Accidentals in Sixteenth-Century Rome. *Analecta Musicologica* 2: 24–40.

Lowinsky, Edward. 1964. Forward to *Musica Nova*. Ed. H. Colin Slim. Chicago: University of Chicago Press.

Mace, Thomas. 1676. *Musick's Monument*. London: T. Ratcliffe and N. Thompson.

Maffei, Giovanni Camillo. 1562. *Delle lettere . . . Libri due*. Naples: Amato.

Manchester. Public Library, Watson Collection, MS 832 Vu 51, c. 1660.

McGee, Timothy, ed. 1996. *Singing Early Music: The Pronunciation of European Languages in the Late Middle Ages and Renaissance*. Bloomington: Indiana University Press.

Melanthonis, Philippi. 1850. *Opera*, Vol. 16. Halle: Schwetschke. Repr., New York: Johnson Reprint, 1963.

Mersenne, Marin. 1623. *Observationes*. Paris: Sebastiani Cramoisy.

Montanos, Francisco de. 1592. *Arte de música theorica y pratica*. Valladolid: Fernandez de Cordova. Trans. Dan Urquhart, Francisco de Montanos's *Arte de musica theorica y pratica*: A Translation and Commentary. Ph.D. diss., University of Rochester, 1969.

Monteverdi, Claudio. 1587. *Madrigali a cinque voci . . . Libro primo*. Venice: Gardano.

More, Sir Thomas. 1516. *Utopia*. Louvain: Martens. Facs., Leeds: Scolar Press, 1966. Trans. Ralph Robinson. London: Abraham Vele, 1556. Ed. George Sampson, *The Utopia of Sir Thomas More*. London: G. Bell and Sons, 1910.

Morley, Thomas. 1597. *A Plaine and Easie Introduction to Practicall Musicke*. London: P. Short. Facs., Amsterdam: Theatrum Orbis Terrarum, 1969.

Morley, Thomas. 1600. *The First Booke of Ayres*. London: William Barley.

Mulcaster, Richard. 1581. *Positions*. London: T. Vautrollier. Facs., Amsterdam: Theatrum Orbis Terrarum, 1971.

Mulcaster, Richard. 1582. *Elementarie*. London: T. Vautroullier. Ed. Ernest T. Campagnac, *Mulcaster's Elementarie*. Oxford: Clarendon Press, 1925.

Munich. Bayerische Staatsbibliothek, Mus. ms. 1512, c. 1533.

Ness, Arthur J. 1970. *The Lute Music of Francesco Canova da Milano (1497–1543)*. Cambridge, Mass.: Harvard University Press.

The New Grove Dictionary of Music and Musicians, 2nd ed.

Novum et insigne opus musicum. 1558. Nürnberg: Berg & Neuber.

Nucius, Johannes. 1613. *Musices poeticae*. Neisse: Scharffenberg.

Ochsenkun, Sebastian. 1558. *Tabulaturbuch auff die lauten*. Heidelberg: Kholen.

Ornithoparchus, Andreas. 1517. *Musice active micrologus*. Leipzig: Valentin Schumann. Trans. John Dowland, *Andreas Ornithoparcus His Micrologus, or Introduction*. London: Thomas Adams, 1609. Facs. of both eds. in one volume, New York: Dover, 1973.

Ortiz, Diego. 1553. *Trattado de glosas sobre clausulas*. Rome: Dorico.

Peacham the Elder, Henry. 1577. *The Garden of Eloquence*. London: H. Jackson. Facs., Menston: Scolar Press, 1971.

Peacham the Elder, Henry. 1593. *The Garden of Eloquence*. London: H. Jackson. Facs., Gainesville, Fla.: Scholars' Facsimiles & Reprints, 1954.

Peacham the Younger, Henry. 1622. *The Compleat Gentleman*. London: F. Constable. Facs., Amsterdam: Theatrum Orbis Terrarum, 1968.

Phalèse, Pierre. 1546. *Des chansons reduictz en tabulature de luc*. Louvain: Phalèse.

Phalèse, Pierre. 1547a. *Des chansons & motetz reduictz en tabulature de luc.* Louvain: Phalèse.

Phalèse, Pierre. 1547b. *Des chansons reduictz en tabulature de lut.* Louvain: Phalèse.

Philip, Robert. 1992. *Early Recordings and Musical Style: Changing Tastes in Instrumental Performance, 1900–1950.* Cambridge: Cambridge University Press.

Pilkington, Francis. 1605. *The First Booke of Songs or Ayres.* London: T. Este.

Pisador, Diego. 1552. *Libro de musica de vihuela.* Salamanca: Pisador.

Playford, John. 1674. *An Introduction to the Skill of Musick.* London: W. Godbid.

Poliziano, Angelo. 1498. *Omnia opera Angeli Politiani.* Venice: Aldus Manutius. Available in microform: *Italian Books before 1601*, Roll 207. Lexington, Ky.: Erasmus Press, 1965–.

Pontio, Pietro. 1588. *Ragionamento di musica.* Parma: Erasmo Viotto. Facs., Kassel: Bärenreiter, 1959.

Pope, Isabel. 1961. La vihuela y su música en el ambiente humanístico. *Nueva revista de filología hispánica* 15: 364–76.

Potter, John. 1998. *Vocal Authority: Singing Style and Ideology.* Cambridge: Cambridge University Press.

Poulton, Diana. 1982. *John Dowland*, 2nd ed. London: Faber.

Powers, Harold. 1981. Tonal Types and Modal Categories in Renaissance Polyphony. *Journal of the American Musicological Society* 34: 428–70.

Powers, Harold. 1992a. Is Mode Real? Pietro Aron, the Octenary System, and Polyphony. *Basler Jahrbuch für Historische Musikpraxis* 16: 9–52.

Powers, Harold. 1992b. Modality as a European Cultural Construct. In *Secondo convegno europeo di analisi musicale: atti*, pp. 207–19. Ed. Rossana Dalmonte and Mario Baroni. Trento: Università degli Studi di Trento.

Praetorius, Michael. 1619. *Syntagma musicum.* Wolfenbüttel: Elias Holwein. Facs., Kassel: Bärenreiter, 1958.

Prizer, William F. 1980. Lutenists at the Court of Mantua in the Late Fifteenth and Early Sixteenth Centuries. *Journal of the Lute Society of America* 13: 5–34.

Prizer, William. 1999. Una "virtù molto conveniente a madonne": Isabella d'Este as a Musician. *Journal of Musicology* 17: 10–49.

Puttenham, George. 1589. *The Arte of English Poesie.* London: Richard Field. Facs., Menston: Scolar Press, 1968.

Quintilian. *The Institutio Oratoria of Quintilian*, ed. and trans. H. E. Butler. Cambridge, Mass.: Harvard University Press, 1920–1922.

Robinson, Ralph. 1641. *An English Grammar.* London: M. Walbank and L. Chapman. Facs., Menston: Scolar Press, 1972.

Robinson, Thomas. 1603. *The Schoole of Musicke.* London: Tho. Este.

Rogniono, Richardo. 1592. *Passaggi per potersi essercitare nel diminuire.* Venice: Vincenti.

Rognoni, Francesco. 1620. *Selva de varii passaggi.* Milan: Lomazzo.

Rosseter, Philip. 1601. *A Booke of Ayres.* London: Peter Short.

Rossetti, Biagio. 1529. *Libellus de rudimentis musices.* Verona: Stefano e fratelli de Nicolinis de Sabio. Facs., New York: Broude, 1968.

Rutgerus Sycamber de Venray. c. 1500. *Dialogus de musica.* Ed. Fritz Soddemann. Köln: Arno Volk, 1963.

Sancta Maria, Thomas de. 1565. *Arte de tañer fantasia.* Valladolid: Francisco Fernandez de Cordova. Facs., Geneva: Minkoff, 1973. Trans. Almonte C. Howell, Jr. and Warren E. Hultberg, *The Art of Playing the Fantasia.* Pittsburgh: Latin American Literary Review Press, 1991.

Seay, Albert. 1965–1970. *Arcadelt, Opera omnia.* Rome: American Institute of Musicology.

Sebastiani, Claudius. 1563. *Bellum musicale.* Strasbourg: Paulus Machaeropoeus.

Shakespeare, William. 1623. *Mr. William Shakespeares Comedies, Histories, & Tragedies.* London: Isaac Iaggard and Ed. Blount.

Sherry, Richard. 1550. *A Treatise of Schemes and Tropes.* London: John Day.

Simpson, Christopher. 1665. *The Division-Viol.* London: Brome.

Smith, John. 1657. *The Mysterie of Rhetorique Unvail'd.* London: George Eversden. Facs., Hildesheim: Georg Olms, 1973.

Snegasius [Schneegass], Cyriacus. 1596. *Isagoges musicae libri duo. Tam theoricae quám practicae studiosis inservire iussi*. Erfurt: Georg Baumann.

Sonnino, Lee A. 1968. *A Handbook to Sixteenth-Century Rhetoric*. London: Routledge & Kegan Paul.

Stoquerus [Stocker], Gaspar. c. 1570. *De musica verbali libro duo*. Madrid, Biblioteca Nacional, MS 6486, fols. 1–40v.

Tertius liber modulorum. 1555. Geneva: Du Bosc & Guéroult.

Toft, Robert. 1983. Pitch Content and Modal Procedure in Selected Motets of Josquin Desprez: A Comparative Study of the Printed Intabulations with the Vocal Sources. Ph.D. diss., King's College, University of London.

Toft, Robert. 1985. An Approach to Performing the Mid 16th-Century Italian Lute Fantasia. *The Lute, The Journal of the Lute Society* 25: 3–16.

Toft, Robert. 1992. *Aural Images of Lost Traditions: Sharps and Flats in the Sixteenth Century*. Toronto: University of Toronto Press.

Toft, Robert. 1993. *Tune thy Musicke to thy Hart: The Art of Eloquent Singing in England 1597–1622*. Toronto: University of Toronto Press.

Toft, Robert. 2009. Limitations of Meaning: Text and Context in Monteverdi's 'Baci soavi e cari' (1587). In *The Sounds and Sights of Performance in Medieval and Renaissance Music: Essays in Honour of Timothy McGee*, pp. 229–51. Ed. Brian Power and Maureen Epp. Aldershot: Ashgate.

Tomlinson, Gary. 1987. *Monteverdi and the End of the Renaissance*. Berkeley: University of California Press.

Towne, Gary. 1990/91. A Systematic Formulation of Sixteenth-Century Text Underlay Rules. *Musica Disciplina* 44 (1990): 255–87 and 45 (1991): 143–68.

Trissino, Giangiorgio. 1524. *I ritratti*. Rome: Arrighi.

Tyard, Pontus de. 1555. *Solitaire second ou prose de la musique*. Lyons: I. de Tournes. Ed. Cathy M. Yandell. Geneva: Droz, 1980.

Vanneo, Stefano. 1533. *Recanetum de musica aurea*. Rome: Valerio Dorico. Facs., Kassel: Bärenreiter, 1969.

Verdelot, Philippe. 1536. *Intavolatura de li madrigali di Verdelotto*. Venice: Scotto.

Vicentino, Nicola. 1555. *L'antica musica ridotta alla moderna prattica*. Rome: Antonio Barre. Facs., Kassel: Bärenreiter, 1959. Trans. Maria Rika Maniates, *Ancient Music Adapted to Modern Practice*. New Haven: Yale University Press, 1996.

Vickers, John. 1984. Figures of Rhetoric/Figures of Music? *Rhetorica* 2: 1–44.

Virgiliano, Aurelio. c. 1600. Bologna, Civico Museo Bibliografico Musicale, MS C. 33.

Vogelsang, Johann. 1542. *Musicae rudimenta*. Augsburg: Valentin Otthmar.

Walther, Johann G. 1708. *Praecepta der musicalischen composition*. Ed. Peter Benary. Leipzig: Breitkopf & Härtel, 1955.

Wilson, Christopher R. 1991. Review of *The Life and Works of Philip Rosseter* by John Jeffreys. *Music and Letters* 72 (1991): 580–81.

Wilson, Thomas. 1553. *The Arte of Rhetorique*. London: Richardus Graftonus. Ed. Thomas J. Derrick. New York: Garland, 1982.

Wright, Thomas. 1604. *The Passions of the Minde in Generall*. London: Valentine Simmes. Facs., of the 1630 ed. [differs from the 1604 ed. mainly in the correction of typographical errors]. Urbana: University of Illinois Press, 1971.

Wulstan, David. 1985. *Tudor Music*. London: J. M. Dent.

Yates, Frances A. 1966. *The Art of Memory*. London: Routledge and Kegan Paul.

Zacconi, Lodovico. 1592. *Prattica di musica*. Venice: Girolamo Polo, Alessandro Vincenti. Facs., Bologna: Forni, 1967.

Zarlino, Gioseffo. 1558. *Le istitutioni harmoniche*. Venice: n.p. Facs., New York: Broude, 1965. Part IV trans. Vered Cohen, *On the Modes*. New Haven: Yale University Press, 1983.

Zarlino, Gioseffo. 1588. *Sopplimenti musicali*. Venice: Francesco de' Franceschi Senese. Facs., Ridgewood, N.J.: Gregg, 1967.

Zenobi, Luigi. c. 1600. Lettere. In Rome: Biblioteca Vallicelliana, MS R. 45 (Raccolta di letterre varie Latine, et Italiane), fols. 199r–204v. Ed. Bonnie J. Blackburn and Edward Lowinsky, *Luigi Zenobi and His Letter on the Perfect Musician. Studi musicali* 22 (1993): 61–114.

Index